Over 1000 creative ideas for memory pages, cards, mini albums, tags, and papercrafts

It's All About
SCRAPBOOKING

Includes *Bonus* tear-out scrapbook papers!

LEISURE ARTS, INC
Little Rock, Arkansas

It's All About
SCRAPBOOKING

NANC & COMPANY

SENIOR DESIGN DIRECTOR Nancy M. Hill
DESIGN DIRECTOR Candice Snyder
SENIOR EDITOR Candice Smoot
GRAPHIC DESIGNERS BLT Design, Rafael
   Nielson, Shannon Ogden, and Ty Thomson
PHOTOGRAPHER Julianne Smoot
COPY EDITOR Sharon Staples

Nancy M. Hill began designing scrapbook pages nearly 35 years ago, and wishes she could retire and scrapbook full-time. Before founding DieCuts With a View and The Scrapbook Institute, she was a college professor and administrator with a Ph. D in business and information systems. She has consulted both nationally and internationally in the corporate and private sector as a marketing and institutional researcher and strategic planner. She is a Board Certified Genealogist and prolific writer with more than 200 publications to her credit. She and her husband, Mike, are fortunate to live close to and work professionally with their nine children and seven grandchildren.

LEISURE ARTS, INC.
EDITORIAL STAFF

VICE PRESIDENT AND EDITOR-IN-CHIEF Sandra Graham Case
EXECUTIVE DIRECTOR OF PUBLICATIONS Cheryl Nodine Gunnells
SENIOR PUBLICATIONS DIRECTOR Susan White Sullivan
DIRECTOR OF DESIGNER RELATIONS Debra Nettles
SENIOR DESIGN DIRECTOR Cyndi Hansen
DIRECTOR OF RETAIL MARKETING Stephen Wilson
SPECIAL PROJECTS DIRECTOR Susan Frantz Wiles
SENIOR ART OPERATIONS DIRECTOR Jeff Curtis
ART PUBLICATIONS DIRECTOR Rhonda Shelby
ART IMAGING DIRECTOR Mark Hawkins
IMAGING TECHNICIANS Stephanie Johnson and Mark Potter
PUBLISHING SYSTEMS ADMINISTRATOR Becky Riddle
PUBLISHING SYSTEMS ASSISTANTS Clint Hanson, Josh Hyatt,
   and John Rose

BUSINESS STAFF

CHIEF OPERATING OFFICER Tom Siebenmorgen
VICE PRESIDENT, SALES AND MARKETING Pam Stebbins
DIRECTOR OF SALES AND SERVICES Margaret Reinold
VICE PRESIDENT, OPERATIONS Jim Dittrich
COMPTROLLER, OPERATIONS Rob Thieme
RETAIL CUSTOMER SERVICE MANAGER Stan Raynor
PRINT PRODUCTION MANAGER Fred F. Pruss

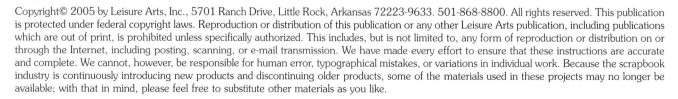

Printed in China.

International Standard Book Number 1-57486-548-X
10 9 8 7 6 5 4 3 2 1

It's All About SCRAPBOOKING

Once you've experienced the thrill of seeing your cherished photos on an awe-inspiring memory page, you understand what the excitement is all about — it's all about scrapbooking! That's why we've compiled this colossal collection of useful ideas, tips, and sample creations. With so much to spark your imagination, you can celebrate your life with unique keepsakes that commemorate special people, favorite places, and unforgettable events. There's help for every aspect of this captivating hobby, from inspiration to finished pages and albums. You'll learn trendy and time-honored techniques, and you'll be filled with great plans for scrapbooking baby faces, school mementoes, family vacations, and pampered pets. There's big fun ahead on a small scale, too, with our mini albums, cards, and tags. And to top it all off, we close with a bonus section of double-sided scrapbooking papers that you can tear out and use for a variety of projects.

Have fun!

CONTENTS

it's all about TEchNiQUE

6

it's all about

TeChNiQuE

Written instructions detailing creative techniques and ideas in scrapbooking

color/tone

embellishments

mesh & metal

decoupage

tinting

mosaic

photography

embossing

journaling

sewing

8

Dear Scrapbooker,

This two-page spread of three of my granddaughters was made from a single photo. The girls and I had been shopping at the mall for a bit and as we were leaving I took their picture with my new digital camera. Their mother was complaining that they were not dressed for picture taking, they were anxious to go swimming and I only had time for one shot before the whining began. Fortunately, that one photo streeeetched a long way. Using a home photo printer, I printed 2 regular 4 x 6 photos, a distorted 4 x 6, and a blown-up and cropped photo of each of the girls. I chose Leisure Arts Memories in the Making paper and asked our designer, Camille Jensen, to do something creative with the photos. I am delighted with the finished two-page design and amazed at what can be done with one, very quick shot!

When we began this technique collecion, I made a very neat working outline of all the possible scrapbooking and paper-crafting techniques I had used or observed. It was my intention to include them all in the 'table of contents' and showcase one or two designs featuring each technique. Boy, was I dreaming! It wasn't very long before I realized that there are far more techniques and creative possibilities than can be featured or described here. An encyclopedia may be more appropriate!

To narrow the scope of this project we chose a variety of techniques to focus on. From the simple to the complex and the trendy to the time-honored we have included detailed instructions for duplicating the techniques highlighted on the pages featured.

Happy Scrapping,

Nancy

NANCY M. HILL

It's All About Technique

Table of Contents

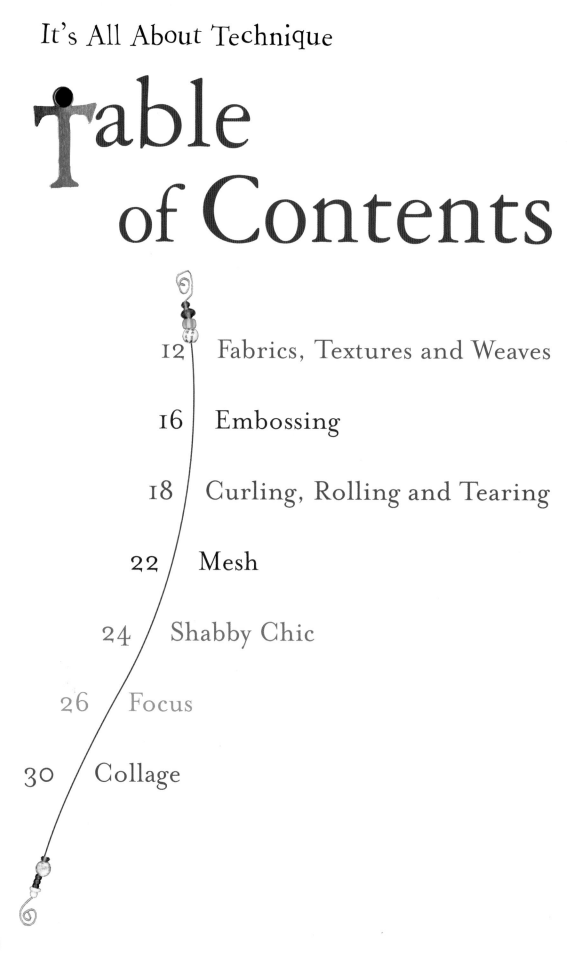

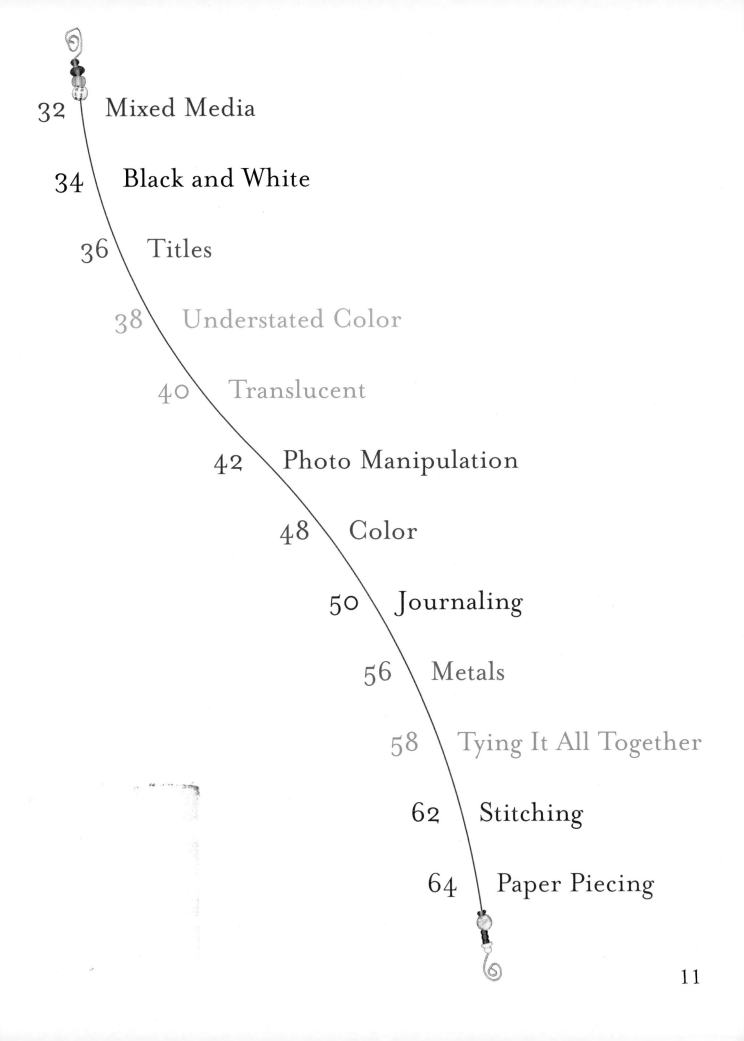

Fabrics, Textures & Weaves

People are likely to spend more time looking at a textured scrapbook page. The eye wanders back and forth between contrasting textures, and the hand is tempted to reach out and feel the page. Using contrasting textures adds dimension and interest. For example, a delicate or shiny, metal embellishment really stands out on a grainy, rustic fabric. Weaving is not only a nice embellishment, but also a great way to combine and layer textures on a page.

Madeline

Supplies - Patterned Vellum: Forget Me Not Designs; Vellum: Laura Ashley; Buckle: Making Memories; Cork: Magic Scraps; Metals: Making Memories; Conchos: Scrapworks; Date Stamp: Making Memories; Buttons: Doodlebug; Die Cut Flowers: Forget Me Not Designs; Beads: Magic Scraps

Construction Tips:

Use cork, paper or other textures in buckle clips instead of always using ribbon.

Designer: Susan Stringfellow

Worth The Wait

Supplies – Patterned Paper: NRN Designs; Die Cuts: NRN Designs; Stickers: NRN Designs; Ink: Stampin' Up; Embossing Powder: Stamps 'n' Stuff; Wire: Artistic Wire; Metallic Rub-ons: Craf-T; Brads: All The Extras

Construction Tips:
Distress fish tags by crumpling and inking tags. Embellish tags with fiber and wire and attach to page with raffia.

Construction Tips:
Fill vellum envelopes with tags that can be removed for a closer look.

Horsin' Around

Supplies – Patterned Paper: Paper Adventures, Leisure Arts, Creative Imaginations; Cardstock: Bazzill; Chalk: Craf-T; Eyelets: Making Memories; Silver Clip: Making Memories; Raffia: Making Memories; Buttons: Making Memories; Vellum Envelopes: Robin's Nest; Charm: The Card Collection; Font: CK Around

Designer: Kelly Litvak

Designer: Wanda E. Santiago

A Moment Of Wonder

Supplies – Stickers: Chatterbox,
Creative Imaginations; Pen: Krylon

Construction Tips:
Use pre-made stickers
to create a textured
background without
the bulk.

Designer: Laura Stewart

Family

Supplies – Patterned Paper: Chatterbox; Stickers: Anna Griffin; Eyelet: Making Memories; Embellishments: K & Co.; Mesh: Magic Mesh

Construction Tips:

Create a common message board with cardstock, buttons and ribbon. Pull the ribbon tight before adhering to the cardstock.

Designer: Debbie Campa

Grandpa's Swing

Supplies – Patterned Paper: Paper Adventures; Stamps: Provo Craft; Fonts: CK Script, Marisa, Sonja

Construction Tips:

To heat stamp vinyl:
1. Cut vinyl to 4 times the size of the image to be stamped.
2. Place vinyl on stamping mat and heat until vinyl begins to melt (heat vinyl evenly to ensure a uniform image).
3. Press stamp into vinyl; don't remove until vinyl cools (approximately 20 seconds).
4. Cut out vinyl to desired shape.

15

Embossing

Embossing adds a nice finishing touch to just about any page element imaginable. The most common forms of embossing are color and clear heat embossing and dry embossing. Clear embossing powder comes in two different forms: 1) regular powder which forms a thin, glass-like coating, and 2) deep powder which is applied in many layers to form a thick, clear coating. The thick coating can then be cracked for an aged look. Dry embossing can give a subtle elegance to a layout or a dramatic look with chalk. Use embossing powder with stamps and clay to add variety. Regardless of what type of embossing is used, the end result adds color, shine or dimension to a layout.

Designer: Janet Hopkins

Smile, Play, Giggle

Supplies – Cardstock: Bazzill; Acrylic Paints: Americana; Brads: Boxer; Embossing Powder: Rubba Dub Dub, Inc.; Metal Words: Making Memories; Stamp Pad: Versamark

Construction Tips:

Heat emboss torn edges by stamping area to be embossed, dusting with copper embossing powder (remove excess powder) and applying heat to the powder with an embossing gun.

Construction Tips:

Create stamped clay leaves by rolling clay to 1/8" thick, covering with metallic rub-ons and stamping with rubber stamps. Dust clay with embossing powder, spray with water and let dry.

Remember When

Supplies – Patterned Paper: Chatterbox; Mulberry Paper: Making Memories; Cardstock: Bazzill, Chatterbox; Rub-ons: Provo Craft, What's New, Ltd., Craft Products, Inc.; Stamps: Stampin' Up; Clay: Provo Craft; Tags: Rusty Pickle; Tiles: Sticko; Crystal Effects: Stampin' Up

Designer: Sherri Allsman

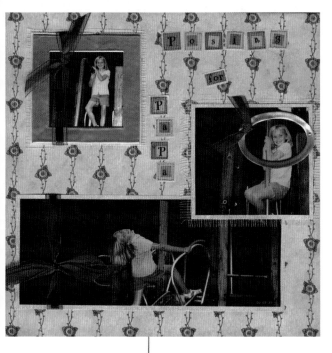

Posing For Papa

Supplies – Patterned Paper: Leisure Arts; Metallic
Frames: DCWV; Embossing Powder: Suze Weinberg

Construction Tips:

Use thick embossing enamel on die cut frames to
create a metallic look. Apply several coats of enamel
until the desired thickness and look is achieved.
Allow each coat to dry before applying the next coat.

Designer: Melissa Smith

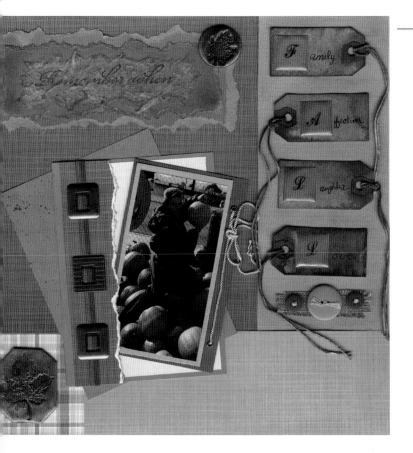

Forever Young

Supplies – Patterned Paper: Karen Foster Design, Misty Teal;
Transparency: 3M; Sand Dollar: Leave Memories; UTEE:
Suze Weinberg; Embossing Powder: Stamps 'n' Stuff, Mark
Enterprises; Re-inkers: Fresco, Stampa Rosa; Fonts: Bradley
Hand, Papyrus

Construction Tips:

Create circle letters by
punching circles from
painted cardstock.
Deep emboss three lay-
ers with clear embossing
powder. Stamp letter
stamps into third clear
embossed layer while
still warm with gold ink.
Dip edges of circles into
gold embossing powder.

Curling, Tearing & Rolling

Curling, tearing and rolling paper are common techniques used to add variety to a layout, yet they are far from commonplace. There are endless ways to use these simple techniques to create extraordinary layouts. Try tearing paper to create designs, rolling paper back to reveal a beautiful photo or curling torn edges of paper for a subtle accent that adds the finishing touch to a layout.

Designer: Maegan Hall

Construction Tips:

Wet scrap paper with water, crumple and tear into various sized circles while still wet. Adhere flowers to layout, chalk edges with metallic rub-ons and finish by adhering beads to the center of each flower.

Cherish

Supplies – Patterned Paper: Sonnets, Daisy D; Cardstock: Paper Garden; Metallic Word: Making Memories; Beads: Bead Heaven

Hooray For Spring

Supplies – Patterned Paper: Deja Views; Black Pen: Creative Memories; Eyelets: Making Memories; Die Cut System: Sizzix; Twistel: Making Memories; Stickers: Jolee's By You; Glue: Tombo

Construction Tips:

Create rolled paper frame by:

1. Cutting out eight pieces of 4" x 5" paper.
2. Tightly roll the 5" edge of the paper around a pencil or rod.
3. Secure the entire seam of the roll with small pieces of tape.
4. Glue rolls to the photo and to each other (if you would prefer not to glue paper to your photo, mat the photo and glue rolls to the mat).

Hooray for Spring

There are so many things about Spring that we love. Even things we do throughout the year (like gardening, picnics or just playing with Derby) seem a little more special during Spring. It's definitely our favorite time of the year.

Spring 2001

Gardening

Picnics

Playing with

Derby

Designer: Leah Fung

Walk Beside Me And Be My Friend

Supplies – Patterned Paper: NRN Designs, Paperbilities; Eyelets: Eyelets Every Month; Fiber: Fibers By The Yard; Definition: Making Memories; Rub-ons: Making Memories; Tags: Making Memories; Snaps: Making Memories; Font: P22 Type Foundry Monet

Construction Tips:

Tear a photo and ink the edges to give an aged look.

friends

love

Don't walk in front of me...
I may not follow.
Don't walk behind me...
I may not lead.
Walk beside me...
And be my friend!
~Albert Camus

Friendship
the state of being friends

Designer: Sam Cousins

19

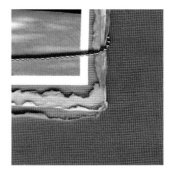

Designer: Leah Fung

I love and I am loved
more than I ever thought possible

Mothers Day
2003

Construction Tips:

Curl torn paper by wetting the torn edges and curling by hand. When the paper dries the curls will remain.

More Than I Ever Thought Possible

Supplies – Cardstock: Bazzill; Beaded Chain: Making Memories; Eyelets: Making Memories

SPLISH SPLASH

Designer: Kim Heston

20

The West

Supplies – Patterned Paper: Leisure Arts,
Design Originals; Eyelets: Making Memories;
Hinge: Demis Products; Glue: Tombo

Construction Tips:

Tear strip of patterned paper,
sand and roll edges. Adhere
to page with a zig-zag stitch.

My dear Andrew,

I have always loved California, but I'm
so happy knowing that you love it too.
The beautiful weather, living on the
coast, and being close to family is such a
blessing. And, I love the fact that I can
walk through our beautiful canyon all
year round with you.

I love you.

Mom

AUG 0 5 2003

Designer: Leah Fung

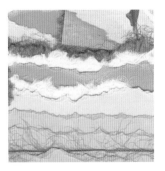

James can't let Corey just sit and play
peacefully. He tries to stir up trouble.
He makes the first move by throwing
wet sand at Corey and the fight begins.
The older Corey gets he is able to give
James a run for his money. Corey
gets tired but is determined. The fight
always seems to turn to me eventually.

Splish Splash

The torn cardstocks and mulberry papers
work really well with the beach theme.

Construction Tips:

Tearing paper is easier when
the paper is wet. Combine
colored fibers and torn
paper to give the layout a
more finished look.

Mesh

Mesh is a versatile element in scrapbooking. It is easy to use and a great way to add texture to a layout. Mesh is often used to mat photos and journaling or as an embellishment to a layout. Mesh can also be used to create elements on your page such as a fishing or basketball net. Experiment with mesh on your next layout and experience for yourself its versatility.

Construction Tips:
Use safety pins to attach the mesh photo mats to one another.

Designer: Martha Crowther

Dream, Believe, Create And Inspire

Supplies — Patterned Paper: Paper Adventures; Fiber: Fibers By The Yard; Metal Accents: Li'l Davis Designs, Rebecca Sower Nostalgiques; Mesh: Magic Scraps; Font: Two Peas In A Bucket Jones Neighborhood

Today I Am Four

Supplies – Cardstock: Bazzill;
Mesh: Magic Mesh; Brads:
Embellish This; Font: Two Peas
In A Bucket Silly

Construction Tips:

Use mesh as a border to add
a lot of texture without bulk.

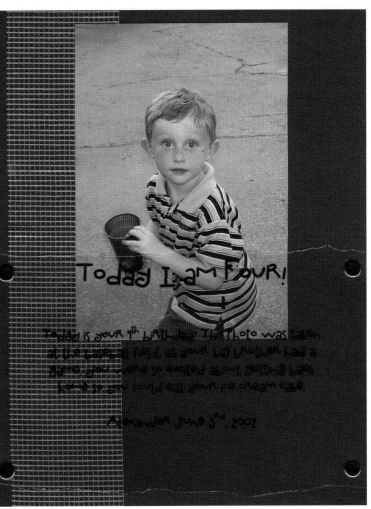

Designer: Jbyne Hanback

Designer: Dee Gallimore-Perry

The Beauty Of Life

Supplies – Textured Paper: Artistic Scrapper; Cardstock:
Bazzill; Netting: Magic Scraps; Starfish: U.S. Shell, Inc.;
Embossing Powder: Ranger; Charm: Embellish It;
Metallic Rub-ons: Craf-T; Tag: Avery; Star: Provo Craft;
Stamps: PSX, Hero Arts; Stamp Pad: Excelsior

Construction Tips:

1. Cut mesh, distress by tearing
   some areas of the mesh and
   adhere to layout.
2. Create bronze portion of tag
   by crumpling beige cardstock, applying metallic rub-
   on and heat embossing with
   bronze embossing powder.

23

shabby Chic

Shabby chic is for all of you who like an antique feel with a fresh twist. It combines the old and new to form a contemporary feel. You can create a shabby chic look by antiquing and distressing your new photos and accents or by combining your old photos and accents with the new. No matter how you create your fresh, vintage look, enjoy the many possibilities of shabby chic.

Happy Hearts

Supplies — Stamps: PSX; Metallic Rub-ons: Craf-T; Nail Heads: Jewel Craft

Construction Tips:

1. Create distressed paper by crumpling and applying metallic rub-ons and ink to the paper.
2. Create 'hearts' portion of title by stamping letters onto tan cardstock, cutting out and adhering to layout. Adhere round page pebbles atop stamped letters.

Designer: Janna Wilson

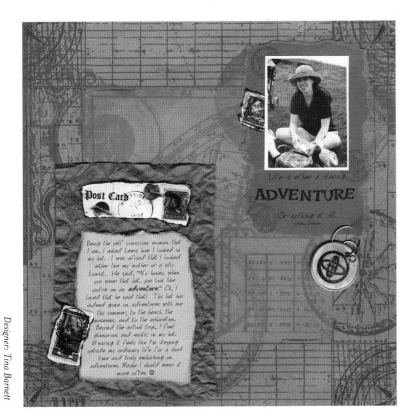

Designer: Tina Barnett

Adventure Hat

Supplies – Patterned Paper: Club Scrap;
Cardstock: Club Scrap; Stamps: Stamp Craft, Club
Scrap; Cutouts: Rebecca Sower; Ink: Vivid!,
Making Memories, Versamark; Chalk: Craf-T

Construction Tips:

Create aged mat by wetting
and crumpling tan card-
stock. When the cardstock
is dry, flatten and chalk.

Construction Tips:

Repeat elements throughout
your layout, such as the mesh,
to pull the page together.

The Smoking Bride

Supplies – Patterned Paper: Paper
Illusions; Netting: Magic Scraps; Stickers:
K & Co., Rebecca Sower; Ribbon: Close
To My Heart; Frame: Anna Griffin Designs

Designer: Sherrill Ghilardi Pierre

25

focus

Focused scrapbook pages really tell a story about a child or event. The photos and journaling take you back to the very moment the page is documenting. Try adding focus to your pages by compiling similar photos onto one layout or by making the background simple to draw attention to the photos and journaling.

Experiencing life's little moments with you is experiencing them for the first time.

Designer: Gina Bergman

Life's Little Moments

Supplies - Patterned Paper: NRN Designs;
Cardstock: National Cardstock; Fiber: Ties
That Bind; Metal Clip: Making Memories;
Wax Seals: Sonnets; Chalk: EK Success;
Brads: Doodlebug; Font: BethsCute HMK

Construction Tips:

1. Match layout colors with the colors in the photo.
2. Adhere fibers to layout with mini glue dots.
3. Place large photos in a row across your layout to keep the focus on the photos.

Andrew, don't move, I need to wash your feet

How lucky am I to get a picture of this? Alex, I've always known that you loved your little brother, but what a joy for me to see you care for him in this way. And, when you told Andrew to stand still while you carefully washed the dirt off his feet, it was the first time that I really saw your father in you.

Love you both very much,

Mom

Don't Move!

Supplies – Stickers: Rebecca Sowers Nostalgique; Fonts: CK Gutenberg, CK Typeset

Construction Tips:
Crop and enlarge photos to emphasize the event being described.

● Please, Andrew ●

Pleeeease, Andrew

Supplies – Cardstock: Bazzill; Punch: Marvy; Beaded Chain: Making Memories

Construction Tips:
Crop the photos to show different parts of the body and to add focus to your subject.

Pleeeease, Andrew, just one picture ●

My dear little Andrew,

Sometimes, I don't know why I even try. It doesn't matter how determined I am to take your picture, you are MORE determined to NOT take a picture. It must look pretty silly seeing a grown woman chase a little boy around the front yard with a camera, begging him to take a picture. Well, one day, I'm going to truly enjoy showing these pictures to YOUR kids, and I'll say "See this silly little boy? That's your dad!"

I love you, Andrew.

Mom

● Please, Andrew ●   ● Don't move ●   ● Please ●

● Just one picture ●   ● No, no, don't move ●   ● Pleeease ●

Designer: Tammy Mellish

Diva In Shades

Supplies – Cardstock: Bazzill; Page
Pebbles: Making Memories

Construction Tips:

Use neutral colors for the
background. Enlarge and crop
photos in different shapes to
make the photos stand out.

Hot Summer Days

Supplies – Patterned Paper:
Wordsworth; Letters: Making
Memories, Simply Stated; Ink:
Close To My Heart

Construction Tips:

Choose a favorite
photo and create a
layout to enhance it.

Designer: Sherrill Ghilardi Pierre

Collage

Collage is often used in creating scrapbook pages. We were probably all given assignments in grade school to make a collage of some sort or another, but who knew how beautiful and fun they could be? Collages are not just a collection of magazine cutouts pasted onto a piece of cardboard; they are a collection of any items you wish. Many scrapbook backgrounds are created from a collage of different pieces of cardstock, paper and fabric. Try creating a collage of photos, paper or embellishments on your next scrapbook page.

Designer: Dawn McDowell

Construction Tips:
Crumple the bandana paper over and over again until it feels like fabric.

Ride Em, Partner

Supplies — Patterned Paper: Paperbilities; Cow Accent: Foofala; Rivet: Chatterbox; Ink: Ranger; Stamps: Hero Arts

Believe In Yourself

Supplies — Patterned Paper: Sarah Lugg, 7 Gypsies; Frame Charm: 7 Gypsies; Tag: Rusty Pickle; Skeleton Leaf: Lacey Paper Co.; Rub-ons: Making Memories; Frames: K & Co.; Label Holder: Making Memories; Clips and Rings: Making Memories; Bubble and Script Words: K & Co.; Clear Tag: K & Co.; Fiber Scraps: Bazzill; Glue Dots: Glue Dots International; Font: Microsoft Mistral

The World Is Before You

Supplies – Patterned Paper: Wordsworth, Karen Foster; Cardstock: Bazzill; Ink: Close to My Heart; Letters: Making Memories

Construction Tips:
When creating a collage use memorabilia items such as a copy of a birth certificate.

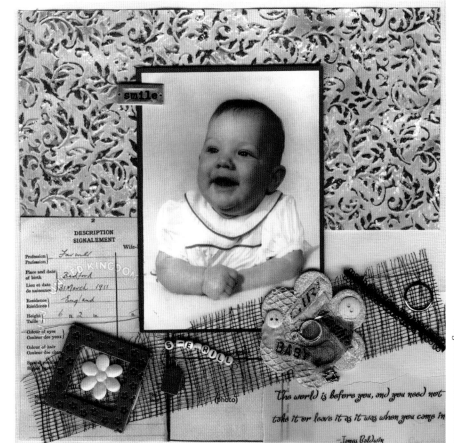

Designer: Sherrill Ghilardi Pierre

Designer: Sharon Laakkonen

Construction Tips:
1. Carry photo and strips of paper over centerline of two-page spread to make it look like one page.
2. Replace the fibers that come with the tag to colors that coordinate with the page.
3. Use metallic rub-ons for corners to give them a gold tone.

31

ixed Media

Create a mixed media look on your scrapbook pages by combining different arts and craft media. On your next layout try using stitching, stamping, inking, and embossing. It is fun to combine elements on a page that people do not expect to see together.

Designer: Ellen Bentley

Scrapbooking

Supplies – Patterned Paper: K & Co., Rocky Mountain Paper Co.; Stickers: NRN Designs; Letters: Foofala, Flavia, Sticko, Creative Imaginations; Quick Kutz: Mini Marissa; Stamps: Hero Arts

Flower Girls

Supplies – Patterned Paper: Bo Bunny, Paper Adventures, The Paper Company; Cardstock: National Cardstock; Tags: Making Memories; Floss: DMC; Flowers: Jolee's By You, My Mind's Eye; Page Pebbles: Making Memories; Eyelets: Making Memories

Look At This Face

Supplies – Patterned Paper: Terri Martin, Creative Imaginations; Transparency: HP; Buttons: Making Memories; Buttons: Making Memories; Bamboo Clips: All The Extras; Tag: KI Memories; Metal Heart: Making Memories; Pink Heart: Foofala; Font: Good Dog Plain

Look at this face

Sometimes I wonder what goes through a four year olds brain. I bet it is "what am I going to play next, Power Rangers or Spiderman or Hulk" or "I want to run, hide, no I want to eat, no I want to roller blade or swim" May you always have simple and happy thoughts.

october 2, 2003

dream ♥ believe

Designer: Martha Crowther

Construction Tips:
Choosing paper that expresses your theme is a great way to save time.

Designer: Dezda Wengler

Construction Tips:
Sew frames and borders with a decorative sewing machine stitch to add a home made feel to a layout.

33

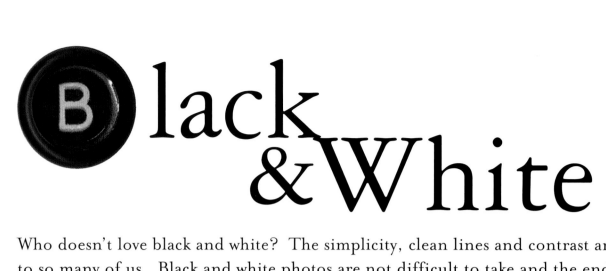

Black & White

Who doesn't love black and white? The simplicity, clean lines and contrast are appealing to so many of us. Black and white photos are not difficult to take and the end result is great. A tip for beginning photographers: keep the backgrounds simple and crop in close to the subject. Black and white is always classy and always in style.

"Know how much I love you mommy?

As big as the sky and more den anyfing

Dat's how much I love you-

As told by Baylee, 3 ½ , Spring 2002

Designer: Sheila Riddle

More 'Den Anyfing'

Supplies – Charm: Making Memories; Font: CK

34

Paparazzi

Supplies – Cardstock: Bazzill; Floss: DMC; Eyelets: Making Memories; Clothespin: Ellsworth Hall; Stamp: 2000 Plus

Construction Tips:

1. Hang the photos and subtitle to give the layout a darkroom feel.
2. Place three photos in a strip with eyelets to look like a film negative.

Designer: Tarri Botwinski

Designer: Martha Crowther

Photo Shoot

Supplies – Patterned Paper: Rusty Pickles; Transparency: HP; Fonts: Two Peas In A Bucket Blissful, Stamp Act

Construction Tips:

Place more photos on a layout by dividing a page into equal sections. Each section can be used for journaling, photos or an embellishment.

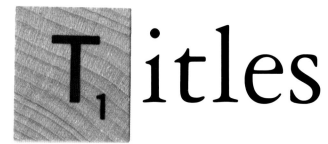

Titles

Titles say so much. They can be long or portray the theme of a page in one word. Take the time to think about what to title your page. They don't need to be cute or elegant, just exactly what you want.

Designer: Jennifer Bourgeault

During a mini photo shoot with Connor, he kept asking me, "what froggy doing?" It seems to be the question of the day...every day! Of course, froggy can be replaced with just about anything. But more often than not, it's mama, daddy, woof-woof and guy. Even though we have to answer the same question over and over again, I know that he is listening to us and learning so much about the world around him. I love that he is so curious about everything and everyone in sight!

july '03

Construction Tips:

Create a title strip that runs across the top, bottom or side of a lay-out. Use jump rings to attach punches that match the theme.

What Froggy Doing

Supplies – Patterned Paper: Magenta, Bo Bunny; Bookplate: Making Memories; Punch: Marvy; Jump Rings: Making Memories; Brads: Making Memories; Floss: DMC; Font: Times New Roman, Two Peas In A Bucket Falling Leaves

Construction Tips:

Scan large photo and use a soft-ware program to duplicate and change the color of the photo.

Original

Supplies – Patterned Paper: Rusty Pickles; Eyelets: Making Memories; Computer Program: Scrapbook Factory; Adhesive: Xyron; Glue: Tombo; Font: CK Typewriter

36

Home Is Where The Army Sends You

Supplies — Patterned Paper: Leisure Arts; Eyelet Letters: Making Memories; Alphabet Beads: Making Memories; Scrabble Tiles: Making Memories; Stickers: David Walker; Punches: Creative Memories, EK Success

Construction Tips:

Create titles using a variety of letter media. Combining the different media will give an interesting look to a page.

7 Wonders Of The World

Supplies — Border Stickers: Club Scraps; Fiber: All The Extras; Charm: All The Extras; Letter Stickers: David Walker, Sonnetts, Treehouse Design, Making Memories, Rebecca Sowers Nostalgique; Poemstone: Sonnets

Construction Tips:

1. Create crayon rubbing by placing white paper over a piece of embossed hieroglyphic cardstock and rubbing with a crayon.
2. The title is from a story where a teacher asks children to list the seven wonders of the world. One girl's response was: touch, love, laugh, taste, see, hear, and feel.

37

U nderstated Color

Understated color gives an easy, restful feel to a layout. They are easy to look at and a nice break from busier, more colorful pages. Monochromatic pages are often understated and reflective of the moment they are documenting. Mix things up in your scrapbook by adding some understated color pages. You will be pleased with the results.

Construction Tips:
Use an oversized frame to give a small photo substance.

Forever Friends

Supplies – Cardstock: Bazzill; Frame: This & That; Metals: Making Memories

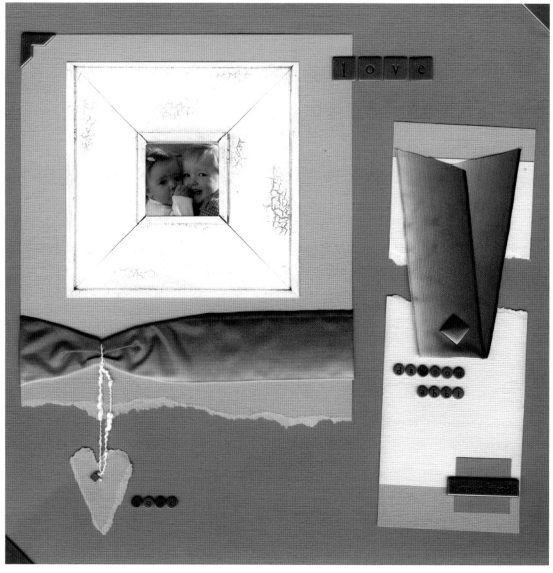

Designer: Jodi Sanford

His Laugh Is Contagious

Supplies – Cardstock: Bazzill; Punches: Paper Shapers; Stamps: Making Memories; Pencils: Primsicolor; Metal Frame: Making Memories; Fonts: Kayleigh, Times New Roman

Construction Tips:

Create a different look by placing photos at the edge of your layout without mats.

JOSEPH DAVID

LOVING   SPIRITED   HAPPY   ADORABLE   CAREFREE

...five words to describe Joseph.
His laugh is contagious, his hugs are
irreplaceable and his smiles are
unforgettable.

APR 2003

Designer: Tracy A. Weinzapfel Burgos

Construction Tips:

A great layout can be made with nothing more than paper and vellum.

Sometimes

Supplies – Cardstock: Making Memories; Tinted Pens: Spot Pens

SOMETIMES...
Let's just blow bubbles,
For no good reason
Let's just blow bubbles
Laugh a little, watch them disappear
Not even wonder where,
Smile and touch the rainbow colors
Watch them float in the air.
No reason why-
No goals, no structure.

SOMETIMES...
Let's just
Blow bubbles

Unknown

Kelly Mieko Nakandakari

Summer 2000

Designer: Brenda Nakandakari

39

ranslucent

So many different looks can be created with translucent paper. Vellum comes in different colors and patterns and transparencies are available, too. Use vellum to create the look of water or to make the background of a photo fade away. Translucent mediums are great for titles and journaling as well.

MY GUYS

My three most favorite guys in the whole world are my beautiful son, Brendan my loving husband, Rob, and my wonderful father, Jack. After a game of miniature golf, The guys decided to take a stroll along the beach while Mimi and Mommy watched from the boardwalk. August 2002

OCEAN BEACH

My Guys

Supplies – Stamps: PSX; Shells: U.S. Shell, Inc.; Metal-Rimmed Tag: Making Memories; Glue Dots: Glue Dots International; Font: P22 Type Foundry Garamouche

Construction Tips:

Cut out holes in the vellum for the subject of the photos to show through. Stitch the vellum to the background.

Bucking Bronco

Supplies – Patterned Paper: Leisure Arts; Cardstock: DCWV; Vellum: DCWV; Rubons: Craf-T Products, Inc.; Frames: Leisure Arts; Leather: Dritz

Construction Tips:

Scan a photo into a software program and print onto a sheet of vellum. Tear the edges and mat with tan cardstock.

Our Buckaroo

The world is but a canvas to the Imagination

Snow in the Park

Kassidy

DEC 0 2 2002

No time like

Snow time

Snow In The Park

Supplies – Patterned Paper: Leisure
Arts; Vellum: Leisure Arts;
Snowflake Brads: Making Memories;
Charms: Leisure Arts; Stickers:
Leisure Arts; Font: CK Elusive

Construction Tips:
Attach torn vellum to
the bottom of a layout
to mimic snow.

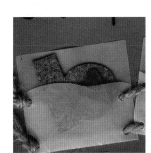

Carpenteria Beach

Supplies – Cardstock: Bazzill; Picture Pebble:
Two Peas In A Bucket; Sea Shells: Magic
Scraps

Construction Tips:

Cut vellum into rectangles, fold
and punch holes to thread jute
through. Cut out corkboard
title with a template and place
into vellum pockets with sea glass
and a sand dollar.

Carpenteria

Summer
of
1999

Photo Manipulation

Manipulating photos is a favorite way to add variety to scrapbook pages. Image transfers, hand tinting, laminating, embossing, cropping and cutting are just a few ways to enhance your photos. This technique produces a lot of impact for your effort, so try new things and see how you can enhance your photos.

Construction Tips:
Use a photo manipulation program to print photos in different forms (artistic, brush strokes, stylized, etc.).

Construction Tips:

Enlarge a photo and crop different sections of the photo. Mat each section and then reassemble the photo.

Designer: Camille Jensen

Girl's Day Out

Supplies – Patterned Paper: Leisure Arts; Cardstock: DCWV; Vellum: DCWV, Leisure Arts; Stickers: Leisure Arts; Brads: Making Memories

43

Pick Of The Patch

Supplies – Patterned Paper: Leisure Arts; Cardstock: DCWV; Leaves: Family Treasures; Square Punches: Family Treasures; Stamps: Hero Arts, Simply Stamps; Beads: Provo Craft; Embossing Powder: Suze Weinberg; Concho: Scrapworks

Construction Tips:

Punch out squares of a double print. Adhere over the same spot on the original photo with pop dots.

Designer: Camille Jensen

44

Children look at the world with their perfect little hearts
Children are gifts to be treasured, which need to be shown love, patience, and fairness, that their value is known. They need freedom to grow, but with a strong guiding hand, to learn honesty, courage, and when to take a stand. Encouragement and praise should be directed their way, so dreams can be reached and goals accomplished each day. September 12, 2003

Children Are Gifts To Be Treasured

Supplies – Patterned Paper: Terri Martin, Creative Imaginations; Transparency: HP; Metal Trinkets: Lil' Davis Designs; Font: Bottled Fart

Construction Tips:
Give the impression of a larger photo by cutting the edge of a photo into strips. Keep the strips in order and reassemble the photo leaving space between each strip.

The Wild Child

Construction Tips:
Hand tint a black and white photo to add as much color as you like.

Designer: Vickie McMillan

45

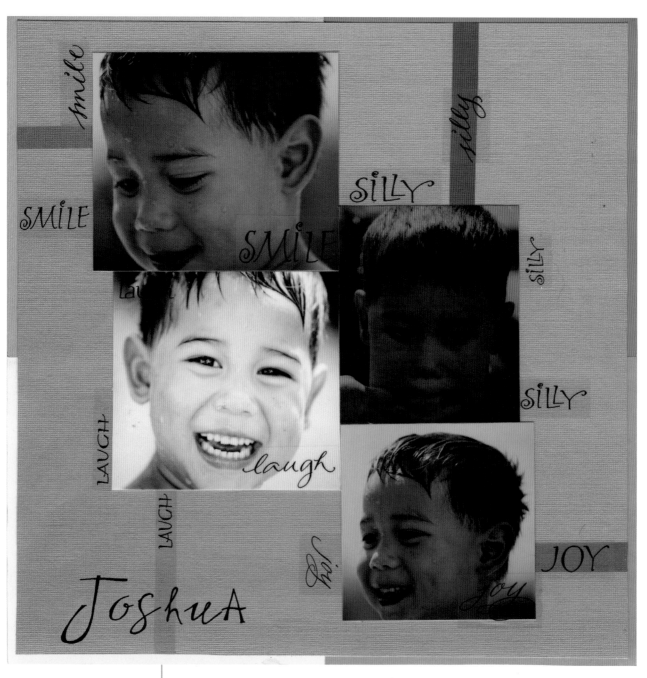

Designer: Sherrill Ghilardi Pierre

Silly, Silly Joshua

Supplies - Cardstock: Bazzill; Stickers: Bo Bunny; Title: Making Memories; Laminate Sheets: Xyron

Construction Tips:
Apply colored laminate sheets to photos with a Xyron Machine.

Mud

Supplies – Title: Wordsworth; Fiber: Fibers By The Yard

Construction Tips:

Create a title background from scrap pieces of photos cut into strips.

The spring mud combined with an odd assortment of clothes to produce this little urchin girl in our backyard. Jaimee was excited to dress herself and venture into the warmer weather.   3/03

Designer: Jane Swanson

Nana's Girls

Supplies – Patterned Paper: Leisure Arts, Made To Match; Mesh: Scrapbook Diva; Font: CK Hustle

Construction Tips:

Adhere ribbon to the edges of the cropped photo and as a border for the layout.

Color

Nothing can grab your attention quite like color. Using lots of color is fitting for joyous occasions, holidays and celebrations. Can you think of a better way to communicate a child's joyful personality on a scrapbook page than color? Don't be afraid to be bold and use the colors you love.

Designer: Janna Wilson

Construction Tips:
Bring a page together by choosing colors for a layout from the colors in the photos.

Sip Of Summer

Supplies – Patterned Paper: Leaving Prints, All About Me Co.; Vellum: The Paper Company; Metal Charms: Maki Memories; Brads: Making Memories; Title: Creative Imaginations; Photo Corners: I & Co.; Font: CK Summer

Designer: Dezda Wenglar

All Girl

Supplies – Patterned Paper: Bazzill; Cardstock: National Cardstock; Gingham: This & That; Buttons: This & That; Eyelets: Doodlebug; Beads: Bead

Construction Tips:

Cover enlarged photo with clear contact paper, dip it in water and gently rub paper off the back of the photo. The resulting image should be transparent. Lightly sand the edges and adhere to the background.

Designer: Ashley Smith

SEP 2 2 2003

Daphne, Pigtails And Cade

Supplies – Patterned Paper: Leisure Arts; Label Holder: Making Memories; Font: CK Curly

Construction Tips:

Triple matting photos with different colors is a great way to add color to a layout.

49

Journaling

Journaling is used on almost every scrapbook page. It says what the photos cannot, like your feelings when you took the photo, the details of special events or even the date. Having children write their own journaling is a fun idea. They will be able to look back at the pages and be amazed at how their handwriting and spelling abilities have changed over the years. Hide journaling behind a tag or in a booklet if you would like to write your thoughts but don't want to share them with every person who looks at your scrapbook. You will be glad you took the time to add journaling to your page as your loved ones cherish what you have written, now and in the future.

Pucker up

Here come Abby's lips! And isn't this her color?! We didn't have to worry about it smudging off everywhere because she was so smart and used the "stay on" formula! These moments are priceless!
-June 2003-

Construction Tips:

Handwrite title onto cardstock with black chalk pencil. Blend colors together with a brush pen and then go over letters with a medium fine black pen.

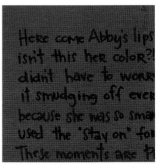

Here come Abby's lips
isn't this her color?!
didn't have to worr
it smudging off ever
because she was so smar
used the "stay on" for
These moments are t

Pucker Up

Supplies – Cardstock: Bazzill, DMD; Vellum: Treehouse Designs, Inc.; Pens: Zig, Sakura; Nail Heads: Jewel Craft; Fibers: Adornments; Tag: Making Memories; Ink: Crafters

Designer: Janna Wilson

Designer: Ashley Smith

Rock Star

Supplies – Patterned Paper: Leisure Arts;
Tags: Leisure Arts; Font: CK Child's Play

Construction Tips:
Create pockets behind
photos to hide journaling.

Merry And Bright

Supplies – Patterned Paper: Leisure Arts;
Frames: Leisure Arts; Rub-on: Making
Memories; Clips: Making Memories; Labels:
Me & My Big Ideas; Font: CK Curly

Construction Tips:
Select a few images that capture the event
you are scrapbooking, then describe the
event in detail with the journaling.

Designer: Ashley Smith

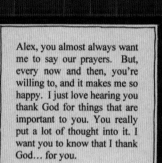

Alex, you almost always want me to say our prayers. But, every now and then, you're willing to, and it makes me so happy. I just love hearing you thank God for things that are important to you. You really put a lot of thought into it. I want you to know that I thank God... for you.

I love you, Alex.

Mom

Designer: Leah Fung

I Thank God For You Too

Supplies — Patterned Paper: K & Co.; Eyelets:
Making Memories; Font: Times New Roman

Construction Tips:

Create journaling by matting child's handwritten paper to the bottom half of a folded piece of black cardstock. Adhere the photo to the top of the other half of the black cardstock, so the photo will lift to reveal the journaling underneath.

Designer: Renee Villalobos–Campa

Family Time Together

Supplies – Patterned Paper: Scrap Ease; Cardstock: Bazzill; Eyelets: Making Memories; Floss: DMC; Die Cut System: Sizzix Fun Serif; Font: Little Trouble Girl

Construction Tips:

Create booklets by folding cardstock in half. Give the look of hinges with eyelets.

Dad took the day off from work so we could go to the Madison Zoo with Cook, Melissa, & Jena. It was such a hot day we had to keep splashing water on you to keep you cool. Except for your bright red cheeks, the heat hardly bothered you kids.

Michael loved feeding the goats pellets from an ice cream cone. The 1st time he tried it, the goat was too quick and ate the entire cone, pellets and all. Michael was so broken hearted; we had to let him buy another cone of pellets. That time he was prepared. Michael was crazy about the wild chipmunks. He crumbled up graham crackers on the ground and watched as they eagerly scurried to the crumbly feast.

Hunter was just happy to be out and about. He was wide-eyed; taking in all of the new sights and sounds.

My favorite thing about the day was the day itself. Spending family time together, with my 3 men, means everything to me.

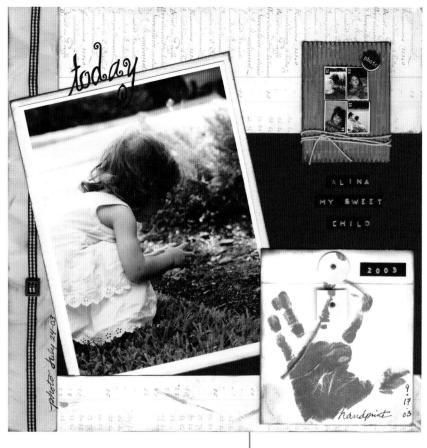

Designer: Anna Estrada Davison

Today, My Sweet Child

Supplies – Patterned Paper: 7 Gypsies; Stickers: Sonnets; Buckle
Charm: Making Memories; Concho: 7 Gypsies; Folding Tag: Paper
Impressions; Ink Pad: Colorbok; Label Maker: Dymo

Construction Tips:

1. Have child press hand into
   chalk inkpad and then onto
   cardstock to create handprint.
2. Use the index print from the
   developer to make a nice, little
   group of photos.

Like A Rock

Supplies – Patterned Paper: Made
To Match; Tag: Paper Loft; Fiber:
Fibers By The Yard; Rub-on:
Making Memories; Metal Word:
Li'l Davis Designs

Construction Tips:

Print journaling onto
vellum, tear the edges
and apply chalk.

54

Designer: Gabrielle Mader

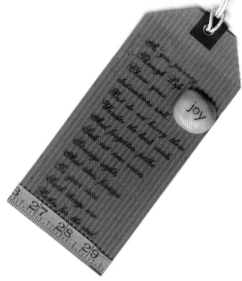

Joyful Journey

Supplies – Patterned Paper: Colorbok; Cardstock: Bazzill; Stamp: Close To
My Heart; Charm: 7 Gypsies; Stickers: Rebecca Sower Nostalgiques

Dance, Cry, Sing

Supplies – Patterned Paper: Design Originals, Rusty Pickle;
Stickers: Sonnets; Photo Corners: Canson; Chain: Making
Memories; Heart Clip: Making Memories; Metal Words:
Making Memories; Buttons: Dress It Up; Stamps: Hero
Arts; Ric-Rac: Memory Lane Paper Co.; Ribbon: May Arts;
Fibers: Rubba Dub Dub, Inc., Art Sanctum; Fonts: Two
Peas In A Bucket Chestnuts, Straight-up, Microsoft
Reference Serif

Designer: Jodi Sanford

Metals

Metals add texture, shine and interest to a page. So many metal embellishments are available to the scrapbooker: metal rimmed tags, brads, eyelets, letters, frames, etc. Embellish your next layout with metal; you will be amazed at how it can transform a page.

Home Is Where The Heart Is

Supplies – Patterned Paper: K & Co., Karen Foster, Daisy D's; Cardstock: Bazzill; Wire: Making Memories; Buttons: Making Memories; Date Stamp: Making Memories; Font: Two Peas In A Bucket Recital

Construction Tips:
1. Create script paper by typing Samuel Woodworth quote repeatedly and printing onto paper.
2. Attach hinges to paper with gold wire.

Designer: Tammy Mellish

Designer: Yasmin Mitchell

Beating The Heat

Supplies – Cardstock: Bazzill;
Vellum: Paper Reflections; Metal
Letters: Making Memories; Circle
Tags: Making Memories;
Poemstones: Sonnets

Construction Tips:

Soak metal tags in water for
a short time to remove the
paper centers easily.

Designer: Angela Marvel

The Most Beautiful Wedding

Supplies – Fiber: Fibers By The Yard; Font:
Two Peas In A Bucket Ringlet

Construction Tips:

Weave wire through
the alphabet letters
in addition to the
floss to keep the let-
ters in place.

Tying It All Together

We love to use fiber and threads in our scrapbook pages to tie everything together. Not only are fibers and threads a great finishing touch to a layout, but they also add texture and color to a page. Use any fiber you can think of from fishing line to raffia to leather to yarn.

It's A Tie Game

Supplies – Patterned Paper: Leisure Arts; Cardstock: DCWV; Walnut Ink: 7 Gypsies; Stamps: Hero Arts; Mesh: Magenta; Fibers: DMC; Crackle Paint: Folk Art; Acrylic Paint: Delta; Baseball Snap: 7 Gypsies

Construction Tips:
Crackle paint frame and ink when dried.

Partners In Grime

Supplies – Transparencies: Clearly Creative; Circle Clips: Making Memories; Fiber: Fibers By The Yard; Fonts: Two Peas In A Bucket Brownies, Two Peas In A Bucket Chatter

Construction Tips:
Use fiber to outline photo and title words.

Designer: Martha Crowther

Designer: Valerie Barton

Little Cowboy

Supplies – Patterned Paper: Paper Loft, Club Scrap; Corrugated Cardboard: Paper Reflections; Star Brads: Magic Scraps; Transparency: Pockets On A Roll; Netting: Magic Scraps; Font: Stagecoach

Construction Tips:
Make a color copy of a toy gun and belt to use in the collage layout.

59

We spent Mother's Day weekend on Long Beach Island. The weather was gorgeous and we stayed at The Engleside Inn in Beach Haven. They had recently redone the rooms, so they were extra nice. We went on the beach, ate at Uncle Will's for breakfast, and took a ride up to Barnegat Lighthouse. It was windy, but warm with sunny, blue skies. Julia was obsessed with picking up tons of little rocks and since Grace was only 9 months old, she was content to hang out in her stroller. But she did try to crawl away from us on the beach! Julia even got to swim in the pool at the hotel which made her very happy. It was a really nice weekend! May 2001

Weekend At The Beach

Supplies – Patterned Vellum: EK Success;
Fiber: Brown Bag Fibers; Metal Snaps: Making
Memories; Paper Crimper: Fiskars; Font:
Creating Keepsakes

Construction Tips:

1. Use the white space on the light-house photo to add journaling.
2. Running paper through a crimper adds subtle texture.
3. Create mock photo hangers with fiber and clip rings.

Cherish

Supplies – Patterned Paper: Paperbilities; Eyelets: Creative Imaginations; Rub-on: Making Memories; Shell Charm: All The Extras; Font: Two Peas In A Bucket Blissful

Construction Tips:

1. Tape-Transfer Method:
   a. Place packing tape on top of script paper, making sure the tape is secure and there are no bubbles.
   b. Run taped paper under warm water while rubbing the back of the paper. The paper will come off and the print will remain on the tape.
   c. Quickly stick the tape onto colored paper and peel off to leave traces of color.
   d. Adhere tape to layout.
2. Braid leather strips together to create a nice accent.

Designer: Sam Cousins

Warm

Supplies – Cardstock: Paper Garden; Stickers: Karen Foster; Key: Jolee's By You; Fiber: EK Success; Tag: Making Memories; Button: Making Memories; Glue Pen: EK Success

Construction Tips:

This technique looks best with different types of fibers. Because the border is small, it is easy to use leftover scraps of fibers.

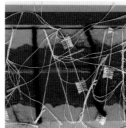

 # titching

Stitching is a creative way to accent pages. You can hand stitch with a needle and thread or use a sewing machine. Stitching can be used functionally or decoratively for embellishments, letters, borders, etc. Make stitching as understated or overstated as you wish.

Jordan - April 2004

Jordan... I love these pictures of you. On this spring morning, I wasn't even planning on taking pictures, but you were full of smiles and you were acting so funny that I thought I would give it a try. The flowers in front of the house were in full bloom and you were the perfect little model with your cowboy hat on. Once again, you filled my day with wonder, like you always do. I am so lucky to have you in my life — I love you!

Designer: Ashley Smith

You Filled My Day With Wonder

Supplies – Patterned Paper: Leisure Arts; Font: CK Hustle

Construction Tips:
Draw flower shape onto back of cardstock. Punch holes for the fibers to go through and stitch with a needle and thread.

Beauty In The Little Things

Supplies – Cardstock: DMD Designs; Vellum: DMD Designs; Thread: DMC; Label: Making Memories; Eyelets: Making Memories; Snowman Charm: Making Memories; Snowflake Charms: Mill Hill Crystal Treasures; Wire: Artistic Wire; Wire Mesh: Paragona; Glass Beads: Create-A-Craft; Fonts: St. Charles, Scrawl of the Chief, Libby Script

Construction Tips:

Draw snowflakes with pencil onto the background. Stitch clear beads to the layout with silver thread.

IT IS NO **WONDER** THAT WE SEE BEAUTY IN THE LITTLE THINGS

January 2000

Designer: Wendy Woodby

secrets secrets secrets

best FRIENDS brother best friends boys

SAM AND JOSH

Secrets

Supplies – Patterned Paper: Rusty Pickle; Twill Strip: 7 Gypsies; Letter Stickers: Rebecca Sower Nostalgiques; Mesh: Magic Mesh

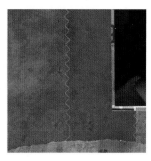

Construction Tips:

Section your layout with zig-zag stitches.

Paper Piecing

Paper piecing is a fun way to add color and design elements to your background. Piecing can also use up those scrap pieces of paper you have been collecting. Don't forget to curl, distress and tear your paper before piecing it together.

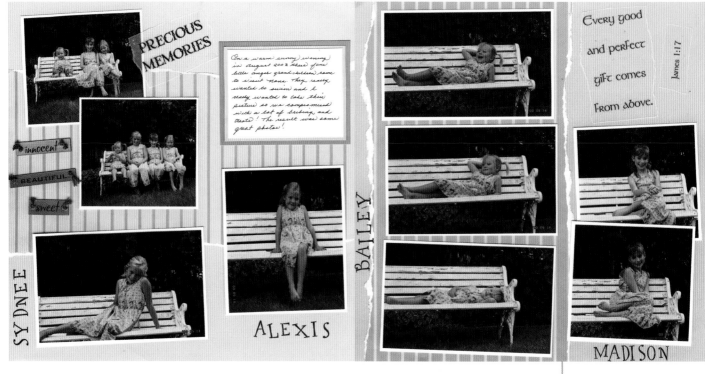

Designer: Ashley Smith

Precious Memories

Supplies — Patterned Paper: Leisure Arts; Cardstock: DCWV; Metallic Words: DCWV

Construction Tips:
Adhere a large torn strip of patterned paper across a piece of cardstock.

Designer: Wanda E. Santiago

A Boy And A Box

Supplies – Patterned Paper: SEI;
Brads: Magic Scraps

Construction Tips:

1. Have photos developed with special borders to add texture without bulk.
2. Use purchased paper that gives the effect of paper piecing to save time.

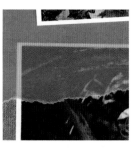

Designer: Ashley Smith

Gray

Supplies – Patterned Paper:
Leisure Arts; Stickers: Leisure Arts

Construction Tips:

Combine torn pieces of vellum and patterned paper. Hide portions of the photo behind the torn vellum.

You're perfect the way you are

Designer: Sherril Ghilardi Pierre

You're Perfect The Way You Are

Supplies – Patterned Paper: 7 Gypsies, Artistic Enhancements; Cardstock: Bazzill; Letters: Making Memories; Ribbon: Close to My Heart; Netting: Magic Scraps; Square with Heart: Foofala; Laminate Sheet: Xyron

Construction Tips:

1. Laminate by running photo with a textured sheet of laminate through a Xyron machine.
2. Offset similar patterned paper with a solid piece of cardstock.

Godspeed Little Man

Supplies – Cardstock: WhirlWin; Vellum: Stampin' Up; Fibers: Fibers By The Yard

Construction Tips:

1. Type words from Dixie Chick's song "Godspeed" and print onto vellum for journaling.
2. Create embellishments for a layout by tearing and piecing scrap pieces of paper together.

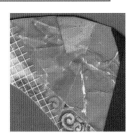

Designer: Stephanie Welsh

Designer: Camille Jensen

Maddie

Supplies – Patterned Paper: Leisure Arts; Cardstock: Bazzill; Conchos: Scrap Works; Punches: EK Success; Buttons: Dress It Up; Floss: Scrap Works; Metal Charms: Lost Art Treasures

Construction Tips:

Create your own patterned paper by piecing together strips of paper.

Tools

Creating a great scrapbook page can become a whole lot easier if you have the right tools and equipment. We asked some of our best designers to give us a list of the scrapbooking tools they could not live without. Here is their list:

1. Sewing Machine
2. Embossing Powder
3. Buttons
4. Wire
5. Pens/Markers
6. Scrappers' Spray
7. Stamps
8. Eyelets & Brads
9. Felt

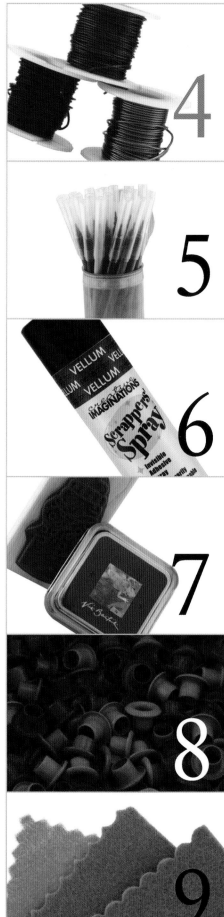

Sources

The following companies manufacture products featured in this section. Please check with your local retail store for these materials. We have made every attempt to identify and give proper credit for the materials used. If by chance we have missed giving the appropriate credit, we would appreciate hearing from you.

3M Stationary
(800) 364-3577 3m.com

7-Gypsies
(800) 588 6707 7gypsies.com

Adornments
adornments.com

Anna Griffin, Inc.
(888) 817-8170 annagriffin.com

Art Sanctum
artsanctum.com

Artistic Scrapper
(818) 786-8304 artisticscrapper.com

Artistic Wire
(630) 530-7567 artisticwire.com

Avery Dennison Corporation
(800) GO-AVERY avery.com

Bazzill Basics Paper
(480) 558-8557 bazzillbasics.com

Bead Heaven
beadheaven.com

Bo-Bunny Press
(801) 771-4010 bobunny.com

Boxer Scrapbook Productions, LLC
(888) 625-6255 or (503) 625-0455 boxerscrapbooks.com

Brown Bag Fibers
brownbagfibers.com

Canson, Inc.
(800) 628-9283 canson-us.com

Chatterbox, Inc.
(888) 416-6260 chatterboxinc.com

Close to My Heart
closetomyheart.com

Club Scrap
(888) 634-9100 clubscrap.com

Colorbok
(800) 366-4660 colorbok.com

Craf-T Products
(800) 530-3410 craf-tproducts.com

Creating Keepsakes Magazine
(888) 247-5282
creatingkeepsakes.com

Creative Imaginations
(800) 942-6487 cigift.com

Creative Memories
(800) 341-5275 creativememories.com

Daisy D's Paper Co.
(888) 601-8955 or (801) 447-9955
daisydotsanddoodles.com

DieCuts With a View
(801) 224-6766 diecutswithaview.com

Design Originals
d-originals.com

DMC
(973) 589-0606 dmc-usa.com

DMD Industries
(800) 805-9890 dmdind.com

Doodlebug Design, Inc.
(801) 524-0050

Dress It Up
dressitup.com

DYMO
(800) 426-7827 dymo.com

EK Success
(800) 524-1349 eksuccess.com

Embellish It
(702) 312-1628 embellishit.com

Eyelets Every Month
eyeletseverymonth.com

Fibers by the Yard
fibersbytheyard.com

Fiskars
(800) 950-0203 fiskars.com

Flavia
(805) 882-2466 flavia.com

FoofaLa
(402) 758-0863 foofala.com

Glue Dots International
gluedots.com

Herma Fix
herma.co.uk.com

Hero Art Rubber Stamps, Inc.
(800) 822-4376 heroarts.com

Hewlett-Packard
hp.com

Hirschberg Schutz & Co.
(800) 543-5442

JewelCraft
(201) 223-0804 jewelcraft.biz

Jolee's By You
jolee'sbyyou.com

K & Company
(888) 244-2083 kandcompany.com

Karen Foster Design
(801) 451-9779 karenfosterdesign.com

KI Memories
(469) 633-9665 kimemories.com

Krylon
(800) 457-9566 krylon.com

Lacey Paper Co.
(877) 775-2239 laceypaper.com

Leave Memories
leavememories.com

Leaving Prints
leavingprints.us

Leisure Arts
(888) 257-7548
business.leisurearts.com

Li'l Davis Designs
(949) 838-0344 lildavisdesigns.com

Magic Mesh
(651) 345-6374 magicmesh.com

Magic Scraps
(972) 238-1838 magicscraps.com

Making Memories
(800) 286-5263
makingmemories.com

Mark Enterprises
(800) 443-3430

Marvy Uchida
(800) 541-5877 uchida.com

May Arts
(800) 442-3950

Me & My Big Ideas
(949) 583-2065
meandmybigideas.com

Memory Lane Paper Co.
(801) 226-1159 memorylanepaper.com

Microsoft
(800) 936-5700 microsoft.com

Mill Hill, Inc.
millhill.com

My Minds Eye
frame-ups.com

National Cardstock
(724) 452-7120
nationalcardstock.com

NRN Designs
nrndesigns.com

P22 Type Foundry
(800) P22-5080 p22.com

Paper Adventures
(800) 727-0699 paperadventures.com

Paper Garden
papergarden.com

Paper Illuzionz
(406) 234-8716 paperilluzionz.com

Paper Impressions
(770) 428-8188 paperimpressions.com

Paper Loft
(909) 694-4420 thepaperloft.com

Paper Reflections
dmdind.com

Pockets On A Roll
pocketsonaroll.com

Provo Craft
(888) 577-3545 provocraft.com

PSX
(800) 782-6748 psxdesign.com

Quickutz
(888) 702-1146 quickutz.com

Ranger Industries
(800) 244-2211 rangerink.com

Rebecca Sower Nostalgiques
mississippipaperarts.com

Rubba Dub Dub, Inc.
(209) 763-2766
artsanctum.com/rubbadubdubhome.html

Sakura Of America
(800) 776-6527 gellyroll.com

Sarah Lugg
sarahlugg.com

Scrap-Ease
(800) 274-3876

Scrapbook Diva
(619) 235-6789 ext. 111 scrapbookdiva.com

Scrapbook Factory Outlet
(800) 739-7277 sfodirect.com

SEI, Inc.
(800) 333-3279 shopsei.com

Sizzix
sizzix.com

Stamp Craft
(08) 8941 1066 stampcraft.com

Stampa Rosa
stamparosa.com

Stampin' Up
(800) 782-6787 stampinup.com

Stamps 'n' Stuff
stampsnstuff.com

Suze Weinberg
(732) 761-2400
schmoozewithsuze.com

The Paper Company
(800) 449-1125 papercompany.com

Tombow
(800) 835-3292 tombowusa.com

Treehouse Designs, Inc.
(877) 372-1109 treehouse-designs.com

Two Peas In A Bucket
twopeasinabucket.com

Un-Du
Un-du.com

U.S. Shell, Inc.
.956.554.4500 usshell.com

What's New, Ltd.
(800) 272-3874 whatsnewltd.com

Wordsworth
(719) 282-3495
wordsworthstamps.com

Xyron
(800) 793-3523 xyron.com

IT'S ALL ABOUT Baby

Get inspired with these great scrapbooking page designs with step-by-step instructions

It's All About Baby

There is very little in this world that parallels the joy that a young child can bring into our lives. With wonder and awe I have gazed adoringly at a brand new baby and have marveled at my child and the miracle of birth. I have counted fingers and toes and kissed little round cheeks and button noses. I have waited eagerly for that first smile, laugh and giggle. And, of course, if I could do it over again, I would never have children, only grandchildren, and they would be allowed to take a bath in 'Nana's' kitchen sink anytime they wished!

It has been said that of all the books we can give our children, the one they will treasure the most will be the one about them. Gathering photos and pages for this section has been a fun project for all of us in the design office. How could we not have fun being surrounded by happy baby photos and scrapbook pages for the past three months?

As we gathered photos, created pages, and reviewed submissions from designers, I found myself focusing not only on the pages, techniques, photography and journaling, but also on the loved ones behind the camera. I thought of those who staged or captured the shots, dressed the child, developed the film, and saved the moment forever with a scrapbook page. I focused on their love of the child and interest in preserving a memory and creating something memorable for the child to look back upon and know they were loved.

It's All About Baby is full of great ideas to help you create memorable pages. This idea section has been designed so you can do some serious "page lifting." We have included detailed descriptions of page construction that can be easily duplicated.

May you find joy in capturing memories of the babies in your life,

Nancy

NANCY M. HILL

Nana & Sydnee

Table of Contents

IT'S ALL ABOUT Birth Day

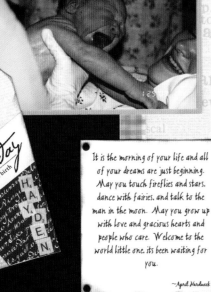

JAN 2 9 2003

It is the morning of your life and all of your dreams are just beginning. May you touch fireflies and stars, dance with fairies, and talk to the man in the moon. May you grow up with love and gracious hearts and people who care. Welcome to the world little one, its been waiting for you.

~April Hardwick

BIRTHDAY

• CREATE BACKGROUND BY ADHERING STRIP OF BABY BLUE PAPER, BLACK WORD PAPER AND BLUE GINGHAM RIBBON TO BLACK TEXTURED CARDSTOCK • MAT PHOTO WITH CARDSTOCK AND ADHERE TO BACKGROUND • PRINT JOURNALING ON CARDSTOCK • ATTACH JOURNALING BLOCK WITH FOUR BLACK BRADS • ADHERE DEFINITION TO LAYOUT • CREATE TAG USING SCRAPS OF PAPER • ADHERE 'BIRTHDAY' DEFINITION • CUT OUT BABY'S NAME USING SCRABBLE LETTER PAPER AND ADHERE TO TAG • CREATE BLACK CIRCLE FOR TAG USING CIRCLE PUNCH AND HOLE PUNCH • RIBBON THROUGH TAG'S HOLE AND TRIM • EMBELLISH TAG WITH CIRCLE CLIP AND CLAY LOVE PEBBLE AND ADHERE TO LAYOUT • STAMP DATE ON SCRAP PIECE OF CARDSTOCK AND ADHERE TO BACKGROUND • INK EDGES OF PAPER, JOURNALING BLOCK, TAG AND DEFINITIONS WITH INK •

SUPPLIES – CARDSTOCK: BAZZILL; PATTERNED PAPER: 7 GYPSIES; INK: CLEARSNAP; CLAY: SCULPEY; STAMP: HERO ARTS; PUNCH: FAMILY TREASURES; DEFINITION TITLE: MAKING MEMORIES; BRADS: AMERICAN TAG; CIRCLE CLIP: MAKING MEMORIES; FONT: TWO PEAS IN A BUCKET BLISSFUL

SPECIAL TIPS:
1. USE A PRE-MADE TAG AS A GUIDE TO MAKE AN EASY CUSTOM TAG. GLUE SEVERAL PAPERS RANDOMLY TO THE TOP AND TRIM AWAY THE EXCESS.
2. MAKE CLAY PEBBLES BY STAMPING DESIGNS AND BAKING AS DIRECTED.

REMEMBER THIS

• BEGIN WITH BLACK CARDSTOCK FOR BACKGROUND • TEAR PHOTO MAT AND PAINT WITH DRY BRUSH TECHNIQUE • MAT PHOTO WITH DRY MAT AND ADHERE TO BACKGROUND • FRAME PHOTO WITH LABELS • FRAME ACCENT PHOTO WITH METAL FRAME • RUB-ON TITLE • STAMP DESIGN WITH FOAM RUBBER STAMP AND ACRYLIC PAINT • ATTACH GINGHAM RIBBON TO LAYOUT WITH STAPLES • ADHERE FRAMED PHOTO WITH METAL GLUE • EMBELLISH WITH METAL PHOTO CORNERS •

SUPPLIES – CARDSTOCK: BAZZILL; STAMP: MICHAEL'S; METAL FRAME: MAKING MEMORIES; TITLE: MAKING MEMORIES; PHOTO CORNERS: MAKING MEMORIES; LABEL MAKER: DYMO

SPECIAL TIPS:
USE A DRY BRUSH TECHNIQUE WHEN USING ACRYLIC PAINTS ON CARDSTOCK. IF THE PAPER WARPS FROM TOO MUCH PAINT, PRESS THE BACKSIDE OF THE CARDSTOCK WITH AN IRON AFTER THE PAINT IS DRY.

Designer: Brandy A. Logan

76

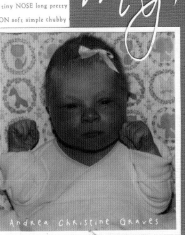

May 12

Andrea Christine Graves

Time: 12:26 am
Hospital: HOLY CROSS
Weight: 8 lbs. 3 oz.
Length: 20 inches
Parents: Terri & Roger
Doctor: L. Dean Day
Pediatrician: Ken Fisher

baby GIRL 1983

Designer: Andrea Graves

BABY GIRL

• CREATE BACKGROUND PAPER BY PRINTING DESCRIPTIVE WORDS IN UPPER AND LOWER CASE • ADHERE COLORED CARDSTOCKS TO PRINTED PAPER • CHANGE BACKGROUND OF BABY PHOTO TO BLACK AND WHITE AND ADD BABY'S NAME TO PHOTO • PRINT OUT PHOTO IN BLACK AND WHITE • ATTACH STICKERS FOR TITLE • PRINT AND CUT OUT DATE AND JOURNALING • TEAR EDGES OF JOURNALING AND ADHERE TO THREE TAGS • ATTACH EYELETS TO EACH TAG AND THREAD WITH WHITE CHENILLE FIBER • CREATE COVER PAGE OF STORY BOOK WITH DESCRIPTIVE WORD PAPER, TEXTURED CARDSTOCK AND MINI PHOTO • CREATE BOOK BY FOLDING A PIECE OF PAPER, INSERTING COVER AND FILLER PAGES AND ATTACHING WITH STAR EYELETS • CUT OUT TWO THIN STRIPS OF CARDSTOCK AND ATTACH TO BACKGROUND WITH BRADS • PENETRATE SURFACE ABOVE STRIPS WITH AN EXACTO KNIFE AND INSERT TAGS • ADHERE THIRD TAG WITH A VELLUM ENVELOPE •

SUPPLIES – CARDSTOCK: BAZZILL; EYELETS: MAKING MEMORIES; STICKERS: SONNET'S; FONT: SCRIPTINA, TWO PEAS IN A BUCKET NEVERMIND, TWO PEAS IN A BUCKET SHACK, TWO PEAS IN A BUCKET SHACK WIDE, TWO PEAS IN A BUCKET COOKIE DOUGH; TWO PEAS IN A BUCKET CHESTNUTS

On the day you were born, the sunlight danced in your hair, stars twinkles in your eyes, the moonbeams kissed your cheeks, and the angels sang your name.

BENJAMIN

• CREATE BACKGROUND BY CUTTING OUT A LARGE SQUARE IN THE CENTER OF PATTERNED PAPER, ADHERING BLUE CARDSTOCK ATOP THE BORDER PIECE AND ADHERING CUT OUT PIECE ATOP THE BLUE CARDSTOCK • ENLARGE AND PRINT PHOTO • CREATE TITLE WITH METAL LETTERS • ATTACH TO BACKGROUND WITH SILVER EYELETS AND FIBERS • PRINT QUOTE ON TRANSPARENCY AND CUT TO FIT PHOTO • EMBELLISH LAYOUT WITH BRADS, LETTER BEAD CHAIN, AND STICKERS •

SUPPLIES – PRINTED PAPER: LEISURE ARTS; EYELET LETTERS: MAKING MEMORIES; BLOCK LETTERS: LEISURE ARTS; BRADS: MAKING MEMORIES; FIBER: FIBERS BY THE YARD; STICKERS: KANGAROO & JOEY

SPECIAL TIP:

PLACE A SPECIAL EMPHASIS ON WORDS BY USING BEADS OR LETTER STICKERS.

IT'S ALL ABOUT
The Lullaby

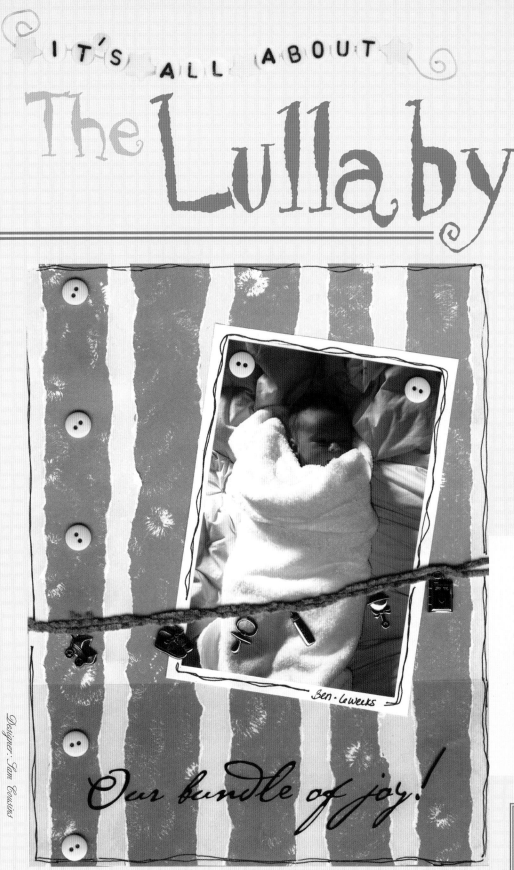

Ben · 6 weeks

Our bundle of joy!

Designer: Jan Coulter

BUNDLE OF JOY

• CREATE BACKGROUND BY ADHERING TORN STRIPS OF YELLOW PAPER TO BLUE PATTERNED PAPER • MAT PHOTO WITH WHITE CARDSTOCK • PRINT TITLE ONTO A TRANSPARENCY AND ADHERE TO BACKGROUND WITH SCRAPPERS SPRAY • WRAP FIBER AROUND LAYOUT • ATTACH BABY CHARMS • ADHERE BUTTONS • OUTLINE PHOTO AND LAYOUT WITH PEN •
SUPPLIES – PAPER: LEISURE ARTS; CHARMS: LEISURE ARTS; FIBER: FIBERS BY THE YARD; BUTTONS: MAKING MEMORIES; FONT: P22 CEZANNE

SPECIAL TIPS:
1. HANDWRITE ONTO A TRANSPARENCY FOR AN EASY ALTERNATIVE TO HANDWRITING DIRECTLY ONTO A PAGE. IF A MISTAKE IS MADE, JUST REPRINT.
2. BUTTONS MAKE A NICE EMBELLISHMENT AND ARE EASY TO FIND.

Designer: MaryDiane Major

GRANDPA AND GRANDMA

• CREATE BACKGROUND BY ADHERING DIAGONALLY RIPPED PATTERNED PAPERS TO A COORDINATING PATTERNED PAPER • MAT AND ADHERE PHOTOS • MAT PRINTED JOURNALING AND ATTACH WITH BRADS • PRINT TAG JOURNALING ON VELLUM • TRIPLE MAT WITH PATTERNED PAPER AND CARDSTOCK • EMBELLISH WITH FIBERS AND CHARMS • SUPPLIES – PATTERNED PAPER: Anna Griffin; BRADS: Doodlebug

SYDNEE AND ISAAC

• BEGIN WITH GREEN PATTERNED PAPER FOR BACKGROUND • MAT PHOTOS WITH GREEN AND BLUE CARDSTOCK • BABY STAMP MATS WITH A WATERMARK PAD • CREATE TITLE BY ATTACHING LETTER STICKERS TO BUTTONS AND ADHERING TO LAYOUT WITH GLUE DOTS • ATTACH LETTER STICKERS TO BLUE AND YELLOW CARDSTOCK TO FINISH TITLE • EMBELLISH LAYOUT WITH STICKERS AND BUTTONS ATTACHED WITH EMBROIDERY FLOSS • SUPPLIES – PATTERNED PAPER: Leisure Arts; STAMP: Imagination; STICKERS: Leisure Arts

IT'S ALL ABOUT Sleep

Designer: Tammy Mellish

'May you never take one single breath for granted'
-Lee Ann Womack

MAY YOU NEVER TAKE ONE SINGLE BREATH FOR GRANTED
• CREATE BACKGROUND BY ADHERING TWO SQUARES OF COORDINATING PAPER TO
A FLOWER PATTERNED PAPER • CHANGE BLACK AND WHITE PHOTO TO SEPIA AND
ENLARGE CROPPED PHOTO TO 5x7 • MAT PHOTO WITH TEXTURED CARDSTOCK AND
GINGHAM PAPER • PRINT LYRICS FROM LEE ANN WOMACK'S SONG ONTO PAT-
TERNED PAPER • ADHERE MATTED PHOTO AND LYRICS TO PAGE • RANDOMLY
ADHERE BUTTONS WITH GLUE DOTS • EMBELLISH WITH RIBBON •
SUPPLIES – PATTERNED PAPER: DAISY D'S, BAZZILL; CARDSTOCK: BAZZILL; BUTTONS:
MAKING MEMORIES

DREAM

- CREATE BACKGROUND FROM TORN PIECES OF CARD-STOCK • PRINT PHOTO ONTO CARDSTOCK USING COMPUTER • MAT PHOTO WITH CARDSTOCK AND MULBERRY PAPER USING POP DOTS • ADHERE TO BACKGROUND • USE STAMPS TO CREATE TITLE • EMBELLISH WITH FIBERS, BUTTONS AND PAGE PEBBLES

SUPPLIES – PAPER: CAROLEE'S CREATIONS; CARDSTOCK: BAZZILL; FIBER: FIBER ACCENTS; BUTTONS: JESSE JAMES & COMPANY; STAMPS: ANITA'S, HERO ARTS; PEBBLES: MAKING MEMORIES

Photo Manipulation

PHOTO MANIPULATION CAN COMPLETELY CHANGE THE LOOK OF A SCRAPBOOKING PAGE. THERE ARE ENDLESS WAYS TO MANIPULATE YOUR PHOTO, SO BE CREATIVE AND HAVE FUN. HERE ARE SOME IDEAS!

- ENLARGE A PHOTO AND PRINT TWO COPIES. USE DIFFERENT SIZED SQUARE PUNCHES TO PUNCH OUT DIFFERENT AREAS OF ONE PHOTO. ADHERE THE SQUARES RAISED ATOP THE UNCUT PHOTO WITH DOUBLE-SIDED FOAM TAPE OR POP DOTS. PLACE THE SQUARES OVER THE SAME PART OF THE UNCUT PHOTO.
- ELONGATE A PHOTO BY CUTTING IT INTO STRIPS AND ADHERING IT TO A LAYOUT WITH SPACE IN BETWEEN EACH STRIP. ADD DIMENSION BY MATTING STRIPS WITH CORRUGATED CARDBOARD.
- PARTIALLY COVER A PHOTO WITH A TORN PIECE OF VELLUM. TEXT CAN EVEN BE PRINTED ONTO THE VELLUM FOR A DIFFERENT LOOK.
- ADHERE A SERIES OF ACTION PHOTOS TO ADD MOTION AND EXCITEMENT TO YOUR LAYOUT.
- LAMINATE PHOTOS WITH TRANSPARENT COLORS USING A XYRON MACHINE. CHANGE THE MOOD OF A LAYOUT BY LAMINATING COPIES OF THE SAME PHOTO WITH DIFFERENT COLORS.
- PARTIALLY COVER A PHOTO WITH MESH AND ATTACH TO PHOTO WITH A BRAD, EYELET OR OTHER EMBELLISHMENT.

SWEET DREAMS

- CREATE BACKGROUND BY MATTING TRIMMED PATTERNED PAPER TO PINK PATTERNED CARDSTOCK • ADHERE PHOTOS TO PAPER FRAMES • DOUBLE MAT TITLE AND JOURNALING WITH CARDSTOCK AND GLITTER • EMBELLISH WITH FLOWER STICKERS •

81

Me

Designer: Lori Gerard

Our Pot of Gold

- CREATE BACKGROUND BY ADHERING TORN STRIPED PAPER TO YELLOW CHECKED PAPER • ADHERE PHOTO AND ATTACH LETTER STICKERS FOR TITLE • WRAP FEATHER FIBER AROUND ENTIRE LAYOUT • OUTLINE PHOTO AND LAYOUT WITH PEN •
SUPPLIES – PATTERNED PAPER: LEISURE ARTS; STICKERS: FLAVIA; FIBER: FIBERS BY THE YARD

SPECIAL TIPS:
DRAW A LINED BORDER WITH A FINE-TIPPED PEN TO ADD DEFINITION TO PHOTOS AND LAYOUTS.

You

- BEGIN WITH YELLOW CHECKED PAPER FOR BACKGROUND • PRINT PHOTO IN PANORAMIC SETTING • TEAR DARK STRIPED PAPER AND ADHERE TO BACKGROUND WITH PHOTO SHOWING THROUGH THE TEAR • ATTACH VARIOUS STICKERS AND WORDS DESCRIBING THE BABY TO THE DARK PAPER • ADHERE FUN FIBER AROUND DARK PAPER USING A TWO-WAY GLUE PEN •
SUPPLIES – PATTERNED PAPER: LEISURE ARTS; STICKERS: LEISURE ARTS, SONNETS, SEI, RENAE LINDGREN, MAKING MEMORIES, KINKADE; FIBER: FIBERS BY THE YARD; BRADS: MAKING MEMORIES; EYELET LETTERS: MAKING MEMORIES

SPECIAL TIPS:
DON'T ALWAYS PRINT YOUR PHOTOS IN TRADITIONAL 3x5 OR 4x6 FORMATS. PRINT LARGE OR PANORAMIC PHOTOS FOR VARIETY.

our POT of GOLD

Ben, you had such a good time at Sherwood's Pumpkin Patch. You rode around in your little red wagon & picked out your very first pumpkin
October 2002

PUMPKIN PATCH KID

• CREATE BACKGROUND BY ADHERING TORN PIECES OF DENIM PAPER TO GREEN CARDSTOCK • FRAME SMALL PHOTO WITH DENIM PHOTO FRAME • TIE DENIM RIBBON AROUND PICTURE FRAME • CUT STRIPES FROM TAG SQUARE SHEET AND ATTACH TO TWO SIDES OF A PHOTO WITH BRADS • USE BEIGE CENTER FROM PHOTO FRAME AND ADHERE TO INSIDE OF DENIM TAG SQUARE FOR TITLE • PRINT TITLE ON TRANSPARENCY AND ATTACH WITH BRADS • ATTACH TWO EYELETS AND STRING DENIM RIBBON THROUGH • ATTACH 'MY FIRST PUMPKIN' METAL TAG TO THE LAYOUT • EMBELLISH WITH BRADS •
SUPPLIES – PATTERNED PAPER: LEISURE ARTS; FONT: BATIK

BEN OCTOBER 2003

• CREATE BACKGROUND BY ADHERING A BLUE PATTERNED PAPER WITH TORN AND CHALKED EDGES TO THE OUTER PIECE OF A BROWN PAPER WITH CENTER CUT OUT • CRUMPLE, SAND, AND INK OUTER AND CENTER PIECE OF CUT BROWN PAPER • FRAME TWO PHOTOS WITH DISTRESSED STICKER FRAMES • ADHERE PHOTOS TO BROWN SQUARE • USE THE CENTER OF ONE FRAME AS THE TITLE BACKGROUND • PRINT TITLE ON TRANSPARENCY • ADHERE FIBER UNDER TITLE AND ACROSS PAGE • ATTACH TITLE ELEMENTS TO BACKGROUND WITH BRADS • TWIST AND ATTACH WIRE TO TITLE • CUT CENTER FROM OTHER FRAME INTO STRIPS • PRINT NAME AND DATE ONTO STRIPS AND ADHERE TO THE PHOTOS • PUNCH PHOTOS OF PUMPKINS WITH SQUARE PUNCH AND ADHERE WITH POP-DOTS OVER FIBER •
SUPPLIES – PAPER: LEISURE ARTS; FRAMES: LEISURE ARTS; FIBER: FIBERS BY THE YARD

SPECIAL TIPS:

1. SAND, CRINKLE, INK AND TEAR YOUR PAPER TO GIVE IT A DISTRESSED LOOK.
2. USE ALL YOUR SCRAPS. THE PUMPKIN SQUARES WERE FROM CUT UP PHOTOS AND THE TITLE BLOCK AND STRIPS INSIDE THE FRAMES WERE FROM THE INSETS OF THE FRAMES.
3. IF YOU ARE USING MULTIPLE PIECES OF PAPER FOR THE BACKGROUND, CUT THE CENTER OUT OF THE BOTTOM PIECE (IT CANNOT BE SEEN BECAUSE THE OTHER SHEET WILL HIDE IT) AND IT CAN BE USED LATER ON THE SAME LAYOUT

IT'S ALL ABOUT
Little Girls

sweet

cutie   girl   baby   beauty

happy

KRYSTAL

Sweetest Thing
• CREATE BACKGROUND BY ADHERING TORN PATTERNED PAPER
TO CARDSTOCK • MAT PHOTO WITH PATTERNED PAPER AND
CARDSTOCK • CREATE TITLE WITH LETTER STICKERS • FRAME
POEM STICKER WITH METAL FRAME • ADHERE CORRUGATED
CARDBOARD ACROSS PAGE • WIND TULLE AROUND PHOTO AND
ADHERE TO LAYOUT • EMBELLISH WITH HEARTS •
SUPPLIES – PATTERNED PAPER: PAPER ILLUZIONZ; HEARTS:
SCRAPWORKS; METAL FRAME: MAKING MEMORIES

Precious McKinley

• CREATE BACKGROUND BY ADHERING TORN CARDSTOCK TO LIGHT BLUE CARDSTOCK • ATTACH PHOTO TO BACKGROUND WITH METAL PHOTO CORNERS • PRINT JOURNALING ONTO LARGE TAG AND INSERT INTO POCKET • ADHERE EYELET WORDS • STAMP DESIGN WITH FOAM RUBBER STAMP AND ACRYLIC METALLIC PAINT • PUNCH HOLES IN LAYOUT AND THREAD WITH FIBERS TIED IN BOWS • EMBELLISH POCKET WITH FIBERS, STAMP AND CHARM •

SUPPLIES: CARDSTOCK: BAZZILL; FIBER: BROWN BAG FIBERS, TIMELESS TOUCHES; EYELET WORDS: MAKING MEMORIES; PHOTO CORNERS: MAKING MEMORIES; TAG: FOOFALA

Designer: Janet Hopkins

Love Bug

• CREATE BACKGROUND BY ADHERING A PIECE OF PATTERNED PAPER AND PINK SPLATTER NET TO PINK CARDSTOCK • DOUBLE MAT PHOTO • CREATE TITLE BY STRINGING METAL LETTER BLOCKS ON FIBERS • ATTACH OVER SPLATTER NET WITH BRADS • ATTACH STICKER LETTERS TO FINISH THE TITLE • PRINT JOURNALING ON CLEAR VELLUM AND TEAR LOWER EDGE • CUT FIBERS AND ATTACH TO JOURNALING BLOCK AND LAYOUT WITH BRAD • CREATE TAG BY MATTING A PUNCHED SQUARE OF PATTERNED PAPER WITH WHITE AND PURPLE CARDSTOCKS • ATTACH FIBERS TO TAG AND LAYOUT WITH TWO SILVER MINI BRADS • EMBELLISH LAYOUT WITH FLOWER STICKERS AND CHARMS • OUTLINE LAYOUT WITH WATERCOLOR PENCILS AND BLACK MARKER •

SUPPLIES – PATTERNED PAPER: LEISURE ARTS; NETTING: SCRAPLOVERS; METAL LETTER BLOCKS: LEISURE ARTS; STICKERS: LEISURE ARTS; CHARMS: LEISURE ARTS; FIBER: FIBERS BY THE YARD; VELLUM: PAPER ADVENTURES; SILVER BRADS: ALL THE EXTRAS; PURPLE BRADS: MAKING MEMORIES; LETTER STICKERS: BEARY PATCH

IT'S ALL ABOUT
Little Girls

Jiulia is so lovely in her beautiful Christening dress.
The dress was given to Jiulia by her God Mother, Rosie Brito.
These photos were taken on Jiulia's first birthday.
Her Christening was performed when she was 9 months old.

First
Birthday

June 14th
2003

JIULIA

• CREATE BACKGROUND BY ADHERING TRIMMED PATTERNED PAPER TO RED CARDSTOCK •
DOUBLE MAT PHOTOS WITH PINK VELLUM AND CARDSTOCK • CREATE TITLE BY ADHERING
ALPHABET STICKERS TO **1**" SQUARES OF PINK VELLUM MATTED WITH CARDSTOCK • PRINT
JOURNALING ON VELLUM • ADHERE TITLE TO BACKGROUND OVER RED THREAD WITH KNOTS
ON BOTH SIDES • WRAP JOURNALING WITH THREAD AND ADHERE TO BACKGROUND • MAT
FLORAL STICKER BORDERS WITH CARDSTOCK • ADHERE BORDERS TO LAYOUT •
SUPPLIES – PATTERNED PAPER: LEISURE ARTS; STICKERS: LEISURE ARTS; FIBER: TWOTWINKLES.COM

LUV MADE VISIBLE

• BEGIN WITH PINK CARDSTOCK BACKGROUND • MAT PICTURE
WITH PATTERNED PAPERS • PRINT AND MAT JOURNALING •
CREATE TITLE BY STRINGING BEADS AND LETTERS ON WIRE •
ATTACH WIRED BEADS BELOW PHOTO • HANG HANDWRITTEN
TAG FROM WIRE USING SAFETY PIN • EMBELLISH JOURNALING
WITH SAFETY PIN AND WIRED BEADS •
SUPPLIES – PATTERNED PAPER: LEISURE ARTS; METAL LETTERS:
LEISURE ARTS

KELLY MIEKO

• CREATE BACKGROUND BY ADHERING PATTERNED
VELLUM TO ROSE CARDSTOCK WITH VELLUM TAPE •
DOUBLE MAT PICTURES WITH CARDSTOCK • TEAR
BOTTOM EDGE OF ONE MAT AND CHALK TORN
EDGE • PRINT TITLE ONTO VELLUM AND MAT WITH
CARDSTOCK • TEAR AND CHALK EDGES AND
ADHERE TO PAGE • CUT TAG WITH TEMPLATE •
SHADE TAG WITH CHALKS • ATTACH EYELET, RIB-
BON, AND PAPER WOVEN LACE TO TAG • ADHERE
TO LAYOUT • CUT MATCHING STRIPS OF CARD-
STOCK AND WEAVE IN ECRU LACE • DAB ENDS OF
LACE WITH TACKY GLUE TO PREVENT FRAYING •
ADHERE LACE TO BACKGROUND WITH GLUE DOTS •
EMBELLISH WITH BUTTONS AND STICKERS •
SUPPLIES – CARDSTOCK: MAKING MEMORIES, CREATIVE
MEMORIES; PRINTED VELLUM: AUTUMN LEAVES;
BUTTONS: DRESS IT UP; TAG: DELUXE CUTS; EYELETS:
DOODLEBUG; FONT: TWO PEAS IN A BUCKET BEAUTIFUL

IT'S ALL ABOUT Little Boys

Human beings can create all manner of Things to bring **joy** But only a Wonderful GOD could have created a Beautiful little boy

Designer: Tammy Gauck

COREY

SPECIAL TIPS:
SPEED UP DRYING TIME BY USING AN EMBOSSING GUN.

COREY

• BEGIN WITH PLAID PAPER FOR BACKGROUND • WET AND CRUMPLE LIGHT BLUE CARDSTOCK • LAY FLAT TO DRY • DOUBLE MAT PHOTO WITH CRUMPLED PAPER AND SANDED TAN PAPER • ADHERE BUTTONS, FIBERS AND TINY EYELETS TO PHOTO MAT • HANDWRITE QUOTE MIXING IN STAMPED AND METAL LETTERS • CHALK WHITE TAGS WITH BLUE AND BROWN CHALK • ATTACH SILVER LETTER STICKERS TO TAGS • ATTACH TAGS TO LAYOUT WITH BRADS • ADHERE PICKET FENCE WITH GLUE DOTS •
SUPPLIES – PATTERNED PAPER: MAKING MEMORIES; CARDSTOCK: BAZZILL; STAMPS: STAMPIN' UP; METAL LETTERS: MAKING MEMORIES; TAGS: MAKING MEMORIES, AVERY; BUTTONS: DRESS IT UP; FENCE: WESTRIM CRAFTS

ONE LITTLE BOY

• CREATE BACKGROUND BY ADHERING GREEN CRACKLED PAPER TO DENIM PAPER • CUT THREE SIDES OF A RECTANGLE (LEAVING THE TOP UNCUT) IN THE DENIM PAPER WITH A PAPER TRIMMER • ROLL UP CUT PAPER • ADHERE GREEN PAPER TO THE WHITE ROLL THAT IS LEFT SHOWING • TIE THE ROLL WITH STRING TO LOOK LIKE A WINDOW BLIND • ADHERE PHOTO BEHIND WINDOW • ADHERE OTHER PHOTO TO LAYOUT • FRAME PHOTO WITH STRIPS OF DENIM PAPER • ATTACH TO LAYOUT WITH A CROSS-STITCH IN EACH CORNER • PRINT TITLE AND JOURNALING ONTO CARDSTOCK AND ADHERE TO LAYOUT •
SUPPLIES – PATTERNED PAPER: LEISURE ARTS; CARDSTOCK: PAPER GARDEN; COMPUTER FONT: CK RUGGED

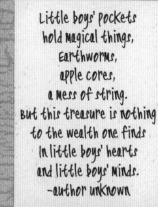

Little boys' pockets
hold magical things,
Earthworms,
apple cores,
a mess of string.
But this treasure is nothing
to the wealth one finds
In little boys' hearts
and little boys' minds.
-author unknown

one little boy
-ocean in sept. 2003

Designer: Tori Anderson

PRECIOUS LITTLE ONE

• CREATE BACKGROUND BY ADHERING BLUE CARD-STOCK TO GREEN CARDSTOCK • MAT PHOTO WITH CARDSTOCK AND ADHERE TO BACKGROUND • ATTACH RUB-ON WORDS TO STRIP OF CARDSTOCK FOR TITLE • PRINT JOURNALING ON WHITE CARDSTOCK • TEAR AND MAT WITH TORN CARDSTOCK AND ATTACH WITH PAPER CLIP AND STRING • CRUMPLE PATTERNED PAPER AND ADHERE TO LAYOUT OVERLAPPING PHOTO • ADHERE METAL FRAME LIKE A BUCKLE •
SUPPLIES – PATTERNED PAPER: CHATTERBOX; CARDSTOCK: BAZZILL; FRAME: MAKING MEMORIES; TITLE: MAKING MEMORIES

Ty Joseph Booms
Aug. 1, 2003
6lbs 4oz

precious little one

IT'S ALL ABOUT

Little Boys

Designer: Peggy Manrique

Aging Techniques

AGING PAPER IS A COMMON SCRAPBOOKING ACTIVITY. THE METHOD CAN TIE AN ENTIRE LAYOUT TOGETHER AND ANY SCRAPBOOKING ELEMENT CAN BE AGED (PAPER, PHOTOS, STICKERS, ACCENTS, FIBERS, ETC.). THE SCRAPBOOKER HAS A VARIETY OF AGING OPTIONS AVAILABLE TODAY.

WALNUT INK IS THE MOST POPULAR AGING MEDIUM AND WORKS VERY WELL. IT IS GREAT FOR STAINING, SPRAYING, BRUSHING AND TEXTURING PAPERS. WALNUT INK IS TAKEN FROM THE SHELLS OF WALNUTS AND COMES IN AN OILY, CRYSTALLIZED FORM. TO USE, JUST ADD WATER. THE COLOR OF THE STAIN DEPENDS ON HOW MUCH WATER IS USED (DARK—LESS WATER, LIGHT—MORE WATER). A QUICK AND EASY WAY TO AGE PAPER IS TO WET PAPER, CRUMPLE, AND DIP IT IN THE INK MIXTURE. LEAVE THE PAPER IN THE INK MIXTURE LONGER FOR A DARKER RESULT. IF THE RESULT IS TOO DARK, THE PAPER CAN BE RINSED. THE INK MIXTURE CAN ALSO BE BRUSHED ONTO PAPER WITH A FOAM BRUSH OR SPONGE. THERE ARE MANY WAYS TO USE THE INK SO EXPERIMENT AND HAVE FUN WITH IT. LET THE INK DRY BY SPREADING PAPER FLAT ON A TOWEL OR IRONING PAPER ON A COTTON SETTING. WALNUT INK WORKS GREAT ON MOST PAPERS, BUT THERE ARE SOME THAT DO NOT ABSORB THE INK.

ACRYLIC PAINT AND SANDING CAN GIVE AN AGED LOOK TO A VARIETY OF PRODUCTS. DRY BRUSH PAPER WITH ACRYLIC PAINT AND LET IT DRY. THEN SAND THE PAPER FOR AN AGED LOOK. SANDING, EVEN WITHOUT THE PAINT, WILL ADD YEARS TO A PRODUCT. JUST BE CAREFUL NOT TO SAND TOO HEARTILY!

TEA BAG DYING IS ANOTHER AGING OPTION. BOIL WATER IN A POT AND ADD A TEA BAG. STAIN PAPER IN A SIMILAR MANNER TO THE OTHER WATER BASED STAINS.

METALLIC AND LUSTER RUB-ONS ARE USED AS AN AGING MEDIUM AS WELL. THEY HAVE THE ADVANTAGE OF ADHERING TO MANY DIFFERENT MATERIALS. RUB-ONS WORK ESPECIALLY WELL ON METAL AND PAPER AND CAN BE BUFFED IF DESIRED. THEY ARE BEST APPLIED WITH A FINGER (COVERED WITH A LATEX GLOVE) OR RAG.

RUB N' BUFF IS ANOTHER RUB-ON MEDIUM WITH A WAX METALLIC FINISH. IT WORKS VERY WELL ON METAL AND IS LONG LASTING. RUB N' BUFF COMES IN A SMALL SQUEEZABLE TUBE AND IS BEST APPLIED WITH A FINGER AND BUFFED WITH A SOFT TOWEL.

AGING CHALKS WORK WELL ON MOST PAPERS AND ARE EASILY APPLIED WITH A COTTON SWAB OR MAKE-UP SPONGE.

FOLK ANTIQUING MEDIUM IS A WATER BASED STAIN USED ON WOOD AND PAPER ALIKE. IT COMES READY TO USE, BUT CAN BE WATERED DOWN FOR A LIGHTER WASH.

LITTLE COWBOY

• CREATE BACKGROUND BY ADHERING STRIPED PAPER, BEIGE PAPER AND COLLAGE PAPER TO RED PAPER • TEAR, CRUMPLE, FLATTEN AND ADHERE TEXTURED LOFT PAPER TO BACKGROUND • PAINT EDGES OF PHOTOS WITH METALLIC RUB-ON AND ADHERE TO BACKGROUND • WEAVE STRING THROUGH TAG LETTER STICKERS FOR TITLE AND KNOT THE ENDS • ADHERE TITLE TO LAYOUT • STRING RAFFIA THROUGH DATE TAGS AND ADHERE TO LAYOUT WITH KNOTS IN CORNERS TO FRAME PHOTO • MAKE PAGE ACCENT WITH COLLAGE PAPER, WISDOM LEATHER, STICKERS AND TINY BUTTONS • ATTACH THE 'J' TAG WITH A SAFETY PIN AND GLUE DOTS • USE A METAL TAG RIM TO FRAME THE AGE OF THE BABY •
SUPPLIES – PATTERNED PAPER: CHATTERBOX, PAPER LOFT, LEGACY COLLAGE; METAL RIM: MAKING MEMORIES; METAL TAG: MAKING MEMORIES; STICKERS: NOSTALGIQUE

SPECIAL TIPS:
1. STRING LETTER STICKERS WHILE STILL ATTACHED TO THE STICKER PAPER.
2. CHALK OR METALLIC RUB-ONS GIVE AN AGED LOOK AND HELP COORDINATE ITEMS ON A LAYOUT.

Couldn't Bee Any Cuter

• CREATE BACKGROUND BY ADHERING TRIMMED PATTERNED PAPER TO PURPLE PATTERNED PAPER
• MAT PHOTOS WITH PURPLE PAPER AND ADHERE TO BACKGROUND • CREATE TITLE BY ATTACHING STICKERS TO SQUARE PIECES OF PURPLE PAPER • PRINT JOURNALING ON VELLUM AND MAT WITH PURPLE PAPER • MAT PURPLE CHECKED BORDER STICKER WITH PURPLE PAPER AND ADHERE TO TOP AND BOTTOM OF LAYOUT
• EMBELLISH WITH BUMBLE BEE STICKERS (ATTACH TO SHEET PROTECTOR MATERIAL AND CUT OUT TO TAKE AWAY THE STICK) AND ADHERE TO LAYOUT WITH POP DOTS •
SUPPLIES - PATTERNED PAPER: LEISURE ARTS; STICKERS: LEISURE ARTS

Designer: Sheila Hansen

"Couldn't BEE any Cuter"

Darling Paul Charles on his first birthday, June 14th, 2003. He is such a happy and loveable little boy! His sweetness is emulated in his countenance of these photographs. Paul Charles is wearing his handsome Christening tuxedo.

P A U L

Moment

• CREATE BACKGROUND BY ADHERING PATTERNED PAPER, CHALKED PAPER AND GINGHAM RIBBON TO BROWN CARDSTOCK • PRINT TITLE ON PATTERNED PAPER AND ADHERE TO BACKGROUND • ATTACH LARGE PHOTO TO LAYOUT WITH PHOTO CORNERS • ADHERE PATTERNED PAPER, WATCH CUT OUT, SMALL PHOTO, GINGHAM RIBBON AND PEWTER LETTERS TO TAG • CREATE SMALL TAG BY TYING A CIRCLE TAG, HEART TAG AND SILVER TOGGLE TOGETHER WITH RIBBON • ADHERE TAGS TO LAYOUT • HANDWRITE AGE ON SQUARE METAL RIMMED TAG AND STRING WITH GINGHAM RIBBON • EMBELLISH LAYOUT WITH HEART CLIPS •
SUPPLIES: PATTERNED PAPER: DMD COLLAGE PAPER, KAREN FOSTER; CARDSTOCK: BAZZILL

Special Tips:
1. MINI GLUE DOTS HELP KEEP HANGING ITEMS IN PLACE.
2. CHALK PAPERS TO HELP THEM COORDINATE.

IT'S ALL ABOUT
Double Trouble

The twins each had their own 8" birthday cake. The party was held at Red Morten Park. Parents, Cousins, Aunts, Uncles, Grandparents, Great Grandparents, and Godparents attended.

June 14th 2003

Jiulia   Paul Charles

Designer: Sheila Hanson

FIRST BIRTHDAY

• CREATE BACKGROUND BY ADHERING TRIMMED GREEN PATTERNED PAPER TO YELLOW CARDSTOCK • MAT PHOTOS WITH COLORED PAPER AND ADHERE TO BACKGROUND • CREATE TITLE BY ATTACHING LETTER STICKERS TO SQUARE PIECES OF YELLOW PAPER • ADHERE TITLE TO BACKGROUND OVERLAPPING THE LETTERS • PRINT JOURNALING ON VELLUM AND ATTACH TO LAYOUT WITH GOLD MINI BRADS • CREATE BORDER AT BOTTOM BY ATTACHING STICKERS TO TWO STRIPS OF YELLOW PAPER •

SUPPLIES – PATTERNED PAPER: LEISURE ARTS; STICKERS: LEISURE ARTS

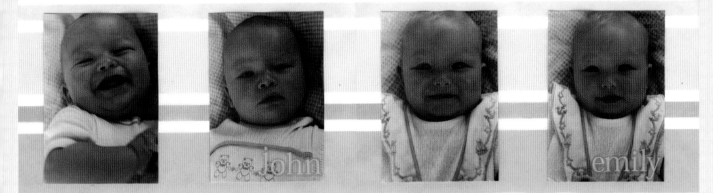

Designer: Lynette Anderson

twice the fun   twice as nice

double the tears   seeing double

SEEING DOUBLE

• BEGIN WITH PATTERNED CARDSTOCK FOR BACKGROUND •
ADHERE PHOTOS TO BACKGROUND • ATTACH LETTER STICKERS
TO BACKGROUND AND PHOTOS FOR JOURNALING AND NAMES •
SUPPLIES – PAPER: SEI

TWINS

• CREATE BACKGROUND BY ADHERING TRIMMED
PATTERNED PAPER TO BLUE CARDSTOCK • MAT PHO-
TOS WITH PURPLE, SAGE AND WHITE CARDSTOCKS •
CREATE TITLE BY ADHERING GREEN ALPHABET
STICKERS TO MATTED CARDSTOCK SQUARES • CUT
OUT SMALL TAGS TO MAT CHARMS • ATTACH BOY
AND GIRL CHARMS WITH THREAD • EMBELLISH LAY-
OUT WITH THREADS •
SUPPLIES – PATTERNED PAPER: LEISURE ARTS; STICKERS:
LEISURE ARTS; METAL EMBELLISHMENTS:
TWOTWINKLES.COM; FIBER: TWOTWINKLES.COM

IT'S ALL ABOUT Smiles

Designer: Anna Estrada Davison

CHERISH—*verb*
1. To have the highest regard for;
2. To recognize the worth, quality, importance, etc., of.
Syns: prize, treasure.—*Idiom* hold dear. Appreciate.

13 months old

ALINA

ALINA

- CREATE BACKGROUND BY ADHERING PATTERNED PAPER, GREEN CORRUGATED CARDBOARD AND RIBBON TO TAN CARDSTOCK • MAT LARGE PHOTO WITH CARDSTOCK AND ADHERE TO BACKGROUND • MAT SMALLER PHOTOS WITH CARDBOARD AND ATTACH TO BACKGROUND WITH CHIFFON RIBBON AND BUTTON • CREATE TITLE WITH LETTER STICKERS • PRINT JOURNALING ONTO CARDSTOCK, TEAR AND INK EDGES AND ADHERE TO LAYOUT • HANDWRITE AGE • CREATE TAG BY CUTTING OUT PATTERNED PAPER AND ADHERING TO BACKGROUND • ADHERE TITLE TO LAYOUT OVERLAPPING TAG • EMBELLISH LAYOUT WITH RIBBON AND CHARM •
SUPPLIES – PATTERNED PAPER: 7 GYPSIES; LETTER STICKERS: NOSTALGIQUE, REBECCA SOWER; STAMP: ECLECTIC OMNIBUS; HEART CHARM: EMBELLISH IT

SMILE

• BEGIN WITH RED CARDSTOCK FOR BACK-
GROUND • MAT PHOTOS TOGETHER WITH
CARDSTOCK • CREATE TITLE WITH STICKERS
AND METAL-RIMMED TAGS • FILL TAGS WITH
DIE CUTS • EMBELLISH LAYOUT WITH PAPER
SHAPES AND STICKERS •
SUPPLIES – CARDSTOCK: BAZZILL, SEI; STICKERS:
SNIP IT'S, BRYCE & MADELINE, REBECCA SOWER;
METAL TAGS: MAKING MEMORIES

SPECIAL TIPS:
MOUNTING SIMILAR PHOTOS
TOGETHER ADDS IMPACT AND
FOCUS.

Designer: Peggy Manrique

SPECIAL TIPS:
1. CHALK THE EDGES OF TORN
   PAPER TO GIVE AN ANTIQUED OR
   BURNT LOOK.
2. JOURNALING CAN SIMPLY BE
   WORDS DESCRIBING A PERSON.
   CHOOSE FONTS THAT FIT THE
   WORD YOU ARE USING.
3. TEXTURE AND DARK COLORS
   HELP CONTRAST PHOTOS.

3 MONTHS

• CREATE BACKGROUND BY ADHERING MESH AND AGED
PAPER TO BROWN CARDSTOCK • ATTACH PHOTO TO
BACKGROUND WITH METALLIC RUB-ON PHOTO CORNERS
• ATTACH ALPHABET BLOCKS WITH SMALL SILVER BRADS
TO CREATE TITLE • PRINT JOURNALING TEXT ONTO
CARDSTOCK • TEAR AND CHALK EDGES OF JOURNALING
PAGE • EMBELLISH WITH FRAME AND TOOTHPICKS TO
CREATE TRAIN TRACKS • TIE GINGHAM RIBBON LIKE A
PACKAGE AND ADHERE TO LAYOUT •
SUPPLIES – PATTERNED PAPER: LEGACY COLLAGE,
CHATTERBOX, PATCHWORK PAPER; MESH: MAGIC MESH;
LETTER BOXES: MY MIND'S EYE, THIS & THAT; BOOKPLATE:
MAKING MEMORIES; PHOTO CORNERS: PIONEER; STICKERS:
BO BUNNY; FONTS: DEAR JOE, BLACK BOYS ON MOPEDS,
GILLIGANS ISLAND, FLOWERCHILD, LOV LETTERS, TYPEWRITER,
FREESTYLE SCRIPT

IT'S ALL ABOUT

Attitude

Designer: Sam Cousins

My Favorite Photo

• CREATE BACKGROUND BY INKING EDGE OF WHITE CANVAS PHOTO PAPER • PRINT PHOTO ONTO CANVAS PAPER AND TEAR EDGES • ARRANGE ABSTRACT ART IMAGES IN TWO DIFFERENT SIZES ON THE COMPUTER • ADD TITLE TO LAYOUT ON COMPUTER • PRINT BLOCKS AND TITLE ONTO TRANSPARENCY • ADHERE TRANSPARENCY TO CANVAS • WRAP FIBER AROUND PHOTO • ADHERE POEM STONE TO HEART CONCH AND ADHERE TO PHOTO • ATTACH RUB-ON LETTERS FOR NAME AND DATE • ATTACH BLACK PHOTO CORNERS TO EDGE OF LAYOUT TO KEEP TRANSPARENCY ATTACHED TO CANVAS •
SUPPLIES – POEM STONE: SONNETS; FIBER: FIBERS BY THE YARD; RUB-ON LETTERS: STAPLES; FONT: CARPENTER

My First Bunny

• BEGIN WITH BLUE CARDSTOCK FOR BACKGROUND • TRIPLE MAT PHOTO AND ATTACH TO BACKGROUND WITH BLUE BRADS • PRINT JOURNALING ONTO CARDSTOCK AND DOUBLE MAT • HANDWRITE MESSAGE ON JOURNALING • ATTACH JOURNAL BLOCK WITH BLUE BRADS • USE TEMPLATE TO CUT OUT HEARTS • ADHERE HEARTS TO CARDSTOCK, DOUBLE MAT AND ADHERE TO LAYOUT •
SUPPLIES - CARDSTOCK: BAZZILL; BRADS: DOODLEBUG; HEARTS: QUICKUTS

MY FIRST BUNNY

IN APRIL OF 2003, WE ALL WENT BACK TO OMAHA TO MEMORIALIZE THE MEMORY OF GREAT GRANDMA ROSE WHO HAD RECENTLY PASSED FROM OUR LIVES. ALL OF HER KIDS AND GRANDKIDS WERE THERE FOR THE SOLEMN EVENT. WE ALL MET ON THE LAST DAY AT THE OMAHA AIRPORT TO SAY OUR GOOD-BYES. THERE WAS GREAT AUNT DEV AND HER DAUGHTER LORI, AND LORI'S KIDS LEXI AND MOLLY, GREAT AUNT BARB AND GREAT UNCLE DICK AND THEIR KIDS, MICHELLE AND WENDY, GRANDMA AND GRANDPA NORTHUP, MY PARENTS SHAWN AND SARAH, AND MY AUNTIE MEAGHAN. GRANDMA MARIDAWN HAD BOUGHT ME MY FIRST BUNNY RABBIT, AND SURPRISED ME WITH THE GIFT AS I SAT ON GRANDPA FRANK'S LAP. AS YOU CAN SEE, I WAS OVERJOYED. THANKS GRANDMA!!

Love You My Joshua!! Grammy

HEARTS FILLED WITH LOVE

• CREATE BACKGROUND BY ADHERING CUT PAT-
TERNED PAPERS AND COLORED CARDSTOCKS
TOGETHER IN STRIPED PATTERN • MAT PHOTO
AND PRINTED JOURNALING BLOCK WITH CARD-
STOCK • FRAME WITH CHIFFON RIBBON AND
ATTACH WITH BRADS • RUN CHIFFON RIBBONS
ACROSS LAYOUT AND ATTACH WITH BRADS •
SUPPLIES – PATTERNED PAPER: ANNA GRIFFIN;
BRADS: DOODLEBUG

Babies
bits of stardust blown from
heaven
to fill our
hearts with hope
and Love

Designer: MaryDawn Mayer

Designer: Penny Morrison

mad

I JUST HAVE TO LAUGH SOMETIMES WHEN I SEE YOU TRYING TO GET MAD. YOU ARE SUCH A LIGHT-
HEARTED AND HAPPY BOY, THAT I DON'T THINK YOU EVEN KNOW HOW TO REALLY GET MAD. I SNAPPED
THIS PHOTO AT A MOMENT WHEN YOU DIDN'T WANT TO BE PHOTOGRAPHED, AND LOOK AT YOUR FACE!
WHAT'S FUNNY IS THAT ONE SECOND LATER WHEN I PUT THE CAMERA AWAY, YOU WERE GRINNING FROM
EAR TO EAR AGAIN. MY LITTLE MAD BOY!

may 03   Jerry

SPECIAL TIPS:

1. USE COORDINATING COLORS IN
   ORDER TO MIX SEVERAL PAT-
   TERNS ON ONE PAGE.
2. CONTINUE CIRCLE THEME FROM
   THE PAPER ONTO THE TAGS.
3. THE PHOTO BLENDS INTO THE
   COLORS OF THE PAGE BECAUSE IT
   IS NOT MOUNTED.
4. SCRAPBOOK IMPERFECTLY POSED
   PHOTOS TO ADD CHARACTER.

MAD

• CREATE BACKGROUND BY ADHERING STRIPED
VELLUM, CIRCLE PATTERNED PAPER AND DARK
BLUE PAPER TO GREEN CARDSTOCK • ADHERE
PHOTO TO BACKGROUND • PRINT TITLE AND
JOURNALING ONTO A COORDINATING SOLID
PAPER AND ADHERE TO BACKGROUND •
ADHERE TWO MATCHING FIBERS ACROSS LAY-
OUT • PLACE RUB-ON CIRCLES AND LETTER
STICKERS ONTO EACH TAG • HANG VELLUM
TAGS FROM FIBERS •
SUPPLIES – PATTERNED PAPER: CHATTERBOX,
AMERICAN CRAFTS, MAKING MEMORIES; TAGWEAR:
CREATIVE IMAGINATIONS; VELLUM TAG: MAKING
MEMORIES; STICKERS: DAVID WALKER; FIBER:
ADORNMENTS; FONT: YOU ARE WHAT YOU EAT

IT'S ALL ABOUT

Seeing The World Through A
Child's Eyes

Designer: Tam Cousins

EXTREME CONCENTRATION

- CREATE BACKGROUND BY PRINTING PATTERNED PAPER USING VARIOUS FONTS FOR ONE WORD AND ADHERING IT TO BLACK CARDSTOCK • ADHERE THREE PHOTOS • ADHERE GINGHAM RIBBON ALONG THE BOTTOM OF THE PHOTOS • ATTACH GREEN STICKERS AND BRADWEAR LETTERS TO METAL-RIMMED TAGS • ATTACH TO BACKGROUND WITH SILVER EYELETS • RUB GREEN BRADWEAR ONTO BRADS • PRINT ONE 'CONCENTRATION' WORD IN GREEN • CUT OUT WORD AND PLACE ON PAGE PEBBLE • ADHERE TO LAYOUT WITH POP-DOT •

SUPPLIES – STICKERS: DOODLEBUG, CREATIVE IMAGINATIONS; EYELETS: MAKING MEMORIES; TAGS: MAKING MEMORIES; PAGE PEBBLE: MAKING MEMORIES

FEEDING DUCKS

• BEGIN WITH DARK GREEN CARDSTOCK FOR BACKGROUND • DOUBLE MAT THREE PHOTOS AND ADHERE TO BACKGROUND • MAT SIX PHOTOS TOGETHER AND ADHERE TO LIGHT GREEN CARDSTOCK • ADHERE MATTED PHOTOS TO BACKGROUND • CREATE TITLE BLOCK FROM RECTANGLE OF CARDSTOCK FRAMED ON TOP AND BOTTOM WITH STRIPS OF LIGHTER CARDSTOCK • REVERSE PRINT TITLE ON CARDSTOCK AND CUT OUT • CUT DUCKS FROM SCRAP PAPER AND ATTACH WITH BLACK BRADS FOR EYES • PRINT JOURNALING ONTO CARDSTOCK AND DOUBLE MAT • ADHERE TITLE AND JOURNALING TO BACKGROUND •
SUPPLIES - CARDSTOCK: BAZZILL

THE WORLD

• BEGIN WITH MAP PATTERNED PAPER FOR BACKGROUND • MAT PHOTOS • PRINT TITLE ONTO A TRANSPARENCY • FINISH TITLE WITH LETTER STICKERS • ADHERE TRANSPARENCY WITH CLEAR DOUBLE-SIDED TAPE • EMBELLISH WITH BOTTLE AND SHIP WHEEL •
SUPPLIES – PATTERNED PAPER: SONNETS; STICKERS: SONNETS; BOTTLE: JOLEE'S BOUTIQUE; SHIPS WHEEL: DRESS IT UP; FONT: TWO PEAS IN A BUCKET DREAMS

Hopes and Dreams

Designer: Jennifer Bourgeault

Dear child. I will care for you, protect you – until you are grown. And then I will let you fly free. But, loving you? That is for always.
~ Charlotte Gray

DEAR CHILD
• CREATE BACKGROUND BY PRINTING JOURNALING DIRECTLY ONTO TAN PAPER •
ADHERE TWO TORN COORDINATING PAPERS TO JOURNALING PAPER AND THEN
ADHERE TO BLACK CARDSTOCK • DEVELOP PHOTO IN SEPIA • ATTACH PHOTO TO
BACKGROUND WITH A STICKER FRAME • EMBELLISH WITH CIRCLE STICKERS •
SUPPLIES – PATTERNED PAPER: CHATTERBOX, ARTISTIC SCRAPPER; CARDSTOCK: BAZZILL;
FRAME: MY MIND'S EYE; BUTTONS: MY MIND'S EYE

Transparencies/Vellum

TRANSPARENCIES ARE A GREAT MEDIUM FOR TITLES,
JOURNALING, GRAPHICS AND EVEN PHOTOS, AND ARE
SO EASY TO USE. A TRANSPARENCY CAN GIVE ANY
LOOK YOU ARE TRYING TO CREATE FROM OLD FASH-
IONED TO SHABBY CHIC. THE KEY TO CREATING THE
PERFECT LOOK IS IN THE FONT AND BACKGROUND
SELECTION. TO MAKE A TRANSPARENCY, JUST MEAS-
URE WHERE THE TITLE OR JOURNALING SHOULD BE
ON THE LAYOUT, PRINT OR HANDWRITE ONTO THE
TRANSPARENCY AND ATTACH IT TO THE LAYOUT.
YOU CAN EITHER ATTACH PIECES OF THE TRANS-
PARENCY TO THE LAYOUT OR THE ENTIRE TRANS-
PARENCY AS AN OVERLAY. YOU CAN ALSO ADD VARI-
ETY TO YOUR TRANSPARENCIES BY PRINTING GRAPHICS
AND PHOTOS, DRAWING WITH MARKERS AND BY
PRINTING TEXT IN COLOR. PRINTING YOUR PHOTOS
ONTO A TRANSPARENCY GIVES THEM A GREAT
TRANSLUCENT QUALITY.

VELLUM IS ALSO A WONDERFUL CHOICE FOR OVER-
LAYS, TITLES, JOURNALING AND QUOTES. VELLUM
COMES IN MANY DIFFERENT WEIGHTS, COLORS,
DESIGNS AND TEXTURES. DON'T BE AFRAID TO PLAY
AROUND WITH THE DIFFERENT OPTIONS TO SEE
WHICH YOU LIKE BEST. MOST VELLUM WILL WORK
FINE WITH AN INK-JET PRINTER BUT DOES EVEN BET-
TER WITH A LASER PRINTER.

VELLUM IS AN EXCELLENT MATERIAL FOR REPRESENT-
ING WATER. CHOOSE WATER COLORED VELLUM, RIP
THE EDGES AND LAYER WITH THE SAME COLOR OR
COORDINATING COLORS. VELLUM'S TRANSLUCENT
QUALITY ALSO GIVES AN ETHEREAL AND PURE LOOK
TO THE SOFT AND HEAVENLY QUALITIES OF A NEW-
BORN BABE, CHILD AND BRIDE.

THE BEST GLUE TO USE IN ADHERING TRANSPAREN-
CIES AND VELLUM TO A LAYOUT IS NONE AT ALL. TRY
ATTACHING THEM WITH BRADS, EYELETS, STITCHES,
NAIL HEADS, FIBERS, OR EVEN WEDGING AN EDGE
UNDER ANOTHER ELEMENT ON A PAGE WITH A DROP
OF GLUE. VELLUM TAPE CAN BE USED BUT USUALLY
SHOWS THROUGH THE VELLUM. YOU CAN USE A
XYRON MACHINE TO ADHERE TRANSPARENCIES AND
VELLUM TO A LAYOUT, BUT BE AWARE THAT IT DOES
CHANGE THE LOOK OF THE MEDIUM.

Designer: Jan Coratti

LEAD, GUIDE, WALK

- CREATE BACKGROUND BY ADHERING PATTERNED PAPER WITH TORN AND CURLED EDGES TO TEXTURED SANDPAPER • SAND AND INK PAPER WITH SEPIA INK
- MAT PHOTOS WITH CARDSTOCK AND INK EDGES • ADHERE TORN VELLUM TO SOME PHOTOS WITH SCRAPPERS SPRAY • PUNCH FOCAL IMAGE FROM ONE PHOTO WITH SQUARE PUNCH • MAT WITH CARDSTOCK AND PARCHMENT PAPER AND RE-ATTACH TO PHOTO WITH POP DOTS • INK AND ADHERE LETTER STICKERS FOR TITLE • PRINT POEM ONTO TRANSPARENCY AND ADHERE OVER PHOTO OF FOOTPRINTS • EMBELLISH LAYOUT WITH SILVER FOOTPRINTS • SUPPLIES – PATTERNED PAPER: CLUB SCRAPS, REBECCA SOWERS; FIBER: FIBERS BY THE YARD; FEET EYELETS: NAME-TRACES; TITLE: FOOFALA; FONTS: CK FLOURISH, TWO PEAS IN A BUCKET BEACHBALL

CHILD OF GOD

- CREATE BACKGROUND BY ADHERING COLORED PAPERS TO WHITE CARDSTOCK • ADHERE PHOTOS TO BACKGROUND • ADHERE JOURNALING TRANSPARENCY OVER LAYOUT • EMBELLISH WITH METAL CHARMS, EYELETS, FLOSS AND METAL LETTERS • SUPPLIES - PATTERNED PAPER: SEI; OVERLAY: ARTISTIC IMPRESSIONS

IT'S ALL ABOUT

The Clean-Up

Designer: Sam Cousins

my dirty little valentine

My Dirty Little Valentine

• BEGIN WITH BLUE CARDSTOCK FOR BACKGROUND • PRINT PHOTO IN PANORAMIC SETTING
• ATTACH PHOTO TO BACKGROUND WITH PHOTO CORNERS • FRAME SMALL PHOTOS WITH
METAL FRAMES • ATTACH LETTER STICKERS FOR TITLE • MAT BORDER STICKER WITH TORN
WHITE CARDSTOCK •
SUPPLIES – STICKERS: SONNETS; PHOTO CORNERS: MAKING MEMORIES; FRAMES: MAKING MEMORIES

We LOVE to see you SMILE!

I only have "FRIES" for you!!!

My Little Fry Guy!!! I don't like giving you french fries, because I don't think they are healthy. But they are your new FAVORITE Food!!! You don't like Ketchup, you like them "naked" as daddy calls it!

I Only Have Fries For You

• CREATE BACKGROUND BY ADHERING YELLOW CARDSTOCK TO RED CARDSTOCK • PRINT TITLE ONTO TRANSPARENCY AND ADHERE WITH GLUE DOTS • PRINT JOURNALING ONTO WHITE CARDSTOCK AND MAT WITH BLUE CARDSTOCK • ATTACH JOURNALING WITH EYELETS • MAT ONE PHOTO • ADHERE ALL PHOTOS TO BACKGROUND • ADHERE A CLEAN McDonald's© FRY BAG • CREATE FRY SHAPES BY CUTTING YELLOW PAPER INTO STRIPS AND RUNNING THEM THROUGH A CRIMPER • SHADE FRIES WITH ORANGE CHALK • ADHERE INSIDE BAG AND RANDOMLY THROUGHOUT LAYOUT •

Popsicle Delight

Jena enjoying her orange popsicle. I think she got more on her then in her mouth. She was a sticky mess. My daughter just put a diaper on her so she could enjoy every single lick. When she was done she had dark orange lips but she looked absolutely adorable.

priceless

Popsicle Delight

• CREATE BACKGROUND BY ADHERING TWO TORN PIECES OF COMPLIMENTARY PAPER TO TEXTURED CARDSTOCK • ADHERE PHOTOS TO BACKGROUND • ATTACH STICKERS FOR TITLE • PRINT JOURNALING DIRECTLY ONTO BACKGROUND • CREATE TAGS WITH BACKGROUND PAPERS • EMBELLISH TAGS WITH TORN EDGES, METAL WORDS AND MINI BRADS • EMBELLISH PHOTOS WITH PHOTO CORNERS AND BUTTONS • SUPPLIES – PATTERNED PAPER: KAREN FOSTER; METAL WORDS: MAKING MEMORIES; BRADS: GOOSE BARN; BUTTONS: MAKING MEMORIES; METAL SQUARE AND TAG: MAKING MEMORIES; STICKERS: K&CO.; FONT: FIRST GRADER

Holiday Fun

Designer: Peggy Manrique

EASTER 2003

- CREATE BACKGROUND BY CUTTING A COORDINATING PAPER INTO EQUAL-SIZED RECTANGLES AND ADHERING THEM EQUALLY SPACED TO PURPLE CARDSTOCK • CROP PHOTOS TO FIT WITHIN RECTANGLES • MAT SOME PHOTOS • CREATE TITLE IN ONE REC-TANGLE WITH STICKERS • PRINT CONTENTS OF EASTER BASKET ON VELLUM FOR JOURNALING • ATTACH JOURNALING ATOP AN EASTER BASKET PHOTO WITH STRIP STICKER ALLOWING VELLUM TO LIFT TO REVEAL PHOTO • FILL REMAINING BLOCKS WITH EMBELLISHMENTS • CREATE PURSE FREEHAND, ADHERE YELLOW FIBER FOR HANDLE AND MAKE BOW FROM LEFTOVER STICKERS • ATTACH PURSE TO BACKGROUND WITH POP-DOT • HAND STITCH GREEN FIBERS ACROSS PAGE WITH RANDOM CROSS-STITCHES •
SUPPLIES – PATTERNED PAPER: DOODLEBUG; CARDSTOCK: BAZZILL; STICKERS: SNIP IT'S, DAVID WALKER, SONNETS

SPECIAL TIPS:

1. THE STITCHING AND PURSE GIVE THE PAGE A HOME-MADE FEEL. THIS IS ESPECIALLY NICE FOR HOLIDAYS.
2. RANDOMLY SPACING PHOTOS KEEPS YOUR EYE MOVING ACROSS AND DOWN THE PAGE.
3. USING A VELLUM OVERLAY ALLOWS FOR JOURNALING WITHOUT DISTRACTING VIEWERS FROM THE PICTURES.
4. USING SIMPLE AND FUN TEXT CAN BE JUST AS MEMO-RABLE AS DESCRIBING THE ACTUAL EVENT.

MY FUNNY BUNNY

- CREATE BACKGROUND BY CHALKING PINK AND GREEN STRIPED PAPER AND TEARING A RANDOM HOLE OUT OF THE CENTER OF THE PAPER • CRUMPLE AND SAND MATCHING CARDSTOCK AND ADHERE TO THE BACK OF PATTERNED PAPER UNDER TORN HOLE • MAT ONE PHOTO WITH WHITE CARDSTOCK • TEAR AND CHALK EDGES OF OTHER PHOTO • CREATE TITLE BY STRINGING LETTER BEADS ON FIBER AND ATTACHING TO LAYOUT WITH BRADS • ATTACH STICKERS TO FINISH TITLE • CREATE TAG FROM WHITE CARDSTOCK AND STRIPED PAPER • EMBELLISH TAG WITH RIBBON AND STICKERS • ADHERE FIBER ACROSS LAYOUT • ATTACH GRASS STICKER, EGGS AND TAG TO LAYOUT • EMBELLISH WITH BLACK PHOTO CORNERS AND ROUND SILVER EYELETS • OUTLINE LAYOUT AND TAG WITH PEN •
SUPPLIES – PATTERNED PAPER: LEISURE ARTS; LETTER BEADS: TARGET; FIBER: FIBERS BY THE YARD; STICKERS: JOLEE'S, LEISURE ARTS

SPECIAL TIPS:

1. TEAR PHOTOS FOR A DIF-FERENT LOOK.
2. ATTACH BRADS AND EYE-LETS TO PHOTOS FOR ACCENTS.

CLOWNING AROUND

- CREATE BACKGROUND BY ADHERING TRIMMED LINE PATTERNED PAPER TO CIRCLE PATTERNED PAPER • ADHERE CUT STRIP OF GREEN CARDSTOCK AND TENT TOP OF CIRCLE PATTERNED PAPER TO BACKGROUND • MAT PHOTO WITH PATTERNED PAPERS AND CARDSTOCKS • REVERSE PRINT TITLE AND CUT OUT
- MAT WITH COLORED CARDSTOCK, CUT OUT AND ADHERE TO BACKGROUND • ADHERE TAG WITH HANDWRITTEN JOURNALING • ADHERE CLOWN EMBELLISHMENT TO LAYOUT •

Designer: Eleanor House

SANTA BABY

- BEGIN WITH RED CARDSTOCK FOR BACKGROUND • MAT PHOTO ON RED AND WHITE CARDSTOCK • MAT THREE PHOTOS IN A STRIP ON WHITE CARDSTOCK • ADHERE PHOTO STRIP TO BOTTOM OF BACKGROUND AND OTHER PHOTO IN UPPER RIGHT CORNER • PRINT TITLE AND JOURNALING ON WHITE CARDSTOCK • USE "NIGHT BEFORE CHRISTMAS" POEM AS BASIS FOR JOURNALING • CUT, MAT WITH RED AND WHITE CARDSTOCK AND ADHERE TO BACKGROUND • EMBELLISH LAYOUT WITH FIBERS TO MIMIC BOA IN PHOTO •
SUPPLIES – FIBER: FIBERS BY THE YARD; FONT: BRADLEY HAND

PEEK-A-BOO: I DONT SEE YOU!

play (pla)
1. to participate in recreation activities
2. to participate in a game or sport
3. a child's pastime

Benny and his sun hat in Cancun   spring 2003

PLAY

Designer: Pam Canavan

PEEK-A-BOO
• CREATE BACKGROUND BY ADHERING A
TORN PIECE OF PATTERNED PAPER TO A
COORDINATING PATTERNED PAPER •
ADHERE CUT CHEESECLOTH ACROSS LAY-
OUT • ADHERE MAIN PHOTO TO BACK-
GROUND • FRAME OTHER PHOTO AND
ADHERE TO BACKGROUND • CREATE TITL
WITH VARYING STICKERS AND A HAND-
WRITTEN TRANSPARENCY FOR 'I SEE YOU
• PRINT JOURNALING ON PATTERNED
PAPER AND TRANSPARENCY AND ADHERE
TO LAYOUT • CREATE TAG WITH PAT-
TERNED PAPER AND STICKERS • ATTACH
WITH BRAD • THREAD BEADS ONTO WIRE
AND ATTACH WITH BRAD • EMBELLISH
CHEESECLOTH BY ATTACHING BEADS WIT
DIAMOND GLAZE •
SUPPLIES – PATTERNED PAPER: NRN DESIGN
STICKERS: NRN DESIGNS, MARY ENGELBRE
REBECCA SOWER, MAKING MEMORIES; FRAMI
NRN DESIGNS; TAG: NRN DESIGNS

TREASURE
• BEGIN WITH BLUE CARDSTOCK FOR BACKGROUND • EMBEL-
LISH PHOTO WITH TORN AND INKED CARDSTOCKS AND PAT-
TERNED PAPER • MAT PHOTO AND INK EDGES • REVERSE PRINT
TITLE AND CUT OUT • ADHERE MESH OVER TITLE • PRINT
JOURNALING ON WHITE CARDSTOCK, INK EDGES AND MAT •
USE A TEMPLATE TO ARRANGE PHOTO AND JOURNALING BLOCKS
AND ADHERE TO BACKGROUND • CUT STRIP OF PATTERNED
PAPER AND ADHERE EMBELLISHMENTS •
SUPPLIES – CARDSTOCK: BAZZILL; STICKERS: JOLEE'S BOUTIQUE;
MESH: MAGIC MESH; FONT: SAFFRON TOO

treasure

Connor has always required a certain
amount of gentleness, especially when
he was brought into any new
situation. People would have to spend
a lot of time just being in the same
room, then talking at a distance, then
communicating close up, before they
made an attempt at physical contact.
Connor's sensitivity has only made me
feel more important and I love
providing Connor with the patience
and understanding he needs.

Be gentle with
all the world's
treasures.

HOME GROWN

- CREATE BACKGROUND BY ADHERING BLACK, RED AND FAWN CARDSTOCKS AND PATTERNED PAPER IN A COLLAGE • DISTRESS BACKGROUND IN SMEARING FASHION WITH BLACK INK • MAT PHOTOS AND ADHERE TO BACKGROUND • CREATE TITLE BY MATTING METAL EYELET WORD WITH GINGHAM RIBBON AND STAMPING FAWN CARDSTOCK WITH BLOCK LETTER STAMPS • TEAR BLOCK LETTERS, CHALK EDGES AND ATTACH TO LAYOUT WITH RED EYELETS • CREATE BORDER BY ADHERING A KNOTTED GINGHAM RIBBON TO FAWN AND RED CARDSTOCKS AND STAMP DATE • EMBELLISH LAYOUT WITH TAN MESH, THREE PEWTER STAR EYELETS AND BUTTON •

SUPPLIES – PATTERNED PAPER: 7 GYPSIES; INK PAD: HERO ARTS; EYELETS: MAKING MEMORIES; DATE STAMP: MAKING MEMORIES; METAL EMBELLISHMENTS: MAKING MEMORIES; STAMP: HERO ARTS; CHALKS: STAMPIN' UP

Designer: Tammy Melish

CLASS OF 2020

- CREATE BACKGROUND BY ADHERING RANDOMLY TORN PATTERNED PAPER TO CORRUGATED CARDBOARD • DISTRESS BACKGROUND WITH SEPIA INK PAD • MAT PHOTO WITH PIECE OF CARDBOARD AND ATTACH TO BACKGROUND WITH MINI METAL BRADS • CREATE NAME PORTION OF TITLE BY ATTACHING INKED LETTER STICKERS TO BACKGROUND • PRINT REST OF TITLE ONTO TRANSPARENCY AND ADHERE OVER CARDBOARD • MAT QUOTE STICKER WITH INKED CARDBOARD • EMBELLISH QUOTE WITH FIBER •

SUPPLIES – STICKERS: CLUB SCRAP JOURNEY KIT; FIBER: FIBERS BY THE YARD; FONT: BATIK

Growing-Up

Designer: Christi Fratini

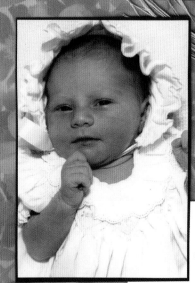

She's finally here, she finally arrived,
A beautiful baby has entered our lives.
Our family is thrilled, as you may have guessed,
We're very thankful that we've been so blessed.

We are proud to announce
the arrival of

Anna Marie

July 2, 2003
7 pounds, 5.8 ounces
20½ inches

Jennifer and Jamie Reardon
& Big Brother Cole

birth (burth) 1. the act of bringing a child into the world 2. bringing forth offspring 3. the beginning of anything   precious (presh′-es) 1. of great worth 2. beloved; cherished

ANNA MARIE

• CREATE BACKGROUND BY ADHERING FLOWER PATTERNED VELLUM TO YELLOW CARDSTOCK • MAT PHOTO WITH BLACK CARDSTOCK AND ADHERE TO BACKGROUND • ADHERE BABY ANNOUNCEMENT TO BACKGROUND • ADHERE PREMADE TAG TO BACKGROUND • EMBELLISH LAYOUT WITH CHALKED BIRTH DEFINITION STICKER AND RAFFIA •

SUPPLIES – VELLUM: WORLDWIN; CARDSTOCK: BAZZILL; TAGS: FRESH TAGS, REBECCA SOWER; STICKERS: MAKING MEMORIES; CHALK: CLOSE TO MY HEART

JOSH

• BEGIN WITH YELLOW CARDSTOCK FOR BACK-GROUND • DOUBLE MAT PHOTOS AND ADHERE TO BACKGROUND • CREATE TITLE CARD BY PRINTING DATE AND AGE ONTO WHITE CARD-STOCK • ATTACH LETTER STICKERS TO TITLE CARD WITH GREEN BRADS • PRINT JOURNALING ONTO CARDSTOCK, DOUBLE MAT AND ADHERE TO BACKGROUND • MAT METAL PLATE WITH TORN PAPER AND DOUBLE MAT WITH CARD-STOCK • ATTACH TO BACKGROUND WITH STAR BRADS • ADHERE GREEN VELLUM ENVELOPE TO BACKGROUND AND INSERT TITLE CARD • EMBEL-LISH LAYOUT WITH ANIMAL STICKERS TO MATCH BABY'S BIB •

SUPPLIES – CARDSTOCK: NATIONAL CARDSTOCK; METAL ACCENT: MAKING MEMORIES; ENVELOPE: EK SUCCESS; STICKERS: EK SUCCESS; STAR BRADS: CREATIVE IMAGINATIONS; LETTER STICKERS: EK SUCCESS; GREEN EYELETS: DOODLEBUG

May 31, 2003
4 Months 3 weeks

CHERUB (cher'-eb) 1. a type of angel characterized as a chubby, rosy cheeked child with wings 2. a child with a sweet, innocent face

Designer: MaryDawn Mayer

2 MONTHS

• CREATE BACKGROUND BY ADHERING CURSIVE PATTERNED PAPER AND NATURAL COLORED CARDSTOCK TO FLOWER PATTERNED PAPER • ATTACH GINGHAM STICKER STRIP TO SEPARATE DIFFERENT PAPERS • MAT PHOTO WITH TORN MULBERRY PAPER AND ADHERE TO PAGE • TRIM PICTURE TO FIT METAL FRAME AND ADHERE WITH GLUE DOTS • ATTACH LETTER STICKERS FOR TITLE • PRINT JOURNALING ONTO VELLUM AND ADHERE TO LAYOUT • EMBELLISH LAYOUT WITH BABY SAFETY PINS AND PHOTO CORNERS •

SUPPLIES – PATTERNED PAPER: ANNA GRIFFIN, 7 GYPSIES; MULBERRY PAPER: BAZZILL; STICKERS: STICKOPOTAMUS, REBECCA SOWER; METAL FRAME: MAKING MEMORIES; BABY PINS: JOLEE'S BY YOU

SPECIAL TIPS:

WET MULBERRY PAPER BEFORE TEARING EDGES TO GIVE IT A SOFT, FLUFFY TEXTURE.

Samuel, at 2 months you are just the sweetest little baby. You are just beginning to smile and we are all doing whatever we can to make you grace us with a grin. You are growing like crazy on mama's milk, weighing in at 12 pounds 14 ounces, and measuring 22.5 inches long. You've just moved into your own crib, since you are sleeping through the night, which we are most grateful for! And as you can see, you are a cloth diapered little baby. The diaper you're wearing here was made for you by one of Mommy's online friends. We think it makes you look like the cutest little diaper butt in town! ~June 2003~

IT'S ALL ABOUT
Head, Shoulders,
Knees And Toes

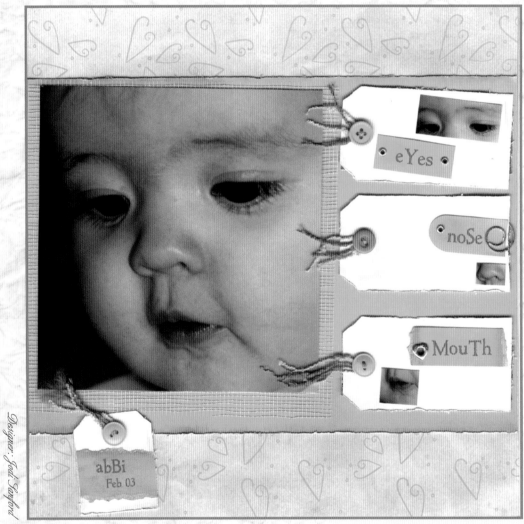

eYes

noSe

MouTh

abBi
Feb 03

Designer: Jodi Sanford

ABBI FACE

• CREATE BACKGROUND BY ADHERING TORN PIECE OF CARDSTOCK WITH INKED EDGES TO PATTERNED PAPER • MAT ENLARGED PHOTO WITH MESH AND ADHERE TO BACKGROUND • CREATE WORD BLOCKS WITH CARDSTOCK AND STAMPS • PRINT JOURNALING ONTO VELLUM AND ADHERE TO LAYOUT • TEAR TAGS AND RUB WITH CHALKS • ATTACH WORD BLOCKS TO TAGS WITH EYELETS • CUT PORTIONS OF PHOTO AND ADHERE TO TAGS • ADHERE TAGS TO LAYOUT OVER JOURNALING VELLUM • EMBELLISH TAGS WITH BUTTONS, FIBERS AND CLIPS •

SUPPLIES – PATTERNED PAPER: PROVO CRAFT; MESH: MAGENTA'S

CHANGES IN YOU

• BEGIN WITH PATTERNED PAPER FOR BACK-
GROUND AND AGE WITH INK • DOUBLE MAT
PHOTOS AND ADHERE TO BACKGROUND •
PRINT TITLE ONTO CARDSTOCK AND ADHERE
TO BACKGROUND • PRINT JOURNALING ONTO
VELLUM, MAT WITH CARDSTOCK AND ADHERE
TO BACKGROUND • HEAT EMBOSS JOURNALING
WITH CLEAR EMBOSSING POWDER • EMBELLISH
LAYOUT WITH CHARM AND BRADS •
SUPPLIES – PATTERNED PAPER: DESIGN ORIGINALS;
BRADS: MAKING MEMORIES; LETTER STICKERS;
SHOTZ; SILVER CHARM: HOBBY LOBBY; FONT:
PROBLEM SECRETARY

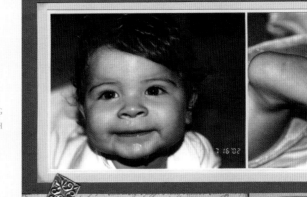

> **SPECIAL TIPS:**
> USE BLACK AND WHITE
> PHOTO PAPER WHEN DEVELOP-
> ING BLACK AND WHITE FILM.
> IT MAY BE MORE COSTLY, BUT
> THE RESULTS ARE STRIKING.

July 18, 2002

Dear Alina,
This evening around 9:50pm, you STOOD up
against the crib railing for the first time.
Briana & I were reading a bedtime story on
the couch and you just had to peek at us.
You were so proud of yourself that after you
stood up, you GRINNED widely. Later you did
it again, but you weren't quite sure how to
get down. You fell backwards into the crib
and scared yourself for just a minute until
you heard us clap & cheer for you! What a
sweet MOMENT to remember. Love, mommy

Designer: Anna Estrada Danion

BEAUTIFUL BOY

• CREATE BACKGROUND BY ADHERING TORN
BLUE NETTING AND A SHEET OF VELLUM TO
PATTERNED PAPER • ATTACH MESH TO PHOTO
WITH STITCHING • PRINT LYRICS TO "BEAUTIFUL
BOY" BY JOHN LENNON ON WHITE VELLUM •
ARRANGE LYRICS THROUGHOUT THE PAGE AND
PRINT IN GRAY TONES • ADHERE VELLUM TO
LAYOUT • PRINT TITLE ONTO VELLUM AND MAT
WITH PATTERNED VELLUM, MATCHING PAPER
AND NETTING • EMBELLISH LAYOUT WITH RIB-
BON, NETTING, STARS AND BRADS •
SUPPLIES – VELLUM: DCWV, LEISURE ARTS;
BUTTONS: DRESS IT UP

IT'S ALL ABOUT
Babies
On The Move

Joshua

• CREATE BACKGROUND BY
ADHERING STRIP OF LIGHT BLUE
PATTERNED PAPER AND ZIPPER TO
PATTERNED PAPER • MAT LARGE
PHOTO AND STRIP OF SMALLER
PHOTOS • SEW TOP EDGE OF
LARGE PHOTO TO ATTACH TO
BACKGROUND • REVERSE PRINT
TITLE LETTERING AND CUT OUT •
MAT LETTERS AND CUT OUT AGAIN
• ATTACH PRINTED JOURNALING
WITH BRADS • EMBELLISH WITH
CHARM AND SILVER LETTERS •
SUPPLIES – CARDSTOCK: BAZZILL;
PATTERNED PAPER: BO BUNNY;
ZIPPER: JUNKITZ; LETTER STICKERS:
MAKING MEMORIES; METAL CHARMS:
LEISURE ARTS; TITLE: QUICKUTZ

CLIMB HIGH

• BEGIN WITH TEXTURED CARDSTOCK FOR
BACKGROUND • MAT AND ADHERE THREE
PHOTOS TO BACKGROUND • ADHERE CLIMB
HIGH QUOTE WITH BRASS EYELETS • STAMP
DATE • CUT TWIG FROM PAPER AND ADHERE
TO BOTTOM OF PHOTOS OVER PORTION OF
QUOTE • EMBELLISH LAYOUT WITH THREE
BRASS EYELETS •

SUPPLIES – PAPER: REBECCA SOWER; QUOTES:
MEMORIES COMPLETE; DATE STAMP: MAKING
MEMORIES

Designer: Pam Cousins

LI'L BABE

• CREATE BACKGROUND BY ADHERING STRIPS OF CARDSTOCK AND PAT-
TERNED PAPER TO TAN CARDSTOCK • DOUBLE MAT PHOTOS AND
ADHERE TO BACKGROUND • ADHERE LETTER DIE CUTS FOR TITLE AND
JOURNALING • EMBELLISH LAYOUT WITH BASEBALL BRADS •

SUPPLIES – CARDSTOCK: BAZZILL; PATTERNED PAPER: DOODLEBUG; BUTTONS:
JESSE JAMES; TITLE: QUICKUTZ

IT'S ALL ABOUT

In Touch With Nature

Designer: Camille Jensen

GROW

- CREATE BACKGROUND BY ADHERING TORN AND EMBOSSED GREEN PATTERNED PAPER (EMBOSS BY STAMPING WITH A CLEAR EMBOSSING PAD AND HEAT EMBOSSING SEVERAL TIMES) TO PURPLE PATTERNED PAPER • ATTACH PICTURE TO BACKGROUND WITH PHOTO CORNERS • CREATE TITLE WITH LETTER STICKERS ON METAL-RIMMED TAGS • EMBOSS EACH TAG WITH DEEP EMBOSSING POWDER • LET TAGS COOL AND CRACK BY GENTLY BENDING TAG • ADHERE GREEN AND YELLOW RIBBON TO LAYOUT • ATTACH NAME TAG TO LAYOUT WITH RIBBON • ATTACH TITLE TO LAYOUT WITH BRADS • ADHERE LAMINATED DRY DAISY WITH SQUARE TAG TO LAYOUT •

SUPPLIES – PATTERNED PAPER: LEISURE ARTS; DEEP EMBOSSING: SUZE WEINBERG; STICKERS: LEISURE ARTS; TAGS: AVERY

BUBBLE

- BEGIN WITH PATTERNED PAPER FOR BACKGROUND
- ALTER ONE PICTURE TO SEPIA TONE • ADHERE PHOTOS TO BACKGROUND • PRINT TITLE ONTO PATTERNED PAPER • PRINT JOURNALING ON VELLUM • REPLACE CENTERS OF METAL TAGS WITH COLORED VELLUM • ADD SPARKLES TO MAKE TAGS LOOK LIKE BUBBLES • ADHERE TITLE, JOURNALING AND BUBBLES TO LAYOUT •

SUPPLIES – PATTERNED PAPER: SONNETS; METAL TAGS: MAKING MEMORIES

May your joys be as deep as the ocean and your sorrows as light as foam.

Designer: Sara Horton

Crystal Lacquer/Clear Embossing

CRYSTAL LACQUER IS A THICK LIQUID THAT DRIES TO FORM A RAISED SOLID. IT WILL DRAW ATTENTION TO WHATEVER IT IS APPLIED TO AND WILL MAGNIFY TEXT OR SHAPES UNDERNEATH IT. BE SURE TO SQUEEZE THE LIQUID ONTO YOUR LAYOUT CAREFULLY TO AVOID AIR BUBBLES. CRYSTAL LACQUER CAN BE USED AS A LACQUER AND AN ADHESIVE. IT IS A GREAT ADHESIVE FOR WATCH CRYSTALS AND OTHER CLEAR PRODUCTS. CRYSTAL LACQUER CAN BE PURCHASED IN A CLEAR OR PRE-COLORED FORM.

CLEAR EMBOSSING POWDER COMES IN TWO DIFFERENT FORMS: 1) REGULAR CLEAR EMBOSSING POWDER HAS A FINE TEXTURE AND CREATES A THIN GLASS-LIKE COATING; 2) THICK CLEAR EMBOSSING POWDER IS HEAT EMBOSSED IN SEVERAL LAYERS TO GIVE A VERY THICK CLEAR COATING.

TO EMBOSS, INK WITH PIGMENT INK, DUST AREA WITH EMBOSSING POWDER, SHAKE OFF EXCESS POWDER AND HEAT. IF USING THICK EMBOSSING POWDER IN A LARGE AREA, REPEAT THE EMBOSSING PROCESS SEVERAL TIMES OVER ONE SMALL AREA AT A TIME. WHEN FINISHED, LET COOL (PUT IN THE FREEZER FOR A MOMENT IF YOU ARE IN A HURRY). TO GET A CRACKLED OR AGED EFFECT GENTLY BEND EMBOSSED AREA BACK AND FORTH. ANY SCRAPBOOKING ELEMENT CAN BE CLEAR EMBOSSED FOR DIMENSION. ADD PAINT OR INK TO CLEAR EMBOSSING TO CHANGE THE LOOK OR COLOR OF AN ELEMENT.

DANDY LION SPRING

• BEGIN WITH GRAY CARDSTOCK FOR BACKGROUND • MAT PHOTOS WITH WHITE CARDSTOCK AND ADHERE TO BACKGROUND • PRINT TITLE ON CARDSTOCK, INK EDGES, MAT WITH DISTRESSED PAPER (CRUMPLE AND SAND PAPER WITH FINE GRAIN SAND PAPER) AND ATTACH TO BACKGROUND WITH SILVER BRAD AND THREAD • PRINT JOURNALING AND INK EDGES • CREATE LARGE TAG FROM WHITE CARDSTOCK, PHOTO AND CRUMPLED PAPER • PLACE A SMALL AMOUNT OF FUN FLOCK IN A WATCH CRYSTAL AND GLUE TO THE TAG WITH DIAMOND GLAZE • SEW ELEMENTS TOGETHER FOR TAG • INK SMALL TAGS • EMBELLISH LAYOUT WITH PIECES OF CRUMPLED PAPER, THREAD, CHARMS, TAGS, SAFETY PINS, BRADS AND EYELETS •

SUPPLIES – CARDSTOCK: CLOSE TO MY HEART, PATCHWORK MEMORIES; BUTTERFLY NAIL HEADS: JEST CHARMING; BRADS: JEST CHARMING: EYELETS: JEST CHARMING; FIBERS: BROWN BAG FIBERS; TAGS: DMD; INK: CLEARSNAP; FUN FLOCK: STAMPIN' UP; WATCH CRYSTAL: TWO PEAS IN A BUCKET; FONT: TWO PEAS IN A BUCKET FLEA MARKET

SPECIAL TIPS:

1. TO MOUNT NAIL HEADS TO TAGS:
   A. PLACE TAGS ON A MOUSE PAD.
   B. PRESS NAIL HEADS INTO TAGS GENTLY. IF NECESSARY, REMOVE NAIL HEADS; USE A CRAFT KNIFE TO CREATE HOLES, THEN PUSH NAIL HEADS THROUGH.
   C. TURN TAG OVER AND USE THE END OF A PEN TO PRESS THE SPIKES TOWARD THE CENTER. MAKE SURE ALL PRONGS ARE COMPLETELY FLATTENED.
2. SAFETY PINS ARE AN INEXPENSIVE AND INTERESTING WAY TO HANG ELEMENTS FROM A SCRAPBOOK PAGE.

115

IT'S ALL ABOUT

Mother Nature

Journaling (within layout):

warm summer sunshine ... rough the sprinkler ice cream sunshine going on a ... watermelon ... ol sipping lemon de watching t e sunset cold water ... sunset Spli ... mping ... n the sand sum ... summer le ... book pool ... ... e dog sunshi ... sunshine an ... ol summer ... mer sun su ... playing in th ... gs on a b ... each nkler ... ike sitting ... sunshin ... sunset ching oing on a c ... ot summer ... nt sand ... n showers ... lemonade spl ... castles ... walk aft ... summer sea ... summer suns ... ugh the sprin er watching the sunset runnin ... the sunset si ... am cool summer nites reading a good book summ ... porch summer ... ching the stars twinkle going on a camping trip an ... rm summer sun ... the sprinkler ice cream roasting hot dogs on ... atermelon w ... ing lemonade sitting by sea shore pool sippin ... ying in the wat ... sunset beach cool summer eating a slice of c ... nset splish splgsh ... rip sea shore warm summer rain showers ... through the sp ... and warm summer sunshine ice cream wat ... mmer laying on ... ol eating an ice cream watching the sunset w ... watermelon hot summer sunh ... ying in the san ... roasting hot dogs on a beach bonfire laying on the sand cool summ ... e sitting by ... sea shore warm summer sunshine sunset watching the stars twinkle pool

Jerry

summer 2003

I couldn't help myself from putting you in the grass. It's not your most favorite thing in fact. I'm not sure what you think of it. You just kind of sit there like a statue at first, not moving at all. Then, you eventually move, but with much uncertainty and with your little toes curled up tight! I'm sure the grass must fell funny against your little legs and feet. You even got adventurous enough to try to pull it after a while. It's just so great watching you discover all these new things in your world. May you always love the feeling of grass between your toes in the summer.   July 2003

SUMMER 2003
• CREATE BACKGROUND BY ADHERING TRIMMED PRINTED VELLUM TO TEXTURED CARDSTOCK • ADHERE MAIN PHOTO TO BACKGROUND • MAT THREE SMALLER PHOTOS AND ADHERE TO BACKGROUND • ADHERE LETTERS TO VELLUM TAGS FOR TITLE • PRINT JOURNALING ONTO ORANGE CARDSTOCK AND ADHERE TO BOTTOM OF LAYOUT • RUN TWO PIECES OF GINGHAM RIBBON ACROSS LAYOUT • STRING VELLUM TAGS FROM TOP RIBBON • STRING SILVER FISH CHARM FROM BOTTOM RIBBON •
SUPPLIES – CARDSTOCK: BAZZILL; PRINTED VELLUM: OVER THE MOON; LETTER STICKER: PROVO CRAFT

SPECIAL TIPS:
1. TO PRINT JOURNALING 12" WIDE, SET THE PAPER SIZE TO LEGAL (81/2X14) AND THE PAPER DIRECTION TO LANDSCAPE ON THE COMPUTER.
2. PULL ACCENTS FOR THE PAGE FROM THE PHOTOS (I.E. THE FISH CHARM ACCENT CAME FROM THE FISH ON THE LITTLE BOY'S SHIRT).
3. MOUNT SEVERAL SMALL PHOTOS CLOSE TOGETHER TO SHOW A SEQUENCE OF EVENTS.

TRUE BEAUTY

• BEGIN WITH PURPLE CARDSTOCK FOR BACKGROUND • CUT 8x10 PHOTO
INTO STRIPS ALONG TOP AND BOTTOM EDGE OF THE PHOTO • ADHERE TO
BACKGROUND SPACING THE STRIPS TO REVEAL CARDSTOCK BACKGROUND •
CUT OUT TITLE USING REVERSE LETTERING AND ADHERE TO BACKGROUND
• PRINT JOURNALING ON GREEN CARDSTOCK AND ADHERE TO LAYOUT •
ADHERE THIN STRIPS OF NAVY CARDSTOCK TO LAYOUT • INK EDGES WITH
BROWN INK • EMBELLISH LAYOUT WITH FLOWERS •
SUPPLIES – CARDSTOCK: BAZZILL; 3-D STICKERS: JOLEE'S; FONT: BROCK SCRIPT,
TWO PEAS IN A BUCKET KATHRYN BROOKS

GOOD OLD SUMMERTIME

• CREATE BACKGROUND BY DECORATIVELY SEWING TRIMMED PATTERNED
PAPER TO RED CARDSTOCK WITH A VINE STITCH • DOUBLE MAT PHOTO •
PUNCH SMALL HOLES ALONG BOTTOM OF MAT EVERY 1/2" • ATTACH
FIBERS AND GLASS BEADS TO MAT BY WEAVING LOOSELY • ADHERE MATTED
PHOTO TO LAYOUT • USE FORTUNASCHWEIN FONT FOR TITLE • PRINT
TITLE REVERSED ON GREEN PAPER AND CUT OUT • ADHERE TITLE TO
BACKGROUND IN A CURVE • PRINT JOURNALING ON VELLUM AND FIT
INSIDE SLIDE HOLDER THAT HAS BEEN COVERED WITH GOLD FABRIC •
WRAP BOTTOM EDGE OF SLIDE HOLDER WITH FIBERS AND BEADS •
ATTACH TWISTED FIBERS ACROSS LAYOUT AND ADHERE SLIDE HOLDER
OVER FIBERS • EMBELLISH LAYOUT WITH SUN CHARM •
SUPPLIES – CARDSTOCK: BAZZILL, MAKING MEMORIES; VELLUM: PAPER
ADVENTURES; FIBERS: FIBERS BY THE YARD; SUN CHARM: ALL THE EXTRAS;
GOLD FABRIC: HOBBY LOBBY; THREAD: COATS; SLIDE HOLDER: ALL THE EXTRAS;
GLASS BEADS: ALL THE EXTRAS; FONT: FORTUNASCHWEIN

Designer: Jason Stringfellow

WHEREVER YOU GO

• CREATE BACKGROUND BY ADHERING STICKER BORDERS
TO THE TOP AND BOTTOM OF A SHEET OF PATTERNED
CARDSTOCK • MAT PHOTOS WITH TAN CARDSTOCK AND
INK THE EDGES • CREATE TITLE BY STAMPING AND
ATTACHING STICKERS TO THE BACKGROUND • ATTACH
VELLUM TO BACKGROUND WITH MINI SILVER BRADS •
SUPPLIES – PATTERNED PAPER: CLUB SCRAPS; STAMPS: PSX;
LETTER STICKERS: STAMPENDOUS, MAKING MEMORIES

Sun, Sea & Sand

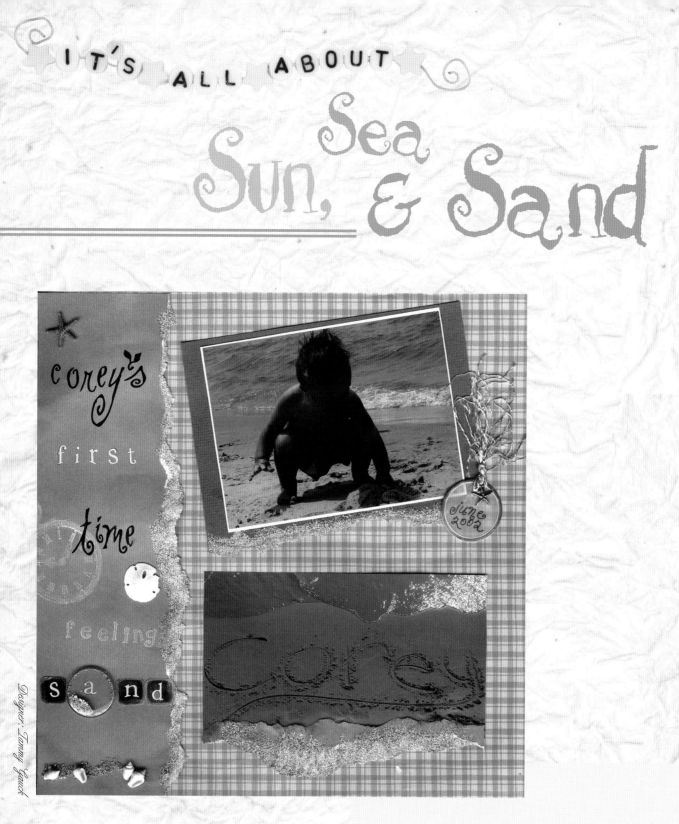

FIRST TIME FEELING SAND

• CREATE BACKGROUND BY ADHERING TORN BLUE PAPER TO PLAID PATTERNED PAPER • MAT TOP PHOTO AND TEAR BOTTOM EDGE • ADHERE TORN AND EMBOSSED PIECE OF PAPER TO SAND PHOTO • EMBOSS EDGES OF TORN PAPERS BEFORE ADHERING TO LAYOUT • ATTACH STICKER LETTERS FOR TITLE • STAMP CLOCK ON TITLE PAPER WITH WHITE INK • HANDWRITE DATE ON VELLUM TAG AND ATTACH TO LAYOUT WITH STARFISH CHARM AND FLOSS • FILL WATCH CRYSTAL WITH SAND AND ADHERE TO TITLE • EMBELLISH WITH SHELLS, SAND, STARFISH AND SAND DOLLAR •

SUPPLIES – PAPER: MAKING MEMORIES, ROBINS NEST; LETTER STICKERS: SONNETS, STAMPIN' UP; TAG: MAKING MEMORIES; FLOSS: DMC; WATCH CRYSTAL: SCRAPSAHOY.COM; STAMPS: INKADINKADOO

Chasing Seagulls

CHASING SEAGULLS

• BEGIN WITH TEXTURED CARDSTOCK FOR BACKGROUND • CROP PORTION OF PHOTO ON COMPUTER, PRINT OUT, TEAR EDGES AND ADHERE TO BACKGROUND • PRINT TITLE IN LANDSCAPE MODE ON WHITE CARDSTOCK • TEAR BOTTOM EDGE OF TITLE PAPER • APPLY LIQUID GLUE TO TORN EDGE AND SPRINKLE WITH GLITTER • ADHERE TO BACKGROUND • TYPE JOURNALING OVER PHOTO, PRINT OUT AND CUT INTO STRIPS • ATTACH JOURNALING STRIPS TO BACKGROUND WITH BRADS • CUT THREE PIECES OF FLOSS AND TIE A KNOT AT ONE END • ATTACH BLUE MOON BEADS, SAND DOLLAR AND MINI METAL FRAMED PHOTO TO ENDS OF FLOSS AND KNOT • EMBELLISH WITH SEASHELL DIE CUTS •
SUPPLIES – CARDSTOCK: BAZZILL; GLITTER: JONES TONES; FLOSS: DMC; BEADS: BLUE MOON; TAG: MAKING MEMORIES; DIECUT: JOLEE'S BOUTIQUE; FONT: CK BELLA

YOU AND ME BY THE SEA

• CREATE BACKGROUND BY ADHERING TORN STRIPS OF BLUE PAPER TO WHITE CARDSTOCK RESEMBLING WAVES OF THE SEA • MAT PHOTOS WITH CARDSTOCK AND ADHERE TO BACKGROUND • CREATE TITLE WITH RUB-ON LETTERS AND LETTER STAMPS • ADHERE DIE CUTS TO THE BACKGROUND • WRAP FIBER AROUND ENTIRE LAYOUT AND TIE OFF • EMBELLISH WITH POEMSTONE AND FLOWER SHAPES •
SUPPLIES – PATTERNED PAPER: LEISURE ARTS; DIECUTS: DELUXE CUTS; METAL FLOWERS: LEISURE ARTS; POEM STONES: SONNETS; TITLE: CREATIVE IMAGINATIONS; STAMPS: PSX; FIBERS: FIBER BY THE YARD

Designer: Sam Cousins

SPECIAL TIPS:

1. USE PRODUCTS FOR A PURPOSE OTHER THAN INTENDED. THE LITTLE FLOWER SHAPES ARE FROM A BABY CHARM KIT.
2. TEAR UP AND RE-PIECE A PAPER TO FIT YOUR NEEDS.

IT'S ALL ABOUT
Water Babies

Designer: Brooke Smith

Water boy

WATER BOY

• CREATE BACKGROUND BY ADHERING
DISTRESSED BLUE CARDSTOCK AND A
STRIP OF DARK BLUE CARDSTOCK TO TEX-
TURED CARDSTOCK • DOUBLE MAT
PHOTO WITH CARDSTOCK AND ADHERE
TO BACKGROUND • REVERSE PRINT TITLE
AND CUT OUT WITH EXACTO KNIFE •
FINISH TITLE WITH DOMINO PIECES
STAMPED WITH LETTERS • EMBELLISH
WITH METALLIC RUB-ONS TO ADD
DIMENSION TO THE DISTRESSED PAPER •
SUPPLIES – CARDSTOCK: BAZZILL; STAMP:
WORDSWORTH

ANYONE WHO SAYS SUNSHINE BRINGS HAPPINESS HAS NEVER *danced in the rain*

DANCED IN THE RAIN
• CREATE BACKGROUND BY ADHERING HALF A SHEET OF BLUE STRIPED PAPER TO WHITE CARDSTOCK • ADHERE A PIECE OF CIRCLE VELLUM ON TOP OF STRIPED PAPER WITH SCRAPPER SPRAY • ADHERE PHOTOS TO BACKGROUND • USE BLUE INK AND LETTER STAMPS FOR TITLE • ADHERE BITS AND BAUBLES FOR THE REST OF THE TITLE • STAMP NAME AND DATE ON CARDSTOCK AND SET IN WATCH CRYSTAL WITH GLASS BEADS • ADHERE CRYSTAL WITH DIAMOND GLAZE • HANG FIBERS FROM TOP OF LAYOUT TO RESEMBLE RAIN • HOLD FIBER DOWN WITH GLUE DOTS IN VARIOUS PLACES • MAKE THE SUN WITH TWISTAL • INK LAYOUT EDGES IN BLUE •
SUPPLIES – PRINTED VELLUM: SEI; STAMPS: PSX; 3-D EMBELLISHMENTS: CREATIVE IMAGINATIONS; FIBER: FIBERS BY THE YARD; TWISTAL: MAKING MEMORIES

GRANDSON

God gave me a special GIFT when you entered my LIFE.

With a bit of MISCHIEF and a twinkle in your eye, you GREET each day with OPEN arms.

You make me SMILE and bring me joy. Thank you for the GIFT of being my GRANDSON.

GRANDPA & JOSHUA 7•4•03

GRANDPA AND JOSHUA
• BEGIN WITH ORANGE CARDSTOCK FOR BACKGROUND • DOUBLE MAT LARGE PHOTO • TRIPLE MAT STRIP OF PHOTOS ALLOWING ROOM FOR TITLE ABOVE PHOTOS • ADHERE PHOTOS TO BACKGROUND • REVERSE PRINT TITLE AND DATE, CUT OUT AND ADHERE TO PHOTO MAT • PRINT JOURNALING ON VELLUM • DOUBLE MAT JOURNALING AND ADHERE TO BACKGROUND WITH SQUARE BRADS •
SUPPLIES – CARDSTOCK: BAZZILL; SQUARE BRADS: MAKING MEMORIES

IT'S ALL ABOUT
A Mother's Love

Designer: Janet Hopkins

A DAUGHTER IS...
• CREATE BACKGROUND BY ADHERING TORN PIECES OF GREEN AND PINK PATTERNED PAPER TO WHITE CARDSTOCK • TRIPLE MAT PHOTOS WITH CARDSTOCKS AND ADHERE TO BACKGROUND • PRINT DAUGHTER POEM AND NAMES ON GREEN VELLUM • TEAR TOP AND BOTTOM EDGES • STAMP EDGES OF VELLUM AND HEAT EMBOSS WITH WHITE EMBOSSING POWDER • ADHERE TO LAYOUT • EMBELLISH LAYOUT WITH ROSE, SILVER PHOTO CORNERS AND DECORATIVE EYELETS • THREAD EYELETS WITH FIBERS • SUPPLIES - PATTERNED PAPER: LEISURE ARTS; METAL EMBELLISHMENTS: LEISURE ARTS; EYELETS: MAGIC SCRAPS

FROM THE HEART
• CREATE BACKGROUND BY ADHERING TORN FLORAL PAPER WITH CHALKED EDGES TO CARDSTOCK • MAT PHOTO WITH TORN CARDSTOCK AND FLORAL PAPER • COVER PHOTO WITH SWATCH OF TULLE FABRIC • ATTACH FABRIC WITH BRADS • PRINT JOURNALING ONTO PAPER AND MOUNT WITH FLORAL PAPER • WRAP JOURNALING WITH STRIPS OF ANTIQUED PAPER AND ADHERE TO PAGE • ANTIQUE SMALL ENVELOPE WITH STAIN AND RUBBER STAMPS • EMBELLISH LAYOUT WITH HEART CHARM, FIBERS AND A FAUX WAX SEAL • SUPPLIES – CARDSTOCK: BAZZILL; PATTERNED PAPERS: ANNA GRIFFIN, KAREN FOSTER; TULLE FABRIC: JOANN'S; ENVELOPE: TWO PEAS IN A BUCKET; FIBERS: ADORNMENTS; BRADS: BOXER; CHALKS: CRAF-T; STAMP: HERO ARTS, STAMPIN' UP; WAX SEAL: SONNETS

SPECIAL TIPS:
USE A GEL ANTIQUING MEDIUM INSTEAD OF WALNUT INK TO GIVE AN AGED LOOK. THE GEL IS EASIER TO USE AND NOT AS MESSY AS THE INK.

122

I AM YOUR MOTHER

• BEGIN WITH BLACK CARDSTOCK FOR BACKGROUND • MAT PHOTO WITH PATTERNED PAPERS, BLACK AND WHITE CARD-STOCKS, AND TRANSPARENCY • ATTACH STICKERS FOR TITLE • TIE BOW AROUND ENTIRE LAYOUT • ATTACH METAL-RIMMED TAG WITH LETTER STICKERS TO RIBBON • EMBELLISH PHOTO WITH 'MOTHER' EYELET •

SUPPLIES – PATTERNED PAPER: KAREN FOSTER, 7 GYPSIES; STICKERS: SONNETS; EYELET WORD: MAKING MEMORIES

Designer: Sam Cousins

LOVE BEING YOUR MOM

• CREATE BACKGROUND BY ADHERING TORN PATTERNED PAPER AND MESH TO BLUE CARDSTOCK • ADHERE PHOTOS TO LAYOUT • CREATE TITLE WITH LETTER STICKERS • BRUSH SMALL ENVELOPE WITH WALNUT INK AND ATTACH LETTER STICKERS • ATTACH ENVELOPE TO LAYOUT WITH HEMP • STAMP DATE AND ADHERE WITH MINI BRADS • ANTIQUE LOVE STICKER WITH WALNUT INK AND ADHERE TO LAYOUT •

SUPPLIES – PAPER: NRN DESIGNS; NAME PLATE: NRN DESIGNS; MESH: CLUB SCRAP; STICKERS: NRN DESIGNS, ALL THE EXTRAS, MAKING MEMORIES; DATE STAMP: MAKING MEMORIES

IT'S ALL ABOUT
A Father's Love

HAND IN HAND

• CREATE BACKGROUND BY ADHERING CORRUGATED CARDBOARD, PATTERNED PAPER, AND SAND PATTERNED PAPER TO BLACK CARDSTOCK • DOUBLE MAT LARGE PHOTO • SINGLE MAT ACCENT PHOTOS • PRINT TITLE AND MAT ON CORRUGATED PAPER • PRINT NAMES AND DATE AND ADHERE TO LAYOUT • TWIST BLACK WIRE FOR ACCENT AND ADHERE TO LAYOUT • SUPPLIES – PATTERNED PAPER: PAPERBILITIES; CORRUGATED PAPER: PAPERBILITIES; CARDSTOCK: KRAFT

SPECIAL TIPS:

ADDING ACCENT PICTURES OF THE MAIN PHOTO IS A GREAT WAY TO USE YOUR DUPLICATE PHOTOS.

Hand in Hand...

Benjamin and Daddy   July 14, 2003

Designer: Melissa Gay

SPECIAL TIPS:

TO GIVE VARIETY TO A PAGE, RANDOMLY CHANGE SOME PHOTOS FROM COLOR TO BLACK AND WHITE.

DADDY'S SWEETHEART

• CREATE BACKGROUND BY CHALKING FLOWERS ONTO CARDSTOCK WITH A STENCIL • MAT PHOTO AND TEAR BOTTOM EDGE • USE SQUARE PUNCH TO CUT UNIFORM PHOTOS • CHALK EDGES OF TORN PHOTO MAT • PRINT TITLE AND JOURNALING ONTO CARDSTOCK • ADHERE PHOTOS TO CARDSTOCK • ATTACH PRINTED CARDSTOCKS TO BACKGROUND WITH EYELETS • EMBELLISH LAYOUT WITH FLOWER CHARMS AND EYELETS •
SUPPLIES – FONT: WORD ART, CHILLER; FLOWER CHARMS: MAKING MEMORIES: EYELETS: MAKING MEMORIES

LOVE IS FOREVER

• CREATE BACKGROUND BY ADHERING TORN HEART PATTERNED PAPER TO WHITE CARDSTOCK • ADHERE PHOTO TO BACKGROUND • TEAR LETTERS FOR 'LOVE' FREEHAND FROM HEART PATTERNED PAPER • ADHERE LETTER STICKERS AND TORN LETTERS TO LAYOUT FOR TITLE • CHALK ENTIRE LAYOUT WITH GREEN CHALK USING RANDOM STROKES • ADHERE WHITE FEATHER FIBERS TO LAYOUT • CHALK FIBERS WITH PINK CHALK • EMBELLISH LAYOUT WITH HEART CHARM •
SUPPLIES – PATTERNED PAPER: LEISURE ARTS; STICKERS: TREEHOUSE DESIGN; FIBER: FIBERS BY THE YARD

SPECIAL TIPS:

USE CHALK TO CHANGE THE ENTIRE LOOK OF A LAYOUT IF YOU DON'T HAVE THE RIGHT COLOR CARDSTOCK.

IT'S ALL ABOUT
Family

Designer: Camille Jensen

WELCOME TO OUR WORLD
- CREATE BACKGROUND BY ADHERING TORN STRIP OF PINK PATTERNED PAPER TOPPED WITH ROSEBUD PINK RIBBON TO YELLOW PATTERNED PAPER • WRAP PHOTOS WITH VARIEGATED EMBROIDERY FLOSS • ADHERE PHOTOS TO BACKGROUND • CREATE TITLE BY SEWING METAL LETTERS TO BACKGROUND WITH PINK FLOSS • ATTACH BUBBLE LETTERS TO LIGHT YELLOW MULBERRY PAPER AND MAT WITH PINK VELLUM AND GREEN MULBERRY PAPER • ATTACH 'SISTERS' ON FUN FOAM TO PINK HANDMADE PAPER, GREEN PATTERNED PAPER AND WHITE VELLUM • SEW TO LAYOUT WITH VARIEGATED GREEN FLOSS • MAT DATE STAMP WITH PINK HANDMADE PAPER AND YELLOW VELLUM AND ATTACH TO LAYOUT •

SUPPLIES – PATTERNED PAPER: LEISURE ARTS; METAL LETTER TAGS: DCWV; MULBERRY PAPER: DCWV

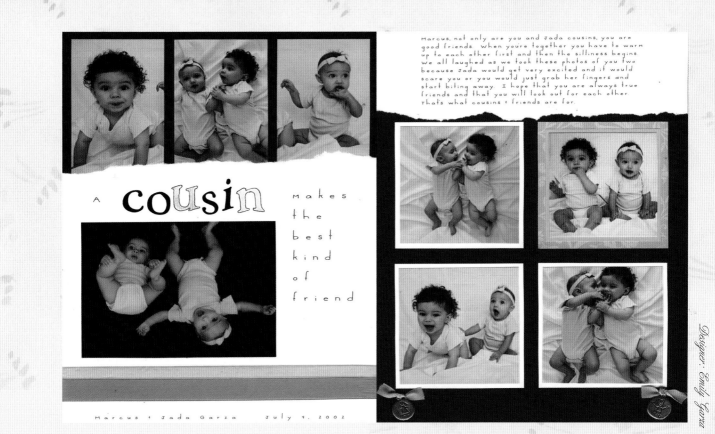

Designer: Emily Garza

COUSINS

• BEGIN WITH BLACK CARDSTOCK FOR BACKGROUND • ADHERE THREE PHOTOS TO BACKGROUND • MAT LARGER PHOTO WITH WHITE CARDSTOCK LEAVING ROOM FOR JOURNALING AND ADHERE TO BACKGROUND WITH TOP EDGE TORN • MAT THREE BLACK AND WHITE PHOTOS WITH WHITE CARDSTOCK • MAT COLOR PHOTO WITH PATTERNED PAPERS • ADHERE PHOTOS TO BACKGROUND • PRINT TITLE AND JOURNALING ON WHITE CARDSTOCK • USE ALPHABET STICKERS AND CHALK TO EMBELLISH TITLE • TEAR BOTTOM EDGE OF JOURNALING AND ADHERE TO LAYOUT • EMBELLISH LAYOUT WITH RIBBON AND CHARMS • SUPPLIES – PATTERNED PAPER: ANNA GRIFFIN; STICKERS: CREATIVE IMAGINATIONS

SPECIAL TIPS:

1. WHEN YOU RUN OUT OF LETTER STICKERS USE THE STICKER SHEET AS A STENCIL. CHALK THE INSIDE OF THE STENCIL OR CUT OUT THE STENCIL, FRAMING THE EMPTY SPACE OF THE LETTER INSIDE AND USE IT AS A STICKER.
2. RUN RIBBON THROUGH A XYRON MACHINE FOR AN EASY WAY TO ADHERE IT TO A LAYOUT.

HOLDING TY

• CREATE BACKGROUND BY ADHERING PATTERNED PAPERS, BLUE CARD-STOCK AND MESH TO TEXTURED CARDSTOCK • MAT PHOTO AND ADHERE TO PAGE • WRAP OTHER PHOTO WITH FELT AND STITCH AROUND EDGES • CREATE FIRST WORD OF TITLE WITH VELLUM STICKERS ON TEXTURED CARDSTOCK • STITCH TITLE BLOCK TO LAYOUT • FINISH TITLE BY CREAT-ING TAG WITH PATTERNED PAPER AND LETTER CHARMS • ATTACH TAG TO FELT WITH SAFETY PIN • PRINT JOURNALING ON VELLUM • ATTACH TO PAGE WITH CROSS-STITCHING • EMBELLISH LAYOUT WITH FIBERS • SUPPLIES – CARDSTOCK: BAZZILL; PATTERNED PAPER: NRN DESIGNS, 7 GYPSIES; FLOSS: DMC; FIBERS: ADORNMENTS; MESH: MAGENTA; LETTER CHARMS: MAKING MEMORIES; TAG: AVERY; FONT: TWO PEAS IN A BUCKET RAGTAG

SPECIAL TIPS:

HOLD FABRIC IN PLACE WITH TEMPORARY ADHESIVE WHILE STITCHING AROUND A PHOTO.

IT'S ALL ABOUT

Love Without

Measure

Designer: Tam Coulter

ALWAYS

- CREATE BACKGROUND BY ADHERING TEXTURED PAPER AND STRIPS OF FLORAL PAPER TO BLACK CARDSTOCK • ADHERE BLACK AND WHITE PHOTO TO BACKGROUND • MAKE BLACK AND WHITE AND COLOR COPY OF OTHER PHOTO • ADHERE COLORED PHOTO TO BACKGROUND • TEAR CENTER SECTION FROM BLACK AND WHITE PHOTO AND ADHERE ATOP COLORED PHOTO • CUT TWO SQUARE PHOTOS AND ADHERE TO SQUARE METAL FRAMES (USE PORTION OF TORN PHOTO FOR ONE FRAME) • CREATE TITLE WITH 'LOVE' TEMPLATE AND CHALK WITH RED AND BLACK CHALK • PRINT 'WITHOUT' ON TRANSPARENCY AND ADHERE TO TAG MADE FROM PATTERNED PAPERS • ATTACH TAG TO LAYOUT WITH THREE STAR CONCHES AND GINGHAM RIBBON • ATTACH EYELET METAL LETTERS TO LAYOUT WITH HEMP • HEAT EMBOSS 'ALWAYS' LETTER WITH RED EMBOSSING POWDER AND ADHERE TO LAYOUT • EMBELLISH LAYOUT WITH HEART EYELET, GINGHAM RIBBON, PHOTO CORNERS, MEASURING TAPE STICKER AND METAL FLOWER PAPER CLIP •

SUPPLIES – PATTERNED PAPER: ANNA GRIFFIN; METAL FRAMES: MAKING MEMORIES, METAL WORD: MAKING MEMORIES; HEART EYELET: MAKING MEMORIES; RIBBON: MICHAELS; PHOTO CORNERS: MAKING MEMORIES; STICKERS: REBECCA SOWER; EYELET LETTERS: MAKING MEMORIES; PIER ONE; LETTER TEMPLATE: MAKING MEMORIES

To the world

you might be

just
one person.

But to
one person

you just might

be

the *World*

ISLAND

THE WORLD

• BEGIN WITH MAP PATTERNED PAPER FOR BACKGROUND • MAT PHO-
TOS • PRINT TITLE ON TRANSPARENCY • FINISH TITLE WITH LETTER
STICKERS • ADHERE TRANSPARENCY WITH CLEAR DOUBLE-SIDED TAPE
• EMBELLISH WITH BOTTLE AND SHIP WHEEL •
SUPPLIES – PATTERNED PAPER: SONNETS; STICKERS: SONNETS; BOTTLE:
JOLEE'S BOUTIQUE; SHIPS WHEEL: DRESS IT UP; FONT: TWO PEAS IN A
BUCKET DREAMS

SPECIAL TIPS:

USE A TRANSPARENCY FOR PRINTING TITLES
AND JOURNALING WHEN YOU HAVE A PRETTY
PIECE OF PAPER TO SHOW THROUGH AND
DON'T WANT IT COVERED BY JOURNAL BOXES.

CHILDREN ARE THE KEY TO PARADISE

• CREATE BACKGROUND BY ADHERING TORN AND DIS-
TRESSED PIECE OF PATTERNED PAPER TO ANTIQUE KEY
PAPER • TEAR EDGES OF PHOTO AND INK • TEAR, CRUM-
PLE, SAND AND INK SMALLER PHOTO • CREATE TITLE
WITH AN ASSORTMENT OF LETTER WORDS • ATTACH KEY
MAGNETS WITH FIBER AND SILVER BRADS • FRAME TITLE
BOX WITH FIBER •
SUPPLIES – PAPER: SEI; FIBER: FIBER BY THE YARD; BRADS:
MAKING MEMORIES; KEY MAGNETS: TARGET; LETTERS:
WORDSWORTH, SONNETS, MAKING MEMORIES, REBECCA
SOWER

LETTER TO MY DAUGHTER SOPHIA

• CREATE BACKGROUND BY ADHERING FLORAL PAPER AND WORD
PATTERNED PAPER TO GREEN CARDSTOCK • MAT LARGE PHOTO
WITH TWILL TAPE • ADHERE PHOTOS TO LAYOUT • ATTACH TWILL
TAPE TO LOWER CORNER OF SMALL PHOTO • ADHERE FRAME OVER
SMALLER PHOTO SKEWED TO ONE SIDE • PRINT TEXT ON SMALL
PIECE OF VELLUM AND TEAR • INK EDGES OF VELLUM WITH PINK
INK • ATTACH VELLUM TAG TO OPEN CARD WITH EYELETS • CRE-
ATE CARD FROM CRAFT PAPER AND ADHERE TORN PIECE OF FLO-
RAL PAPER TO CORNER OF CARD • CREATE WAX SEAL BY MELTING
A COLORED GLUE STICK ONTO A SCRAP PIECE OF CARDSTOCK •
STAMP WAX WITH DESIRED STAMP • HANDWRITE PRIVATE LETTER
AND SLIDE INSIDE CARD • GLUE BACK OF CARD TO LAYOUT •
EMBELLISH WITH CLIP, RUB-ON WORDS AND RIBBON •
SUPPLIES – TWILL TAPE: 7 GYPSIES; RUB-ON WORDS: MAKING
MEMORIES

CHILDREN

ARE THE KEY TO

PARADISE

SPECIAL TIPS:

SEPIA STAMP INK IS AN EXCEL-
LENT WAY TO "ANTIQUE" A
LAYOUT WITHOUT THE MESS
OF WALNUT INK.

Designer: Amy Goldstein

129

IT'S ALL ABOUT
Ties That Bind

Designer: Peggy Manrique

Computer Education:

THE SKY IS THE LIMIT WHEN COMPUTERS AND THE INTERNET ARE USED IN SCRAPBOOKING. HERE ARE SOME WAYS YOU CAN USE THE COMPUTER TO IMPROVE YOUR LAYOUTS.

THE FONTS USED FOR TITLES AND JOURNALING CAN CHANGE THE ENTIRE FEEL OF A LAYOUT. THERE IS AN ENDLESS SUPPLY OF FONTS TO CHOOSE FROM ON THE COMPUTER. THEY CAN BE FOUND IN WORD PROCESSING PROGRAMS, OTHER PURCHASED SOFTWARE PROGRAMS AND THE INTERNET. MANY INTERNET SITES PROVIDE FREE DOWNLOADABLE FONTS OR PURCHASABLE FONTS. TRY USING MANY DIFFERENT FONTS ON ONE LAYOUT TO DRAW ATTENTION TO YOUR TEXT.

PRINT TEXT IN VARYING SIZES AND COLORS WITH ITALICS, BORDERS AND BOLD LETTERING TO ADD INTEREST TO A LAYOUT. LAYER TEXT BOXES TO ADD DIMENSION AND CREATE BACKGROUNDS TO ADD TEXTURE. HIGHLIGHT WORDS WITH COLOR, FONT AND SIZE.

ALTER DIGITAL OR SCANNED PHOTOS WITH PHOTO SOFTWARE PROGRAMS. THE COLOR OF A PHOTO CAN BE CHANGED FROM COLOR TO BLACK AND WHITE OR SEPIA. THE SHAPE AND SIZE OF THE PHOTO CAN BE ADJUSTED TO FIT THE LAYOUT. SOFTWARE PROGRAMS CAN LAYER PHOTOS, ADJUST COLOR TONES, CHANGE THE TEXTURE OF A PHOTO AND PRINT JOURNALING ONTO THE PHOTOS AS WELL. THE MEDIUM ON WHICH PHOTOS ARE PRINTED CAN AFFECT THE LOOK OF THE PHOTO AS WELL. TRY PRINTING ONTO PHOTO PAPER, REGULAR PAPER, CANVAS, VELLUM, TRANSPARENCIES, AND OTHER MEDIUMS.

SCANNING PHOTOS AND IMAGES INTO A COMPUTER OPENS NEW POSSIBILITIES FOR THE SCRAPBOOKER. PHOTOS CAN BE ALTERED WITH A PHOTO SOFTWARE PROGRAM, SENT TO FRIENDS OVER THE INTERNET, ETC. IT IS MOST COMMON TO SAVE PHOTOS AS A JPEG FILE BECAUSE THEY ARE EASIER TO SAVE, REQUIRE LESS STORAGE SPACE AND ARE EASIER TO SEND OVER THE INTERNET. PHOTOS CAN ALSO BE SAVED AS EPS, TIFF OR PICT FILES. A SCANNED PHOTO CAN BE SAVED TO WHATEVER SIZE DESIRED. JUST REMEMBER THAT IT TAKES SOME PATIENCE AND WORK TO GET THE SAME COLOR TONES YOU SEE ON YOUR SCREEN TO APPEAR ON THE PRINTED PHOTO.

THERE ARE MANY DIFFERENT GRAPHICS AVAILABLE TO THE SCRAPBOOK AND PAPER ARTIST. CLIP ART AND OTHER GRAPHICS ARE WIDELY AVAILABLE ON THE INTERNET. MOST GRAPHICS COME WITH A SET OF INSTRUCTIONS ON HOW TO USE THEM AND SHOULD BE AVAILABLE TO BOTH IBM COMPATIBLE AND MACINTOSH USERS. THERE ARE SOME AMAZING PRODUCTS AVAILABLE, JUST BE SURE TO READ THE FINE PRINT BEFORE PURCHASING PRODUCTS.

GROWING CLOSER

• CREATE BACKGROUND BY ADHERING STRIPS OF STRIPE, COLLAGE AND CRUMPLED RED LINEN PAPER TO CARDSTOCK
• RUB RED PAPER WITH BROWN INK TO DEFINE WRINKLES •
ADD THE DATE TO THE PHOTO, PRINT ONTO WHITE CARDSTOCK AND ADHERE PHOTO TO BACKGROUND • CREATE TITLE WITH LETTERING STICKERS • ATTACH LETTER STICKERS TO TAGS FOR JOURNALING • STRING TAGS WITH BROWN GINGHAM RIBBON AND ADHERE TO PAGE • EMBELLISH LAYOUT WITH BROTHER AND SISTER WISDOM STICKERS, CIRCLE CLIPS AND SILVER HINGES •
SUPPLIES – CARDSTOCK: BAZZILL; PATTERNED PAPER: CHATTERBOX, LEGACY COLLAGE, K & COMPANY; STICKERS: NOSTALGIQUE, SCRAPBOOK STICKERZ; CIRCLE CLIPS: MAKING MEMORIES; SILVER HINGES: MAKING MEMORIES

Designer: Renee Villalobos-Campa

EVOLVING AS BROTHERS

- CREATE BACKGROUND BY ADHERING TRIMMED CARDSTOCK STAMPED WITH SHADOW INK TO BLACK CARDSTOCK • TRIM NINE PHOTOS TO DESIRED SIZE AND MAT WITH BLACK CARDSTOCK • ADHERE PHOTOS TO BACKGROUND LEAVING 1\2" BORDER BETWEEN EACH PHOTO • MAT TWO PHOTOS WITH WHITE CARDSTOCK AND DOUBLE MAT LARGE PHOTO WITH JOURNALING • REVERSE PRINT TITLE AND SUPPORTING WORDS • CUT OUT AND ADHERE TITLE TO BLACK CARDSTOCK • PRINT JOURNAL BLOCK AND HIGHLIGHT KEY WORDS WITH A PEN • ADHERE PHOTOS AND TITLE TO LAYOUT •

SUPPLIES – STAMPS: HERO ARTS, STAMPABILITIES, PAPER INSPIRATIONS; FONT: AMAZON BT

DEAR DAWSON AND ABBI

- BEGIN WITH STRIPE PATTERNED PAPER FOR BACKGROUND • PUNCH OUT FOUR PHOTOS WITH SQUARE PUNCH • DOUBLE MAT MAIN PHOTO AND RUN GINGHAM RIBBON ALONG BOTTOM OF MAT • PRINT JOURNALING AND MAT WITH GINGHAM RIBBON ALONG TOP • ADHERE ELEMENTS TO BACKGROUND • EMBELLISH WITH METAL-RIMMED TAGS AND STRING •

SUPPLIES – PATTERNED PAPER: AMERICAN CRAFTS; STAMP: HERO ARTS

Our Designers' Favorite Tools

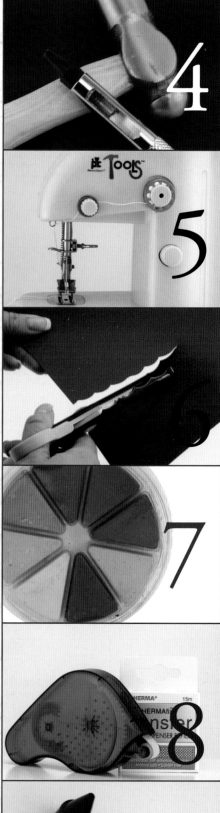

CREATING A GREAT SCRAPBOOK PAGE CAN BECOME A WHOLE LOT EASIER IF YOU HAVE THE RIGHT TOOLS AND EQUIPMENT. WE ASKED SOME OF OUR BEST DESIGNERS TO GIVE US A LIST OF THE SCRAPBOOKING TOOLS THEY COULD NOT LIVE WITHOUT. HERE IS THEIR LIST:

1. CARDSTOCK
2. EMBOSSING POWDER
3. PAPER TRIMMER
4. EYELET TOOL
5. SEWING MACHINE
6. DECORATIVE SCISSORS
7. CHALK
8. HERMAFIX
9. HOLE PUNCHES

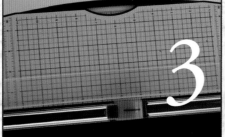

And Scrapbooking Tips

PAPER CURLING

Add dimension to your scrap-booking pages with curled paper. Just wet the edges of torn paper with a cotton swab and gently roll paper with your fingers. Let the paper dry and it will stay curled. Paper curling is easy to do and a great way to use single and double sided paper and cardstock. Add variety to your paper curling by layering paper curls and framing photos and journaling.

FABRIC

Incorporate fabric into your layouts to add dimension, texture and interest to your pages. The color and texture of fabric help set the theme of a layout and make the viewer want to touch the page. Try using some of the following fabrics in your next scrap-booking page:

- Felt
- Vinyl
- Netting
- Denim
- Velvet
- Corduroy

STITCHING

Try stitching on your scrapbook pages with a needle and thread or sewing machine. Stitching gives a finishing touch to your pages that shows attention to detail and makes the entire layout look even better. Add any stitches you can think of as a border, frame, decoration, or even to attach elements together. Here are some other ideas:

- Stitch letters to create words or decorations
- Use a straight, zig-zag or vine stitch for a border
- Stitch designs to embellish layout
- Use cross stitches to adhere element to background
- Thread beads, charms and tags to background

Sources - It's All About Baby

The following companies manufacture products featured in this section. Please check with your local retail store for these materials. We have made every attempt to identify and give proper credit for the materials used. If, by chance, we have missed giving the appropriate credit, we would appreciate hearing from you.

3L Corp.
(800) 828-3130 3lcorp.com

3M Stationary
(800) 364-3577 3m.com

7 Gypsies
(800) 588 6707 7gypsies.com

Adornments
adornments.com

American Craft
(800) 642-4314 americancraft.com

American Tag Company
(800) 223-3956 americantag.net

Anna Griffin, Inc.
(888) 817-8170 annagriffin.com

Avery
(800) GO-AVERY avery.com

Bazzill Basics Paper
(480) 558-8557 bazzillbasics.com

Bluemoon Beads
(800) 377-6715 bluemoonbeads.com

Brown Bag Fibers
brownbagfibers.com

Boxer Scrapbook Productions, LLC
(888) 625-6255 or (503) 625-0455
boxerscrapbooks.com

Carolee's Creations
(435) 563-1100
caroleescreations.com

Clearsnap
(888) 448-4862 clearsnap.com

Club Scrap
(888) 634-9100 clubscrap.com

Coats & Clark
coatsandclark.com

Creative Imaginations
(800) 942-6487 cigift.com

Daisy D's Paper Co.
(888) 601-8955 or (801) 447-9955
daisydotsanddoodles.com

Deluxe Cuts
(480) 497-9005 deluxecuts.com

DieCuts with a View
(801) 224-6766
diecutswithaview.com

DMC
(973) 589-0606 dmc-usa.com

DMD Industries
(800) 805-9890 dmdind.com

Dress It Up
dressitup.com

DYMO
(800) 426-7827 dymo.com

Eclectic Products, Inc.
(800) 767-4667 eclecticproucts.com

EK Success
(800) 524-1349 eksuccess.com

Ellison
(800) 253-2240 ellison.com

Embellish It
(702) 312-1628 embellishit.com

Family Treasures
(661) 294-1330 familytreasures.com

Fibers by the Yard
fibersbytheyard.com

Flavia
(805) 882-2466 flavia.com

Herma Fix
Herma.co.uk.com

Hero Art Rubber Stamps, Inc.
(800) 822-4376 hearoarts.com

Jest Charming
(702) 564-5101 jestcharming.com

Jones Tones
(719) 948-0048 jonestones.com

Junkitz
(212) 944-4250 junitz.com

Junque
Junque.net

K & Company
(888) 244-2083 kandcompany.com

Kangaroo & Joey
(480) 460-4841
kangarooandjoey.com

Karen Foster Design
(801) 451-9779
karenfosterdesign.com

Leisure Arts
(888) 257-7548
business.leisurearts.com

Making Memories
(800) 286-5263 makingmemories.com

Mrs. Grossman's
(800) 429-4549 mrsgrossmans.com

National Cardstock
(724) 452-7120
nationalcardstock.com

NRN Designs
nrndesigns.com

Paper Garden
papergarden.com

Paper Illuzionz
(406) 234-8716 paperilluzionz.com

Provo Craft
(888) 577-3545 provocraft.com

PSX Design
(800) 782-6748 psxdesign.com

Quickutz
(888) 702-1146 quickutz.com

ScrapLovers
scraplovers.com

Scrapworks, LLC
scrapworksllc.com

Sculpey
Sculpey.com

SEI, Inc.
(800) 333-3279 shopsei.com

Stampin' Up!
(800) 782-6787 stampinup.com

Stickopotamus
(888) 270-4443 stickopotamus.com

Timeless Touches
(623) 362-8285 timelesstouches.net

Treehouse Designs
(877) 372-1109 treehouse-designs.com

Two Peas In A Bucket
twopeasinabucket.com

TwoTwinkles.Com
(760) 961-2500 twotwinkles.com

Un-Du
Un-du.com

Westrim Crafts
(800) 727-2727 westrimcrafts.com

Words Worth Stamps
(719) 282-3495
wordsworthstamps.com

Xyron
(800) 793-3523 xyron.com

LET ME PLAY IN THE SUNSHINE; LET ME SING FOR JOY; LET ME GROW IN THE LIGHT; LET ME SPLASH IN THE RAIN, AND REMEMBER THE DAYS OF CHILDHOOD FOREVER.

ten little
fingers
&
ten little
toes

Sweet Dreams

LOOK
out
world,
here I
come

A sweet, new blossom of Humanity, Fresh fallen from God's own home to flower on earth.

—Gerald Massey,
Wooed and Won

There is no cure for birth & death save to enjoy the interval.

—George Santayana

134

MOMS HOLD
LITTLE HANDS
NOW—HEARTS
FOREVER.

PRECIOUS
MEMORIES

Cute as a bug

bundle of joy

SCHOOL IS OUT

• begin with blue patterned paper for background • enlarge photo and mat with green patterned paper • apply a pre-colored crystal lacquer along edge of photo • let dry for three hours • attach photo to background over blue mesh with cross stitches and embroidery floss • print title onto transparency • attach to background over metal strips with green eyelets and black brads • attach letter stickers to large metal rimmed tag • attach to background over blue mesh with large blue brad • stamp names and grade on metal-rimmed tags and attach to layout with large brads • stamp date onto metal tag and attach to photo with black brad •

Supplies – Patterned Paper: Leisure Arts; Stickers: Leisure Arts; Tags: Making Memories; Stamp: Hero Arts; Stamp Pad: Staz-on; Font: CK Constitution, CK Newspaper

it's all about

School

COOKING UP FUN

KINDERGARTEN
DAY ONE

DATE AUG 2002   ISSUED TO ALEXANDER

a b c

WOW. THIS IS SCHO

A

Alex, you had a great first year in school! No one ever said Kindergarten was going to be easy. You learned how to read, write, add, subtract, and so much more! We are very proud of you. We love you, Alex.

d e f

SOMEONE DIDNT WANT TO GO HOME

137

138

it's all about school

Yep, that's me! This is our annual 1st day of school photo, back before color film was available to the masses.   By the look on our faces at nine and eleven years old my brother and I have definitely outgrown this drill. I can't tell if we are not smiling because:

> (a) School is starting and summer is over
> (b) We don't like our new clothes
> (c) My mother is making my brother and
>   I hold hands
> (d) All of the above

Maybe it is just that I don't like my ringlet bangs, and my brother is a little disturbed by his brand new "grow into" Levi's with 6-inch cuffs and a gathered waist. Oh, the things our mothers made us do.

While a lot has changed since this late 1950's photo, one thing has not changed at all. Mothers are still taking photos of their children leaving home on the first day of school.

They are also taking photos of classroom activities, field trips, learning adventures and class parties and trying to find something to do with package A, B or C of the annual school pictures they purchased.

It's All About School is designed to spark your creativity and imagination. Our designers have captured their children in a variety of school activities using techniques and designs that can be easily and quickly "lifted" onto your own scrapbook pages. We have provided step-by-step instructions to help you recreate the designs in this idea book.

Reading, writing and arithmetic have never been so fun!

Happy Scrappin',

Nancy

Nancy M. Hill

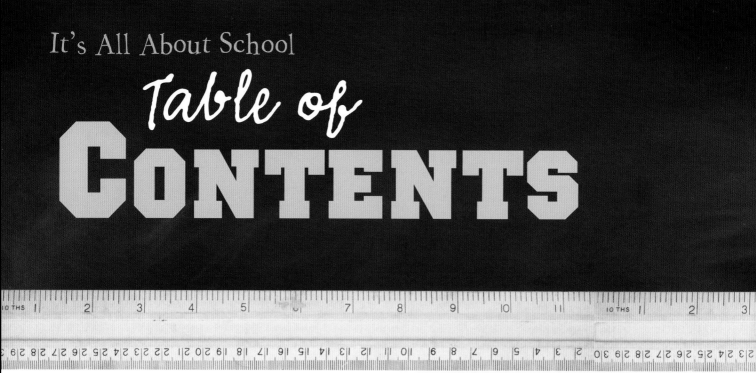

Table of Contents

Designer: Wendy Malichio

THE ABC'S OF BACK TO SCHOOL

• create background by adhering black cardstock, gingham ribbon and torn corkboard patterned paper to red cardstock • mat one photo with black cardstock • adhere photos to background • create and print title block paper • attach letter stickers for title • make labels for journaling with label maker • attach pebble letter stickers to metal-rimmed tags • attach tags to layout with brads • embellish layout with paper clips, stickers and string •

Supplies – Cardstock: Bazzill; Cork Paper: Magenta; Apple Seal: Amscam; Ribbon: Offray; Label Maker: Dymo; Letter Sticker: Sticker Studio, Kamset; Rub-on: Making Memories; Tags: Making Memories; Twistal: Making Memories; Metal Letters: Magic Scraps; Pebble Letters: Sonnets; Slide Mount: Two Peas in a Bucket

BITTERSWEET TIME OF YEAR

• create background by adhering stripe patterned paper and homemade paper to green cardstock • mat photo with green cardstock, tear bottom edge and adhere to background • attach letter stickers for title • print journaling onto vellum • emboss journaling block while ink is still wet • paint frames with acrylic paint, apply crackling medium and another coat of paint • add twill tape to dry frames • adhere to layout with calendar stickers • stamp leaf image with clear ink onto cardstock and vellum • emboss leaves •
Supplies – Patterned Paper: Chatterbox; Cardstock: Bazzill; Stickers: Creative Imaginations, EK Success

I have always have mixed emotions this time of year. I want to keep you home and with me forever. But, I know I cannot teach you everything you need to know, so I have to let go. Don't get me wrong, I am ready for more free time, time for me. The house will be tidier, and I'll even get that long needed nap every now and then. My errands will get done more quickly and I won't have to stop at the toy section of the store "just to look", then tell you "no, you don't need another toy". But I will miss you both. I'll miss having you with me, helping me in the kitchen and with chores. I'll miss hearing "Watch me just one more time Mom", or the spontanious hugs & sometimes smooches I get from you. I know, there will always be next summer, and I'll be anxiously waiting for you. Until then, I am going to ENJOY every peaceful minute I can scrapbooking!

Designer: Marsha Musselman

SCHOOL DAYS

• begin with green patterned paper • mat three photos together with dark purple paper, colored with white pencil and smeared with chalk • adhere matted photos to chipboard • create title and accents by stamping letters with white pigment stamp pad onto dark purple cardstock • mat title block and accents with corrugated cardboard • embellish layout with white linen thread •
Supplies – Patterned Paper: Leisure Arts, DCWV; Stamps: Hero Arts

> **SPECIAL TIPS:**
> Corrugated cardboard adds texture and dimension to a layout.

Designer: Camille Jensen

143

October 7, 2002

Children's Inc. Class fieldtrip to **Leads Farm** just north of where we live. The children got an authentic **hayride** with tractor pulling the wagon, saw many **animals** along the way, stopped at a pumpkin/gourd **patch** to pick, then off to the fun **barn** with hay slides and trucks in corn pits and and **petting**/feeding area.

Designer: Debbie Coe

RIDING THE BUS

• create background by adhering yellow cardstock and black mesh to black cardstock • mat photos with black cardstock and adhere to background • create title with black letters and printed cardstock • use black eyelets to adorn the printed cardstock • print journaling highlighting words with color • cut line of school buses from patterned paper • mat buses and journaling with black cardstock and adhere to layout • adhere bus charm to metal-rimmed tag with a pop dot • adhere to layout with string • embellish layout with school bus cut from printed paper •
Supplies – Mesh: Magic Mesh; Stickers: Provo Craft, Two Busy Moms

BUS STOP BEAUTY

• create background by adhering torn magenta paper and ribbon to floral patterned paper • mat photos and adhere to background • reverse print title and cut out with exacto knife •
Supplies – Patterned Paper: Karen Foster; Cardstock: Colormatch; Font: Two Peas in a Bucket Gingersnap

SPECIAL TIPS:
1. Run delicate letters through a Xyron machine.
2. Reverse print title in a graphics program.

Designer: Maegan Hall

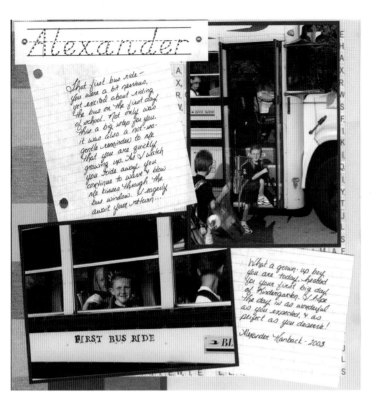

FIRST BUS RIDE

• create background by adhering patterned papers to yellow cardstock • mat photos with black cardstock and adhere to background • cut out child's name from schoolwork for title • attach with gold eyelets • handwrite journaling on notebook paper and adhere to layout • stamp 'first bus ride' onto the photo •

Supplies – Patterned Paper: Leisure Arts, 7 Gypsies; Cardstock: Bazzill

PHOTO TIPS:

Photos are often the focal point of a page. Improving your photos is one of the best ways to improve your scrapbook pages. Our number one photo suggestion is to keep a camera with you at all times to capture unexpected, wonderful moments. Here are some additional suggestions to help improve your photo taking abilities.

POSING

• Take photos that are not posed to give variety and a natural look to your photos. Allow people (especially kids) to be themselves.
• If a posed look is desired, put your subjects at ease by giving them suggestions for poses or providing them with a prop.
• Crop in close and focus in on a detail or object.
• Bring the subject in close to the camera when you are taking a photo of a person in front of a large object (a building or landscape, etc.).
• Photograph the little things that aren't typically photographed!

LIGHTING

• Get out of the bright sunlight and keep the sun out of your subject's eyes. The best light is early in the morning or just before the sun goes down. If you can't get out of the bright light, find shade. If there's no shade, use a flash.
• The most flattering lighting is low-contrast lighting; it makes people look thinner and younger with clearer skin. The larger the source of light, the lower the contrast will be (window light is more flattering than a flashlight).

FILM

• Low-speed film requires more light than high-speed film to be exposed properly, but is less grainy, and the colors are more saturated. A good all-purpose film speed is 200 or 400.
• Color negatives can be printed in color, black and white or sepia, whereas, black and white negatives can only be printed in black and white or sepia.
• All color and most black and white photos are printed on resin-coated paper (RC) and will last 30-60 years before fading or color-shifting, if stored properly. If you have an important photo you would like to last for hundreds of years, have a fiber-based black and white print made.
• Have your film developed promptly and keep it out of the heat.

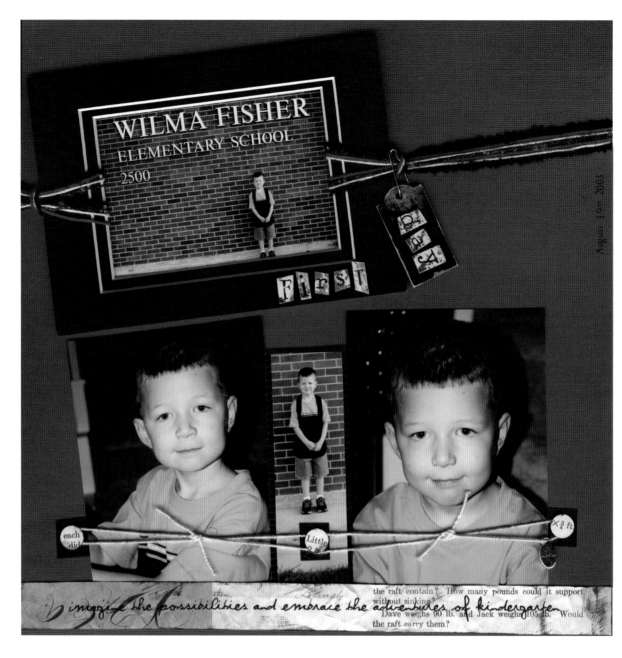

IMAGINE THE POSSIBILITIES
• begin with textured cardstock for background • frame photo with photo mat • attach fibers that reach around back of layout to framed photo • mat small photo with corrugated cardboard and adhere all photos to background • create title by painting metal letters and tag with acrylic paint • print journaling onto collage paper and adhere to layout • stamp date onto background • embellish layout with fibers, charm, safety pin and raised paper circles •

Supplies – Patterned Paper: Legacy Collage; Cardstock: Bazzill; Fibers: Trimtex; Metal Letters: Making Memories; Metal Tag: Making Memories; Date Stamp: Making Memories

SPECIAL TIPS:
Layer the metal tag and letters with different colors. When each coat is dry, sand it to reveal the color beneath.

NEW
Backpack
shoes
Jeans

All for your
very f i r s t
Day of School
oct. 2001

ALL FOR YOUR VERY FIRST DAY OF SCHOOL

• create background by adhering torn yellow patterned paper to red patterned paper • mat photos with patterned paper and adhere to background • handwrite journaling onto white cardstock • accent journaling with letter stickers • attach school-themed stickers onto 1" white squares matted with red cardstock • adhere embroidery floss over yellow paper • attach squares over floss with pop dots • embellish layout with swirl clips •

Supplies – Patterned Paper: Provo Craft; Floss: DMC; Stickers: Provo Craft, Mrs. Grossman's; Swirl Clips: Making Memories

SPECIAL TIPS:
Place swirl clips on layout so the largest amount of swirl is visible.

FIRST DAY AT PRESCHOOL

• create background by attaching homemade paper and trimmed black cardstock to checked paper with photo corners • mat photo with cardstock and adhere to background • create title with letter stickers and alphabet stamps • adhere part of title on vellum envelope holding journaling tag • handwrite journaling onto white cardstock • embellish journaling block with eyelet and ribbon •

Supplies – Patterned Paper: Frances Meyer

SPECIAL TIP:
1. Make apple background from child's finger-painting artwork.
a. Scan artwork and save as a TIFF file.
b. Use photo-editing software to cut and paste specific parts of artwork you wish to duplicate.
2. Enhance with polka dots or other accents and print onto photo paper.

Designer: Janna Wilson

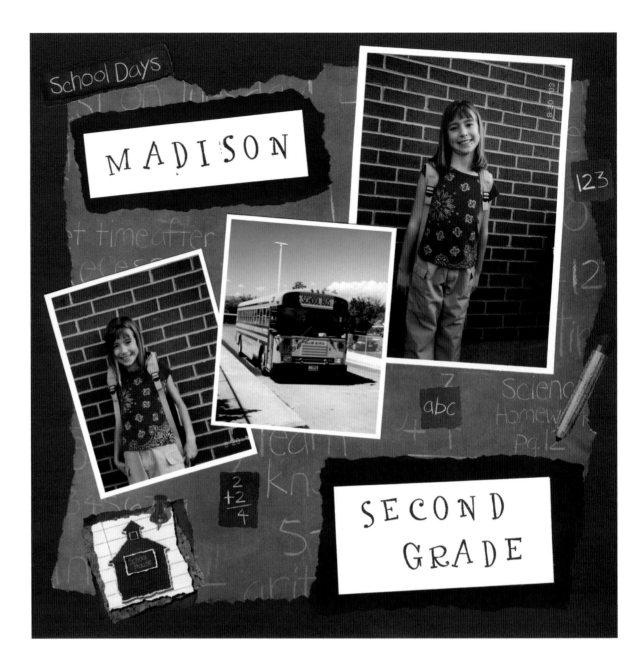

School Days

MADISON

SECOND GRADE

SECOND GRADE

• create background by adhering torn patterned paper to red cardstock • mat photos with white cardstock and adhere to background • stamp title on white cardstock and mat with torn black cardstock • adhere title to background • embellish layout with school stickers •

Supplies – Patterned Paper: Karen Foster Designs; Stickers: Karen Foster Designs

BRAVE JAMESON

• create background by adhering piece of patterned paper and gingham ribbon to black cardstock • mat photos • print title and journaling onto white cardstock • ink edges of white cardstock and adhere to background • cut strips of patterned paper and adhere to layout over journaling block • adhere letter stickers for name • adhere photos to layout • embellish layout with die cut heart and floss •

Supplies – Patterned Paper: 7 Gypsies, KI Memories; Cardstock: Bazzill; Stickers: Rebecca Sower, Provo Craft; Ribbon: Ofrey; Floss: DMC; Ink: Colorbox; Stamp: 2000 Plus; Font: Harting

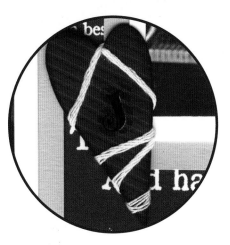

Brave

JAMESON

BRAVE: Four years old, first day of school, leaving mom, getting on the bus.

SEP 0 8 2003

149

THE HERO

• create background by adhering green cardstock to blue cardstock • print photo in panoramic setting • create title frame by attaching sticker to a piece of glass • attach strips of foil tape as frame around sticker and then emboss with blue and silver embossing powder • attach to background with nail head and string • print journaling onto cardstock, adhere photo to journaling block and mat with blue cardstock • attach to background with nail heads • stamp name and date onto metal strip and fill in stamps with blue glass paint • mat with blue cardstock and adhere to background •

Supplies – Metal: ArtEmboss; Metal Stamps: Foofala; Foil Tap: Leave Memories; Font: Papyrus

SPECIAL TIP:
Incorporate glass into your scrapbook pages for a unique look. Try embossing, etching, painting and stamping glass.

BEAUTIFUL

Aspire

Imagine

achieve

Dream

Believe

Take a Look Through My Eyes

Kelly...You are ready. I am not. Your first day of kindergarten and I see my baby, in typical style leading the pack, full of confidence and curiosity. You would be amazed at the other wonderful things I see in you...just take a look through my eyes. I love you my Bella.   mommy

THROUGH MY EYES

• create background by adhering trimmed patterned paper to blue cardstock • mat large photo with blue cardstock • frame small photo with metal frame • print title onto vellum, trim and attach to background over large photo with silver eyelets • tear vellum to show child • print journaling onto vellum and adhere to background • attach metallic accent words to background with silver eyelets • adhere framed photo to layout • embellish layout with metal stars and fibers •
Supplies – Cardstock: DCWV; Vellum: DCWV; Metallic Words: DCWV; Metallic Accents: DCWV; Font: Scriptina, Andale Mono

KINDERGARTEN STRIDE

• begin with quadrant paper for background • double mat photos and zig-zag stitch with sewing machine • adhere photos to background with foam tape • adhere metal letters for title • print journaling onto white cardstock • double mat journaling and poem block and zig-zag stitch • embellish layout with gingham ribbon and small and large mosaic stickers •
Supplies – Patterned Paper: The Robin's Nest; Cardstock: Bazzill; Metal Letters: Making Memories; Tile Stickers: Sticko; Poem Block: The Robin's Nest

SPECIAL TIP:
Coordinate page elements and embellishments with colors in photo.

Your first day of kindergarten was much more exciting to you than to me. Your teacher, Mrs. Davis, let you pick your chair and a cubby for your Hulk back-pack. As I left the school, feeling un-needed, I was a bit teary but you didn't see. My baby boy is in real school now.

You left for school
In a grin so wide
Strutting a new
Kindergarten stride
You walked away,
Backpack in tow.
It was hard for me
To let you go...
Jackie A. Colton

Designer: Brenda Nakandakari

MONTESSORI A GREAT START

• create background by stitching trimmed and torn tan cardstock to red cardstock • mat photo with blue cardstock and adhere to background • create title by matting punched squares from red cardstock with navy cardstock • hand write letters in each square and adhere to page • hand write journaling on tan card stock • highlight words and edges with chalk • create sign with chalked cardstock and hemp • hang from button sewn to page • embellish layout with school stickers •

Supplies – Cardstock: DCWV; Chalk: Craf-T; Stickers: Creative Memories

ATTITUDE, ATTITUDE, ATTITUDE

• begin with checked paper for background • mat picture with mulberry paper, frame and adhere to background • print title onto vellum and mat with white cardstock • run sheer ribbon through metallic accent and adhere to layout • adhere journaling to page • embellish layout with burlap, button and pearl cotton •

Supplies – Patterned Paper: DCWV; Vellum: DCWV; Mulberry Paper: DCWV; Metallic Words: DCWV; Font: Two Peas in a Bucket Falling Leaves

CLASSMATES

• create background by adhering home-made striped paper (run compressed sponge with re-inkers along the edge of a ruler to make straight lines) to navy cardstock • mat photo with white cardstock and attach to background with photo corners from red cardstock • tear piece of white cardstock for title and sponge edges with navy blue ink • attach title to tag made from red cardstock • embellish tag with sponged metal-rimmed tag, buttons and red and blue raffia • adhere metal quote to layout •
Supplies – Cardstock: Close to my Heart; Re-inkers: Close to my Heart; Buttons: EK Success; Metal Quote: Making Memories

Designer: Lisa Lang

JIMMY NEUTRON BACKPACK

• create background by attaching torn mustard cardstock to brown cardstock with gold brads • adhere natural netting to mustard cardstock • mat photos with mustard cardstock and torn mulberry paper • print journaling onto mustard cardstock and cut to tag shape • tear edge, attach mustard colored eyelet and fibers and adhere to background • attach charms with gold mini brads to tag • adhere cutouts to cardstock and mulberry paper and adhere to page •
Supplies – Cardstock: Bazzill

SPECIAL TIPS:
Wet edges of cut mulberry paper to make torn edges more controllable.

153

Designer: Camille Jensen

MEG'S PRESCHOOL

• begin with green patterned paper for background • mat photos with pink mulberry paper and frame with ribbon and trim • create title by stamping letters with clear resist ink onto glossy coated paper • sponge letters with ink from a kaleidoscope pad • cut out letters and adhere to layout • print journaling onto vellum using different fonts • ink the back of the vellum with fingertips and kaleidoscope ink pad • adhere vellum to white tag • attach to layout with green brad •

Supplies – Patterned Paper: Leisure Arts; Mulberry Paper: DCWV

THE GRADUATE

• create background by adhering trimmed patterned paper to black cardstock • mat photo with red cardstock and adhere to background • attach alphabet stickers and graduation die cut for title • print journaling onto white cardstock and adhere to background • attach premade graduation tag to layout • adhere 3-D graduation cap sticker to layout •

Supplies – Patterned Paper: Colorbok; Cardstock: Bazzill; Tag: EK Success; Stickers: Darico; Font: Two Peas in a Bucket Flea Market

SPECIAL TIPS:

1. Use the Xyron machine to apply adhesive to delicate letters.
2. The pre-made tag made this an easy project and gave it a great finishing accent.

PRE-SCHOOL Graduation

CLASS OF 2003

Kyle, you graduated from preschool on May 30, 2003. This picture is when your teacher, Miss Priscilla gave you your diploma. All of our class marched out to the stage area with their graduation caps on and sat patiently waiting as their names were called by either Miss Amanda or Miss Priscilla.

Your class sang a number songs including the Rainbow song which is one of your favorites. Many of the other childrens families were there taking pictures and video along with Momma and Grandma Bishop.

We are so proud of you and all that you have learned in school. We are grateful to have Miss Priscilla as your teacher the last 2 years. She has taught children for over 30 years, 12 of which at your school.

Now my big boy is ready for kindergarden. Daddy and I are so proud to see you grow and become such a wonderful boy.
CONGRADULATIONS!

the Graduate

Designer: Kim Kaiser

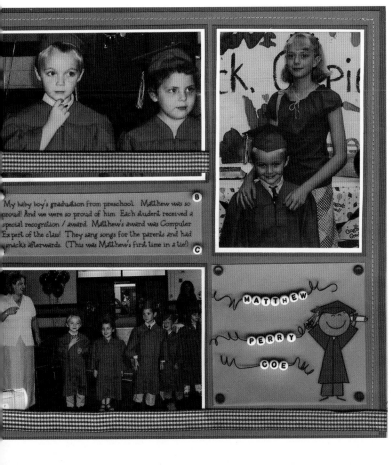

My baby boy's graduation from preschool. Matthew was so proud. And we were so proud of him. Each student received a special recognition / award. Matthew's award was Computer Expert of the class! They sang songs for the parents and had snacks afterwards. (This was Matthew's first time in a tie!)

MATTHEW PERRY COE

Designer: Debbie Coe

GOOD LUCK, GUPPIES

• create background by stitching trimmed blue paper and gingham ribbon to red cardstock • double mat photos with white and red cardstocks and adhere to background • cut out and adhere graduation title • print journaling onto vellum and adhere with glue dots topped with alphabet brads • thread alphabet beads with wire and curl the edges • adhere beads over title and onto vellum with graduate sticker • attach vellum with flat red eyelets • apply shine to graduation cap and adhere to layout • embellish layout with graduation tassel •

Supplies – Title: Li'l Davis Designs; Stickers: Provo Craft, Me and My Big Ideas; Shine: Paper Glaze

SPECIAL TIPS:

Before sewing your layout paper, run two sheets of scrap paper through your sewing machine. Adjust the tension and stitch size as needed before sewing your layout paper.

Today I woke up chanting
"I will not cry! I will not cry!"

Today you woke up very
excited about getting on the
big yellow school bus that
would take you to your first
day of Kindergarten.

Today I counted the minutes
until I could go back to the bus
stop and see you again.

Today you got off the bus
with the biggest smile on your
face and could not wait to tell
me all about your teacher,
classroom, and new friends.

Today I breathed a sigh of
relief.

Designer: Tracey Papano

I WILL NOT CRY

• create background by
adhering torn and rolled
white cardstock to green
cardstock • frame small
photo and adhere all photos
to background • stamp title
with lettering stamps onto
small tags • tie embroidery
floss through each tag and
knot • adhere tags to background with pop dots •
print journaling block onto
vellum and adhere to background • stamp date onto
background • rip vellum out
of metal tag and adhere to
page • adhere bus charm to
center of metal tag •

Supplies – Stamps: Hero Arts;
Tags: Paper Reflections; Floss:
DMC; Metal Tag: Making
Memories; Bus Charm:
Treasured Memories; Ink: Close
to my Heart

Designer: Maegan Hall

LAUGH, DISCOVER, PLAY

• create background by inking green patterned paper • mat photo with cardstock and crumpled and inked brown patterned paper • adhere photo to background • reverse print name onto cardstock and cut out • attach three word stickers to background over oval designs • print journaling onto clear vellum • tear top and bottom edges and ink • attach to layout with distressed punched squares and mini brads • attach distressed, punched squares to each corner of the photo mat •

Supplies – Patterned Paper: Leisure Arts; Stickers: Bo Bunny; Brads: All the Extras

SPECIAL TIPS:
Crumple cardstock or paper with water, flatten paper and dry with an iron or heat embossing tool. The crumple gives the paper a leathery and aged look.

Designer: Susan Stringfellow

FIRST DAY OF KINDERGARTEN

• create background by adhering plaid paper and box paper to daisy background • mat photos with cardstock • rip out center of cardstock to create frame for one photo • fold and chalk edges and make fake stitches with pen • print title onto computer paper and use as template to cut out title • run letters through a Xyron machine and adhere to vellum • outline letters with pen and adhere vellum to background • finish title with stamps and attach to layout with eyelets • print journaling, chalk edges and attach with eyelets •

Supplies – Patterned Paper: Chatterbox; Cardstock: Crafter's Workshop; Flowers: Jolee's By You; Eyelets: Making Memories; Stamp: PSX; Fonts: Tintibulation, Cheri

SPECIAL TIPS:
1. If a photo has dead space in the background, frame it with a torn mat.
2. Let your child journal his/her first day of school to have two different points of view.

157

Designer: Valerie Barton

BIG SCHOOL IS COOL
• begin with blue cardstock for background • triple mat photos • create bulletin board for title by framing corkboard with strips of corrugated paper • print title onto white cardstock using Primary Lined font • cut title into strips to look like sentence strips • adhere die cuts to title • adhere title block to layout • print journaling and date onto vellum using Kidscript font • create folder by adhering vellum to green cardstock • embellish layout with vellum tag die cut, pre-made tag and crayons •

Supplies – Patterned Paper: Paper Adventures; Corkboard: Magic Scraps; Corrugated Paper: Paper Reflections; Tag: Making Memories; Die Cut: AccuCut; Crayons: Jolee's By You; Fonts: Primary Font III, Kidscript

Designer: Leah Fung

KINDERGARTEN 2003

• create background by adhering check, red, and cork patterned papers to blue cardstock • adhere two small triangles to bottom corners of background • mat photo with black cardstock and attach to background with eyelets • attach letter stickers for title • print journaling onto patterned paper and attach to cork paper with alphabet brad • attach bookplate to cork paper with two brads • embellish layout with paper clip, die cut and alphabet stickers •

Supplies – Patterned Paper: Leisure Arts; Brad: Making Memories; Die Cut: Creative Imaginations; Stickers: Colorbok

Designer: Leah Fung

CHAPTER TWO

• create background by attaching torn and crumpled blue paper and checked paper to brown cardstock with silver brads • mat photos with cardstock and adhere to background • trace edge of letter die cuts with metallic pen for title • adhere to background over red paper blocks with foam tape • handwrite journaling onto cardstock and draw line around edges with metallic pen • adhere large journal box to layout • adhere small journal box to metal tag • insert metal chain and adhere tag to layout with foam tape • attach strip of cork to layout with eyelets and glue dots • attach three photos to corkboard with brads • string alphabet beads onto wire and curl ends with wire pliers • adhere beads to layout • adhere homemade booklet to layout •

Supplies – Patterned Paper: K & Company; Brads: Making Memories; Title: Provo Craft; Metal Tag: Making Memories; Eyelets: Making Memories

JACOB GOES TO SCHOOL

• create background by adhering chalkboard patterned paper and a strip of black cardstock to red cardstock • mat picture with black cardstock and adhere to layout • print journaling block onto white cardstock and mat with black cardstock • chalk and outline journaling block • adhere journaling block to background • bead name and letters onto black wire with red divider beads • adhere beads to journaling block • handwrite onto metal tag to finish title • chalk tag and attach to layout with red brad • attach red eyelets to four metal tags • chalk tags and adhere school buttons to tags • hang three tags from red brads with white floss • attach two red eyelets to photo • attach fourth tag to photo with string •

Supplies – Cardstock: Paper Loft; Tags: Making Memories; Buttons: Dress it Up; Eyelets: Making Memories; Brads: Doodlebug; Alpha Beads: Western Craft; Beads: Western Craft; Wire: Western Craft; Floss: DMC

UNIQUE EMBELLISHMENTS

There are countless embellishments to use on your scrapbook pages. Just go into a local scrapbooking store and you will be amazed by the possibilities. These embellishments have not only made scrapbooking easier, but more fun.

Here is a list of some embellishments to spark your interest and give you ideas: beads, metal letters, metal looking letters, rocks with or without letters, wood in multiple designs, paints (watercolor, acrylic, glass paint, etc), fibers, twines, watch glass, rub-ons, wax seals, diamond glaze, heat embossing, cold embossing, papers, sandpaper, cardstock, rice, corrugated cardboard, handmade paper, modeling paste, shrink art plastic, transparencies, screen material, mesh, ribbons, buttons, stamps and inks, walnut ink, lazertran paper for decals, envelopes of every shape and material, old type writer keys, feathers, wire, glitter, paper clips, tags, clay, and stickers made to look like most of these things without the bulk!

Scrapbooking stores are not the only place to find embellishments. Try hardware, fabric, thrift and jewelry stores as well. It is fun to use embellishments that you would not expect to find on a scrapbook page. Don't be overwhelmed by all the possibilities, just use what you like, try new things and enjoy the process.

ALL I REALLY NEED TO KNOW I LEARNED IN KINDERGARTEN

• begin with textured cardstock for background
• print journaling onto textured cardstock •
enlarge photo to 5x7 and punch two holes in
top • fit fiber through holes and knot at ends •
adhere to background with silver star brad •
Supplies – Fiber: On the Surface; Fonts: CK Primary,
Penmanship Print, Times New Roman, Californian FB

SPECIAL TIPS:
Simple pages really focus on
the child.

Designer: Tracy A. Weinzapfel Burgos

WOW, THIS IS SCHOOL

• create background by attaching torn
patterned papers and check patterned
paper to black cardstock with silver snaps
• adhere photos to page • attach library
card and envelope to background with
eyelets for title • create labels with label
maker and attach to layout • stamp journaling onto library card with black ink •
attach alphabet stickers onto six cardstock squares • draw line around edges
with black pen • mat squares with patterned paper and cardstock • adhere to
page with foam tape •
Supplies – Patterned Paper: Leisure Arts;
Stamps: Hero Arts; Stickers: Leisure Arts; Snaps:
Making Memories; Eyelets: Making Memories;
Label Maker: Dymo

GROOVY KELLY

• create background by adhering trimmed and torn patterned paper, yellow cardstock and flower stickers to green cardstock • mat photo with green cardstock and frame with border stickers • adhere photo to background • mat a yellow tag with green cardstock • handwrite journaling and attach heart sticker to corner • embellish tag with wired beads and fibers • adhere to layout • thread seed beads with wire and make curly-q • adhere to flower centers • embellish layout with heart stickers •
Supplies – Patterned Paper: Leisure Arts; Cardstock: DCWV; Tag: DCWV; Stickers: Leisure Arts

FIRST GRADE

• create background by adhering strips of purple cardstock and vellum to blue cardstock • tear holes in purple cardstock for lettering and flowers • frame photo with torn, patterned vellum and chalk edges • attach to layout with fibers strung through eyelets • mat class photo and attach to layout with paper clips attached to fiber • attach eyelet letters for title • print name, age and date and adhere to book plate • attach eyelet flowers with fibers as stems • chalk layout for depth •
Supplies – Vellum: Fiskars; Eyelet: Making Memories; Fiber: Fibers by the Yard; Chalk: Craf-T

INSPIRE. CREATE. DREAM.

• begin with blue cardstock for background • double mat photo with patterned and textured paper • print journaling with Garamouche font onto white cardstock • adhere journaling to background • tear patterned paper and adhere to background • attach photo to layout with silver snaps • attach stickers to metal-rimmed tags • thread beads onto craft thread and tie to rectangular tag • adhere tag to layout • create booklet with white cardstock strips folded in half • cover booklet with blue cardstock • tie booklet together with craft thread and one bead • attach square tag to cover of booklet • adhere photos and journaling inside booklet • embellish layout with stickers, snap, and word eyelet •
Supplies – Patterned Paper: Karen Foster, Creative Imaginations; Stickers: Creative Imaginations; Word Eyelet: Making Memories; Beads: On the Surface; Tags: Making Memories; Font: Garamouche

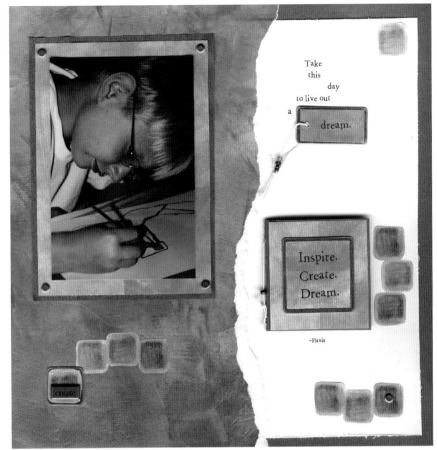

Designer: Dee Gallimore-Perry

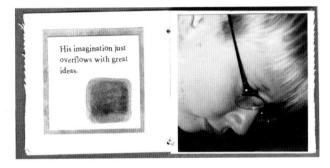

163

Designer: Camille Jensen

JAKE — OUR SECOND GRADE BOY

• begin with green textured cardstock stenciled with a marker for background • frame photo with cut strips of copper • use metal stamps to stamp name, grade and teacher onto frame • ink copper with fingers • attach frame together with large snaps and to background with glue dots • mat class picture with tan and green cardstock and corrugated cardboard • ink edges and adhere to background • print journaling onto light yellow vellum and sew to patterned paper • rub pre-made tag with black, green and orange ink pads • handwrite journaling with calligraphy pen • embellish tag with cut copper and cotton string aged with walnut ink • adhere tag, journaling and string to layout •

Supplies – Stamp: Foofala, Staz-On; Tag: DCWV; Marker: Versamark

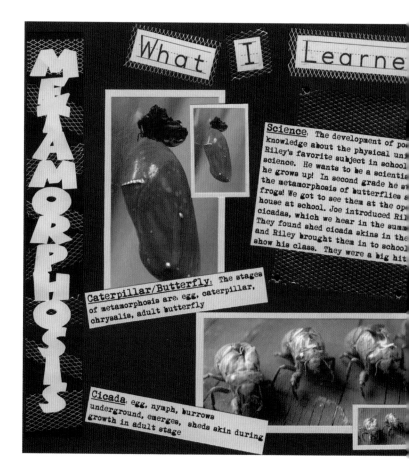

FALL BACK TO SCHOOL

• create background by attaching torn blue vellum and white cardstock to red cardstock with silver brads • single and double mat photos and adhere to layout • frame small photo • attach two black eyelets to bottom of one photo • create title with alphabet stickers and cursive handwriting • embellish title with red buttons • print journaling onto vellum • double mat and attach to layout with silver brads • adhere framed photo to journaling block • adhere school stickers to vellum metal frames • replace string in frames with metal chains • thread through photo eyelets • embellish layout with raffia bow •

Supplies – Patterned Paper: Leisure Arts; Stickers: Leisure Arts; Metal Chain: Leisure Arts; Tags: Making Memories; Metal Frame: Making Memories

Designer: Erin Madsen

Designer: Tami Boturinski

METAMORPHOSIS

• create background by attaching mesh to black cardstock with silver brads • enlarge and change color of photos, mat and adhere to background • reverse print title and cut out letters • print rest of title with Primary Lined font • adhere title to background over mesh • print journaling with Typewriter font and adhere to layout • embellish layout with magnifying glass and butterfly •

Supplies – Cardstock: Bazzill; Fonts: Penmanship Print, Bomk Letters, Mom's Typewriter

165

COOL CONFIDENCE

• create background by adhering blue patterned paper and torn green patterned paper to white cardstock • mat photo and adhere to background • print title and journaling onto vellum, tear and attach to layout with eyelets • thread ribbon through eyelets • adhere torn patterned paper and beaded and curled wire to a vellum metal rimmed tag • embellish tag with fibers and a green, wood tile • adhere tag to layout • stamp dragonfly image onto white background • stamp one dragonfly image onto scrap piece of paper, scan, enlarge and print onto back of blue patterned paper • cut out and adhere to layout over sheer fabric •

Supplies – Patterned Paper: Making Memories, Karen Foster; Vellum: Paper Adventures; Tag: Making Memories; Green Wood Square: Gotta Notion; Wire: Artistic Wire; Stamps: Stampin' Up; Fiber: Fibers by the Yard; Beads: All the Extras; Eyelets: All the Extras

COOL CONFIDENCE

Alexander David Stringfellow
Spring 2001 ~ 3rd Grade

TRANSPARENCIES/VELLUM

Transparencies are a great medium for titles, journaling, graphics and even photos, and are so easy to use. A transparency can give any look you are trying to create from old fashioned to shabby chic. The key to creating the perfect look is in the font and background selection. To make a transparency, just measure where the title or journaling should be on the layout, print or handwrite onto the transparency and attach it to the layout. You can either attach pieces of the transparency to the layout or the entire transparency as an overlay. You can also add variety to your transparencies by printing graphics and photos, drawing with markers and by printing text in color. Printing your photos onto a transparency gives them a great translucent quality.

Vellum is also a wonderful choice for overlays, titles, journaling and quotes. Vellum comes in many different weights, colors, designs and textures. Don't be afraid to play around with the different options to see which you like best. Most vellum will work fine with an ink-jet printer but does even better with a laser printer.

Vellum is an excellent material for representing water. Choose water colored vellum, rip the edges and layer with the same color or coordinating colors. Vellum's translucent quality also gives an ethereal and pure look to the soft and heavenly qualities of a newborn babe, child and bride.

The best glue to use in adhering transparencies and vellum to a layout is none at all. Try attaching them with brads, eyelets, stitches, nail heads, fibers, or even wedging an edge under another element on a page with a drop of glue. Vellum tape can be used but usually shows through the vellum. You can use a Xyron machine to adhere transparencies and vellum to a layout, but be aware that it does change the look of the medium.

THIRD GRADE

School: Greenhills
Teacher: Mrs. Jackson
Best Friends: Brian,
Conor, and Dan
Favorite Subject: gym
Favorite color: yellow
Favorite pastime: baseball

Matthew had a great
third grade year at
Greenhills School. He had
a wonderful teacher and
made many, many new
friends.

First Day Of 4th Grade

• create background by adhering red vellum to stripe patterned paper • adhere photo to background • print journaling onto white cardstock • draw line with loops above title and adhere journaling block to background • embellish layout with pencil sticker •

Supplies – Patterned Paper: Leisure Arts; Cardstock: Bazzill; Stickers: Paper Bliss

SPECIAL TIPS:

There is an endless supply of fonts to choose from on the computer. They can be found in software programs and on the Internet. Try to match a font with the event you are trying to describe. It is also fun to use many different fonts on one layout.

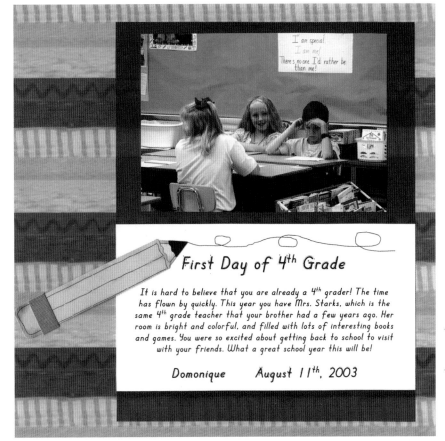

First Day of 4th Grade

It is hard to believe that you are already a 4th grader! The time has flown by quickly. This year you have Mrs. Starks, which is the same 4th grade teacher that your brother had a few years ago. Her room is bright and colorful, and filled with lots of interesting books and games. You were so excited about getting back to school to visit with your friends. What a great school year this will be!

Domonique   August 11th, 2003

Designer: Jayne Hanback

School Day Memories

Designer: Betsy Sammarco

SCHOOL DAY MEMORIES

• create background by adhering black paper and attaching cork patterned papers to brown cardstock with eyelets • mat one photo and adhere all photos to cork paper with brads • attach alphabet letters for title • print journaling onto white cardstock, punch holes, ink edges and attach to corkboard with brads • create booklet by backstitching pages and cover together • ink edges of book title and adhere to cover • adhere cut brad to cover with glue dot • fill pages with photos and journaling •

Supplies – Cork Paper: Magenta; Stickers: Making Memories; Brads: Cut-it-Up, Deco; Frame on Book: Sierra Print Artist; Floss: DMC; Chalk: Craf-T; Font: Two Peas in a Bucket Chicken Shack

SPECIAL TIPS:

1. Using products that resemble a bulletin board and chalkboard enhances the school theme.
2. A mini book is a great way to add more school photos to a layout.

BACK TO CLASS

• create background by cutting 'back to class' overall in half and adhering to top and bottom of cork patterned paper • mat photo and attach to background with brad • have child journal their school experience and attach to layout • embellish layout with ruler ribbon, pencil, paperclips and stickers •
Supplies – Cork Paper: Glad Tidings; Cut Outs: EK Success, Cockadoodle Design; Stickers: Stickopotomus

SPECIAL TIPS:
Have children write their own journaling each year to see their writing skills progress over time. Leave mistakes on the layout for them to look back at in the future.

FOURTH GRADE

• create background by stitching torn purple and green patterned papers to purple patterned paper • curl top edge of bottom strip • adhere photos to background • stamp title inside die cut frame and adhere to background • print journaling onto white cardstock • highlight 'fourth grade' with pen and chalk • stitch around journaling block, double mat, roughen edges and adhere to background • stamp date onto background • punch apples from solid paper • crumple apple punches and adhere to metal-rimmed tags with colored circles • adhere to layout •

Supplies – Patterned Paper: KI Memories; Chalk: Craf-T; Die Cuts: KI Memories; Stamps: PSX; Stamp Pad: Excelsior; Tags: Avery; Punch: Carl; Font: Garamouche

How proud we are to have such a handsome, smart and enthusiastic young man for our son. Brendan couldn't wait for the first day of [Fourth Grade] He was so excited! He just loves school. Even though he was going to be starting a whole new experience because he would be going to the Intermediate School this year, he just couldn't wait to get there! He was all set for his first day...wearing his new clothes and his new Nike Audacious sneakers (that he picked out himself)...and his new L.L. Bean backpack (he chose the color, Light Plum).
We are so proud of him and we hope that he always has as much enthusiasm for school and learning as he does now.

Designer: Dee Gallimore-Perry

RILEY — AGE SEVEN

• create background by attaching torn notebook paper to black cardstock with white brads • double mat photo and adhere to background • attach letter stickers for title • have child handwrite journaling onto background paper • ink and crumple strip of red cardstock and attach to layout with eyelets • embellish layout with school stickers •

Supplies – Patterned Paper: Karen Foster; Cardstock: Bazzill; Stickers: Karen Foster; Ink: Colorbox; Eyelets: Making Memories

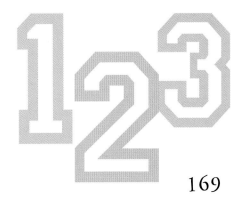

Designer: Tarri Botwinski

A+ Zach

• create background by adhering two torn green patterned papers and cotton binding tape to green stripe patterned paper • stamp pre-made frame with clear embossing ink, cover with deep embossing powder and heat • repeat process five times • let cool and carefully bend and crack • frame photo and adhere to background • double mat class photo and adhere to background • stamp title onto stripe paper and date onto manila library pocket • attach metal phrases with black brads, cotton string and glue dots •
Supplies – Patterned Paper: Leisure Arts; Frame: Leisure Arts; Deep Embossing Clear Powder: Suze Weinberg; Stamp: Hero Arts; Brad: Lasting Impressions; Metallic Words: DCWV

Fifth Grade Alex

• create background by adhering green patterned paper and inked brown patterned paper to brown cardstock • stamp decorative square image onto cardstock • frame photo with strips of inked brown patterned paper, fold under corners and attach to background with silver brads • reverse print title and cut out • print journaling onto clear vellum and tear and ink edges • mat journaling block with brown paper • crumple cream patterned paper and heat emboss with gold embossing powder • adhere die cut to distressed cream paper • adhere title letters to cream paper • attach journaling block with brads to die cut • frame decorator fabric with die cut frame embellished with sticker words • adhere to layout • embellish layout with brass circle clip, bookplate and brads •
Supplies – Patterned Paper: Leisure Arts; Vellum: Paper Adventure; Stamp: Stampa Rosa; Frame: Leisure Arts; Stickers: Bo Bunny; Brass Clip: Making Memories; Brads: Making Memories, All the Extras

Designer: Susan Stringfellow

• create background by adhering patterned papers to cursive patterned paper • mat one photo, roughen edges and adhere all photos to background • attach rub-on for title • print journaling onto sheet of white cardstock • highlight word with large font, chalk and pen • adhere journaling to layout • attach ruler stickers to layout • sand portion of large ruler and attach letter and number stickers • adhere mini jute to photo • embellish layout with sticker and number charm •

Supplies – Patterned Paper: 7 Gypsies, The Paper Patch; Rub-on: Making Memories; Metal Charm: Making Memories; Chalk: Craf-T; Stickers: EK Success; Font: Garamouche

6TH GRADE – FALL 98'

• create background by adhering trimmed blue patterned paper and a strip of sanded red patterned paper to blue cardstock • double mat photo with white cardstock and sanded red paper • adhere to background • reverse print title onto cardstock and cut out • stamp compass shape randomly over tag and stamp date and grade with letter stamps • mat tag with blue cardstock and attach to layout with square brad adorned with red paper • attach four eyelets to layout • tie fibers through eyelets • attach charms with silver thread •

Supplies – Patterned Paper: Leisure Arts; Stamps: Stamp Craft, Stampabilities; Eyelets: All the Extras; Concho: Scrapworks; Ink: Stampin' Up; Fiber: Fibers by the Yard; Font: Imprint MT Shadow

SPECIAL TIPS:
Alter paper by chalking, coloring, embossing, crumpling, aging, rolling, curling, folding, sanding and tearing. The possibilities are endless, so do anything and everything imaginable.

Designer: Susan Stringfellow

171

Madison first day of school was anticipated with the worry of meeting a new teacher and friends. Previous she had gone to Tiny Tots in the city of La Mirada but this was Pre-school. We got a new Crayola backpack with wheels(just like Mom's!) from Sam's club to make it more fun and exciting. MacKenzie, Madison and I all walked into Hillcrest school that morning. MacKenzie was ready to stay but Madison was not too sure. But when we came to pick her up at the end of the day she was all smiles. Not at all like this picture. She didn't want to come home.

School Days

Designer: Gabrielle Mader

SCHOOL DAYS WITH MADISON

• begin with yellow cardstock for background • double mat photo and adhere to page with corkboard photo corners • print title onto white cardstock • print journaling onto white cardstock • mat with cork paper and attach to background with brads • create pocket tag by cutting one tag in half at an angle and stitching to full tag • fill folder with school items • adhere tag to layout with ribbon •
Supplies – Ruler: Rebecca Sower

SPECIAL TIPS:

Create a pocket tag by cutting one tag in half at an angle and stitching it to a full tag. Fill the pocket tag with school supplies and notes from the child (it is fun to see the child's handwriting).

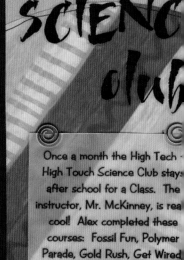

SCIENCE club

Once a month the High Tech - High Touch Science Club stays after school for a Class. The instructor, Mr. McKinney, is rea[l] cool! Alex completed these courses: Fossil Fun, Polymer Parade, Gold Rush, Get Wired, Gas Blast, & Lab 101.

Alex

LETTING MY BABY GO

• create background by adhering strip of clock patterned paper and black cardstock to yellow cardstock • adhere photo to background • print journaling onto cardstock • adhere gingham ribbon to layout • embellish with inked poetry dog tags •

Supplies – Patterned Paper: KI Memories; Cardstock: Bazzill; Ink: Staz-on

I wonder what you're doing right now and if everyone is treating you kind.
I hope there is a special person, a nice friend that you can find.
I wonder if the teacher knows just how special you are to me.
And if the brightness of your heart is something she can see.
I wonder if you are thinking about me and if you need a hug,
I already miss the sound of your voice and how you give my leg a tug.
I wonder if you could possibly understand how hard it is for me to let you grow.
On this day know that my heart breaks, for this is the first step in letting my baby go.

Alex - 8/11/2003

Designer: Layne Hamback

HIGH TOUCH — HIGH TECH

• create background by adhering circular cuts of stripe patterned paper and torn strips of word patterned paper to brown cardstock • double mat photos and adhere to background • attach letter stickers to layout for title, name and grade • print journaling onto clear vellum and cut out • attach to layout with circle clips • scan and reduce class certificate • print onto white cardstock and attach to layout • attach fibers to layout with large circle clips and adhesive • embellish layout by drawing a primary colored border and stitching lines around edges of circles with markers •

Supplies – Patterned Paper: Leisure Arts, KI Memories; Vellum: Paper Adventures; Stickers: All the Extras, Bo Bunny, Leisure Arts; Clips: All the Extras, Work.org; Chalk: Craf-T; Fiber: Fibers by the Yard

Designer: Susan Stringfellow

MEMBERSHIP

makes all the difference

Books are for looks
a look for a tale
Of possibly a lion
a tiger or whale
A look for adventure
exciting intense
With mystery unfolding
and growing suspense
A look for a fact
to inform or relate
A picture a poem
or a word to locate
You never can tell
when you start to look
What interesting things
may come in a book

Designer: Stephanie Welsh

MEMBERSHIP MAKES ALL THE DIFFERENCE

• create background by adhering cut pieces of brown paper to light brown cardstock • adhere photos to background • attach letter stickers to torn white cardstock for title • print rest of title onto brown paper and tear edges • adhere title to layout • print journaling onto cardstock, tear and ink edges and adhere to layout • make book embellishments with strips of paper • round ends and accent with pen and small strips of cardstock •
Supplies – Cardstock: Bazzill; Poem: Two Peas in a Bucket; Font: Two Peas in a Bucket Vintage, AdineKirnberg Regular

HAPPINESS IS BOOKS

• begin with inked patterned paper for background • mat photo with lavender cardstock, ink edges and adhere to background • attach rub-on title to strip of coordinating patterned paper matted with cardstock • thread letter beads with wire to finish title • ink edges of title block and adhere to layout • print journaling with 2 Peas Yoyo font onto vellum • adhere journaling to layout • embellish layout with stickers •
Supplies – Patterned Paper: Chatterbox; Cardstock: Bazzill; Stickers: Sonnets; Rub-on: Making Memories; Ink: Staz-on; Font: Two Peas in a Bucket Yoyo

Designer: Jfayne Hansbach

PIONEER BOY

• create background by adhering red patterned paper to chalkboard patterned paper • mat photos and adhere to background • ink tags and attach letter stickers for title • attach title to background with eyelets • attach labels made from label maker to layout • mat ruler sticker with red paper and adhere to layout • ink brown bag and attach to layout with floss in corners • embellish tag with school stickers •
Supplies – Patterned Paper: Karen Foster; Stickers: Karen Foster; Tags: 2 International; Ink: Colorbok; Eyelets: Making Memories; Floss: DMC; Label Maker: Dymo

Designer: Sam Cousins

LEAD ME, GUIDE ME

• create background by adhering patterned paper cut into squares to blue cardstock • outline squares with pen and attach orange brads to background • triple mat photo and adhere to layout • attach letter stickers for title • print journaling onto transparency and adhere to tag • attach tag to layout over fibers with brads • embellish layout with butterfly charms •
Supplies – Patterned Paper: Leisure Arts; Metal Charms: Leisure Arts; Brads: Making Memories; Fibers: Fibers by the Yard; Font: CK Script

SCHOOL FRIENDS

• begin with white cardstock for background • size photos to frame perimeter of layout and adhere to background • cut out title from template onto blue cardstock, mat with black cardstock, cut out and adhere over mesh to blue cardstock • attach title block to background with eyelets • handwrite names of friends by photos • embellish title block with handwritten journaling and metal tag •
Supplies – Letter Template: Pagerz; Mesh: Magic Mesh

Designer: Tracy A. Weinzapfel Burger

What a Special **Teacher**

There is a special teacher I know.
Each morning she greets me with a glow.
She is no ordinary teacher.
She taught me how to be a reacher.
Someone kind, someone nice.
Someone full of life.

One thing that I know for sure.
She wants me to be a leader.
And always reach for the stars.
She cares for whom I fool around with,
Hoping I don't get distracted.
Distracted from my lessons, my education,
My chance on being someone important in life.

My Special Teacher...Mrs. Snyder
Thank you from the bottom of my heart.
For being just who you are.
The best teacher.
I learned so much in your classroom.
When I needed that challenge
You were the one to keep me motivated.
To learn and read as much as I could,
Thank you for going that extra mile
In my heart you will always be
A very special teacher to me.

Tyler

A SPECIAL TEACHER

• begin with purple cardstock for background • enlarge photo and mat with mesh and black cardstock • print title and journaling onto cardstock and attach to background with star eyelets • cut out 'teacher' from purple cardstock and adhere to title block • highlight teachers name and have child sign bottom of poem •

Supplies – Patterned Paper: Magenta; Cardstock: Bazzill; Snaps: Making Memories; Font: Yippy Skippy; CK Handprint; CK Journaling

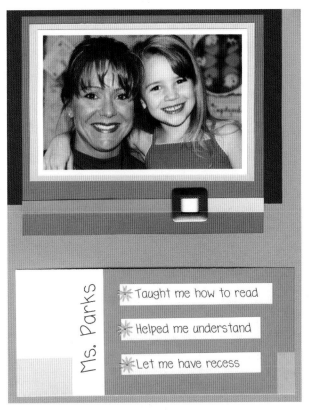

Ms. Parks

✳ Taught me how to read

✳ Helped me understand

✳ Let me have recess

Designer: Maegan Hall

MS. PARKS

• create background by adhering dark brown cardstock to light brown cardstock • triple mat photo with pink papers and adhere to background • print title and journaling onto white paper and cut into strips • adhere to collage of pink papers • adhere title block to layout • embellish layout with strips of pink paper, metal clip and flower stickers •

Supplies – Patterned Paper: SEI; Cardstock: Paper Garden; Clip: Making Memories; Flowers: Jolee's By You; Font: CK Girl

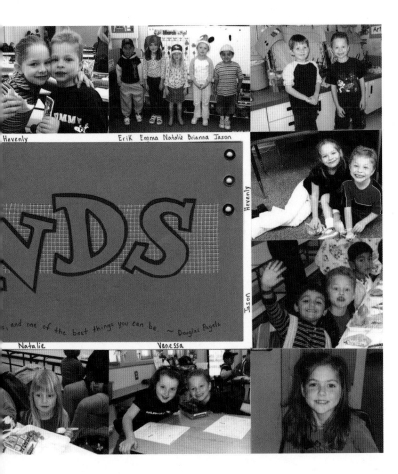

Hevenly

EriK Emma Natalie Brianna Jason

Hevenly

Jason

...and one of the best things you can be. ~ Douglas Pagels

Natalie   Vanessa

Designer: Brenda Nakandakari

CLASS FRIENDS
• create background by attaching birdhouse stickers to stripe patterned paper • mat photo with torn mulberry paper and adhere to background • print journaling onto vellum and adhere to bottom of photo with vellum tape • embellish layout with stickers •
Supplies – Patterned Paper: Leisure Arts; Mulberry Paper: DCWV; Vellum: DCWV; Stickers: Leisure Arts

SCHOOL DAYS WITH SIS
• create background by adhering torn check patterned paper to purple patterned cardstock • adhere photos to background • print title with Yippy Skippy font and LD Boxed font • attach bradwear to brads for 'big' and cut out 'sis' with template • mat title with white and purple cardstock, chalk part of title • handwrite journaling and stamp date onto vellum, mat with purple cardstock, tear edges and attach to background with eyelets • embellish layout with die cuts •
Supplies – Patterned Paper: KMI; Template: Pagerz; Bradwear: Creative Imaginations; Die Cut: Sue Dreamer Doo-Dads; Fonts: Yippy Skippy, LD Boxed

Designer: Tracy A. Weinzapfel Burgos

TEACHERS GIFTS

• begin with red textured cardstock for background • mat three photos together with cardstock • double mat large photo with cardstock and wrap fiber around bottom • secure fiber with flower eyelet charm • print title onto cardstock and mat with red cardstock • print journaling onto cardstock and mat with black cardstock • adhere journaling block to background • attach title block to journaling block with circle clip •

Supplies – Cardstock: Bazzill; Fibers: On the Surface Fibers; Eyelet Flower: Making Memories; Font: First Grader

Designer: Ramona Greenspan

SPECIAL TIPS:
1. Center the design before trimming patterned paper from 12x12 to 8x11.
2. Trim the fibers on the tag so they don't cover the journaling.

MEET THE TEACHER

• create background by adhering trimmed patterned paper to black cardstock • double mat photo and adhere to page • attach letter stickers to layout for title • print journaling onto vellum and attach to layout with photo corners • adhere school days tag • embellish layout with fibers •

Supplies – Patterned Paper: Rebecca Sower; Cardstock: Bazzill; Tag: Rebecca Sower; Vellum: Stampin' Up; Stickers: Deluxe Cuts; Photo Corners: Making Memories

TREASURES FROM THE SEA

• create background by adhering trimmed patterned paper to cardstock • single and double mat photos and ink edges • adhere photos to background • print title onto cardstock, ink edges and stitch to background with mesh • print journaling block and strip onto cardstock • highlight journaling block words with chalk and larger font, ink edges and double mat • adhere to layout • ink edges of journaling strip and attach to layout with brads • tear piece of corrugated cardstock • stain cardstock and quotation sticker with walnut ink • spray with mist of water after ink dries to create watermarks • adhere cardboard, mesh, faux wax seal and sea glass to layout • attach quotation sticker with mini brads • embellish photo with letter sticker •

Supplies – Patterned Paper: Mustard Moon; Walnut Ink: Foofala; Faux Wax Seal: Creative Imaginations; Natural Netting: Jest Charming; Rub-on: Making Memories; Quotation: My Mind's Eye; Chalk: Craft-T; Stamp Pad: Stampin' Up; Font: Two Peas in a Bucket Jack Frost, Garamouche

ANATOMY 101

• create background by adhering blue cardstock and pieced tree and window (make to look like window in photo) to white cardstock • adhere photo to background • dress and label paper doll to match teacher in photo • print title and journaling onto cardstock, cut out and adhere to layout •

Supplies – Doll Kit: Paperkins

SPECIAL TIPS:

Use pieces of clothing from a kit to make clothes for the paper doll. Trace clothing on the backside of a piece of paper and cut out.

Designer: Miranda Isenberg

COOKING UP FUN

• begin with red patterned paper for background • mat one photo with white cardstock and trim other photo to size of overlay frame • adhere photo to underside of overlay • handwrite title and adhere to underside of overlay • print journaling and adhere to underside of overlay • adhere vellum to underside of overlay and attach overlay to background with brads • handwrite onto tags and tie to matted photo with string • trim metallic accent, double mat and adhere to layout • embellish layout with charms attached with brads and string •

Supplies – Patterned Paper: Leisure Arts; Overlay: DCWV; Charms: Leisure Arts; Adhesive: Zots; Metallic Words: DCWV

AGING TECHNIQUES

Aging paper is a common scrapbooking activity. The method can tie an entire layout together, and any scrapbooking element can be aged (paper, photos, stickers, accents, fibers, etc.). The scrapbooker has a variety of aging options available today.

Walnut Ink is the most popular aging medium and works very well. It is great for staining, spraying, brushing and texturing papers. Walnut ink is taken from the shells of walnuts and comes in an oily, crystallized form. To use, just add water. The color of the stain depends on how much water is used (dark–less water, light–more water). A quick and easy way to age paper is to wet paper, crumple, and dip it in the ink mixture. Leave the paper in the ink mixture longer for a darker result. If the result is too dark, the paper can be rinsed. The ink mixture can also be brushed onto paper with a foam brush or sponge. There are many ways to use the ink so experiment and have fun with it. Let the ink dry by spreading paper flat on a towel or ironing paper on a cotton setting. Walnut ink works great on most papers, but there are some that do not absorb the ink.

Acrylic Paint and Sanding can give an aged look to a variety of products. Dry brush paper with acrylic paint and let it dry. Then sand the paper for an aged look. Sanding, even without the paint, will add years to a product. Just be careful not to sand too heartily!

Tea Bag Dying is another aging option. Boil water in a pot and add a tea bag. Stain paper in a similar manner to the other water based stains.

Metallic and Luster Rub-ons are used as an aging medium as well. They have the advantage of adhering to many different materials. Rub-ons work especially well on metal and paper and can be buffed if desired. They are best applied with a finger (covered with a latex glove) or rag.

Rub n' Buff is another rub-on medium with a wax metallic finish. It works very well on metal and is long lasting. Rub n' Buff comes in a small squeezable tube and is best applied with a finger and buffed with a soft towel.

Aging Chalks work well on most papers and are easily applied with a cotton swab or make-up sponge.

Folk Antiquing Medium is a water based stain used on wood and paper alike. It comes ready to use, but can be watered down for a lighter wash.

LEARNING IS FUN!

• create background by adhering school-themed fabric and ribbon to red cardstock • mat three photos with torn white cardstock • double mat main photo and tear bottom edge • print title and journaling onto vellum and tear • attach title and journaling with star eyelets •

Supplies - Fonts: David Walker, CK Girl

181

CHRISTMAS PROGRAM

• begin with stripe patterned paper for background • frame two photos with sticker frames and mat the rest with red vellum • adhere all photos to background • adhere title sticker to background • attach letter stickers to green patterned paper for journaling • double mat and attach to background with mini snaps • mat stickers with red vellum and embellish stickers with glitter • adhere stickers to background • print vellum copy of large photo, trim smaller than actual print and attach to photo with large red snaps • attach page pebbles to sticker frame •

Supplies – Patterned Paper: Leisure Arts; Vellum: Leisure Arts; Letter Stickers: Leisure Arts; Glitter: Close to My Heart; Snaps: Making Memories; Page Pebbles: Making Memories

Designer: Camille Jensen

Hevenly, Tyler & Joshua

Stocking Time!

Hevenly & Tyler

Designer: Tracy A. Weinzapfel Burges

HOLIDAY PARTY

• create background by adhering torn and crumpled red cardstock to green cardstock • adhere photos to background • reverse print title onto green cardstock and cut out • mat title with brown cardstock, chalk edges and adhere to background • print journaling onto brown cardstock, chalk and adhere to background • embellish layout with eyelets, pre-made tag and felt stocking •

Supplies – Tag: Rebecca Sowers; Fonts: CK ClipArt, Courier New, American Classic

ORIENTAL FEAST

• create background by adhering strips of gold paper to red cardstock • mat photos, oriental images and Chinese characters and adhere to background • reverse print title with Chow Mein font, cut out and adhere to background • print journaling, mat and adhere to layout with brad • attach chopsticks to background with fishing line • adhere beads to layout • embellish layout with string, eyelets and paper animal •

Supplies – Cardstock: Bazzill; Buttons: Making Memories; Fiber: Making Memories; Beads: Westrim Crafts; Eyelets: Making Memories; Floss: DMC; Fonts: Chow Mein, Bonzai

Designer: Tammy Bortorinsky

183

DELIGHTFULLY FRIGHTFUL HALLOWEEN

• create background by adhering four torn pieces of textured cardstock together • adhere torn green strip to background • frame two photos and purple cardstock with sticker frames • mat third photo and sticker frames with cardstock • adhere photos to background • attach stickers to orange patterned paper for title, punch into circles and attach title to layout with brass and silver circles • stamp journaling onto drafting paper, tear edges and mat with torn mulberry paper • attach to page with embroidery floss • create 'parade' by painting tags with yellow acrylic paint • attach letter stickers and heat emboss several times with clear embossing powder • attach to sticker frame with purple floss • create ghost shrinky dinks with ghost stamps and ink • embellish layout with Halloween buttons, floss and stickers matted with cardstock and torn mulberry paper •
Supplies – Patterned Paper: Leisure Arts; Cardstock: Bazzill; Stickers: Leisure Arts; Sticker Frames: Leisure Arts; Stamp: DJ Inkers, Imaginations; Ink: Staz-on; Embossing Powder: Suze Weinberg; Brads: Scrapworks; Silver Circles: Scrapworks

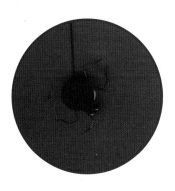

Designer: Tracy A. Weinzapfel Burges

SPIDERMAN HALLOWEEN

• begin with red cardstock for background • draw web pattern onto background • hermafix back of cardstock • punch holes every 1/8" to 1/4" to form outline of web • stitch web with needle and floss • single and double mat photos and adhere to background • print title onto red cardstock, mat with black cardstock and adhere to background • adhere spider to web •

Supplies – Floss: DMC; Stickers: Jolee's; Font: 1979

COSTUME PARADE

• create background by adhering patterned paper to gold cardstock • mat photos with gold cardstock and adhere to background • stamp title and journaling onto background • embellish layout with Halloween stickers •

Supplies – Patterned Paper: Leisure Arts; Stickers: Leisure Arts

Designer: Jane Swanson

EVERY CHILD IS AN ARTIST

• create background by adhering check patterned paper and trimmed pink cardstock to blue cardstock • attach photos to background with black photo corners • scan and print two copies of child's drawing and double mat with pink and blue cardstocks • create title with letter stickers and printed transparency • adhere title to background • print journaling onto transparency • adhere to blue patterned tag • adhere tag to layout • adhere fiber to layout with glue dots to simulate the flow of watercolors • adhere paintbrush to layout • embellish layout with sticker dots •

Supplies – Patterned Paper: Provo Craft; Stickers: Renae Lindgren; Photo Corners: Canson; Fiber: Fibers by the Yard

SPECIAL TIPS:

Attach fiber to layout where it falls to give a natural look.

Designer: Tracy A. Weinzapfel Burgos

EASTER 'EGG'SPERTS

• begin with patterned paper for background • mat four photos and adhere all photos to background • reverse print title onto patterned paper, cut out, outline with black pen and mat with pink cardstock • handwrite journaling onto green cardstock and attach stickers to green cardstock • outline journaling and sticker block with black pen and mat with pink cardstock • adhere title, journaling and sticker blocks to layout • embellish layout with stickers, tags and string •

Supplies – Patterned Paper: Creative Memories; Templates: EK Success, Deluxe Cuts; Stickers: Stickopotomus

Designer: Brenda Nakandakari

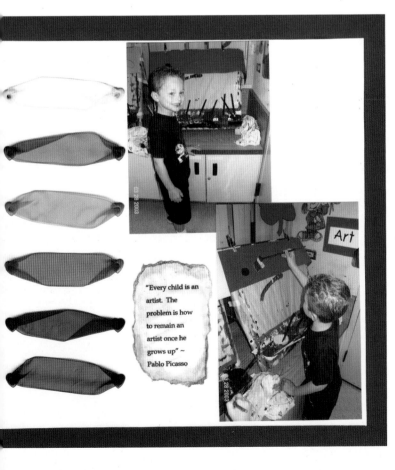

LITTLE ARTIST

• create background by adhering trimmed white cardstock to black cardstock • adhere photos to background • print title and journaling onto white cardstock, chalk edges and use water brush to run chalked colors together • adhere title and journal blocks to background • attach heart eyelets to background • string matching ribbon through each set of eyelets •

Supplies – Fonts: CK Artisan, DJ Crayon, Book Antiqua

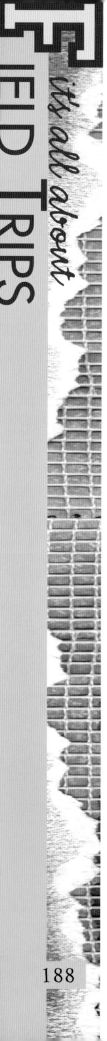

FEILD DAY 2003

• create background by stitching green patterned paper and mesh to brown cardstock with floss • frame and mat photos • handwrite title onto smooth side of clear shrinky dink with black pen • draw a border with pen onto each shrinky dink • stamp journaling onto cardstock and mat • texture torn water colored paper with a stamp and three different color ink pads • ink paper in a striped pattern • stamp flowers along bottom of water colored paper • punch out three flowers to use as reverse stencil • temporarily adhere to water colored paper and sponge around each flower with different colors • remove stencil and adhere water colored paper to background • attach black brads to the center of flowers • adhere title and journaling to layout • adhere and attach photos to layout with brads • embellish layout with waxy floss •
Supplies – Patterned Paper: Leisure Arts; Mesh: Magenta; Metal Frames: DCWV

WILDLIFE

• create background by adhering strips of green cardstock to light green cardstock • mat three photos with cardstock and corrugated cardboard and adhere to background • attach letter stickers to inked and matted cardstock for title • finish title by reverse printing letters onto brown cardstock, cut out and adhere to torn and inked cardstock • adhere title to background • print journaling onto cardstock, ink and cut to form tags • adhere to layout • embellish layout with fiber and an eyelet •

Supplies – Paper: Serendipity Paper; Stickers: David Walker; Chalk: Craf-T; Fiber: On The Surface; Eyelet: HyGlo; Fonts: Dreamer One, American Typewriter

Designer: Betsy Sammarco

Designer: Tracy A. Weinzapfel Burgos

ANIMALS ON THE RANCH

• create background by adhering torn and chalked cardstock to white cardstock • single and double mat photos • tear and chalk bottom edge of one photo • trace letters with template, cut out and mat with black cardstock for title • attach title to background with eyelets as center of letters • print rest of title and journaling onto white cardstock • tear and chalk edges • attach title block to layout with eyelets • adhere journaling block to background • embellish layout with jute and buttons •

Supplies – Cardstock: Bazzill; Button: Dress it Up; Twistal: Making Memories

Designer: Camille Jensen

POSTING THE COLORS

• create background by adhering distressed paper to tan cardstock • create distressed paper by crumpling, running under water and soaking tan cardstock in walnut ink for one minute • let paper dry and lightly sponge upper left corner with blue paint in a rectangle • apply ink to rectangle with a blue ink pad and fingers • stamp stars onto the blue rectangle with white pigment ink • lightly wash paper with walnut ink and rub in red ink stripes • mat photos with tan cardstock with inked and roughened edges • adhere photos to background with inked metal cut into photo corners • tie red waxy floss around each corner • print title and journaling onto transparency • mat journaling with red vellum and blue pinstriped paper • sew title, journaling and silver tags to background with red waxy floss •

Supplies – Patterned Paper: Leisure Arts, 7 Gypsies; Cardstock: DCWV; Ink: Staz-on

Designer: Tracy A. Weinzapfel Burges

FIELD DAY

• create background by adhering trimmed and torn blue and yellow patterned paper to black cardstock • single and double mat photos and adhere to background • reverse print title onto white cardstock, cut out and adhere to background • attach letter stickers to background to finish title • print journaling onto vellum and adhere to tag made from torn cardstock • punch four holes across top of tag and weave fibers through holes • adhere tag to layout • print date onto vellum and attach to layout with a circle clip •

Supplies – Patterned Paper: Making Memories, Colorbok; Cardstock: Making Memories; Vellum: Paper Adventures; Stickers: All the Extras; Circle Clips: All the Extras; Fiber: Fibers by the Yard; Font: Rausch

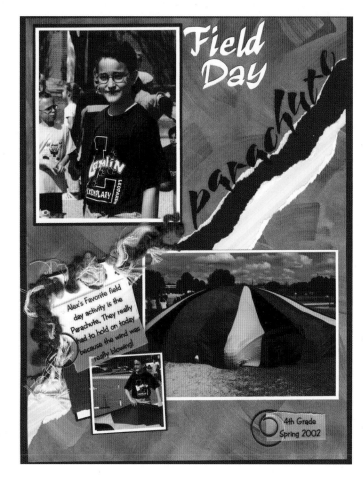

Designer: Susan Stringfellow

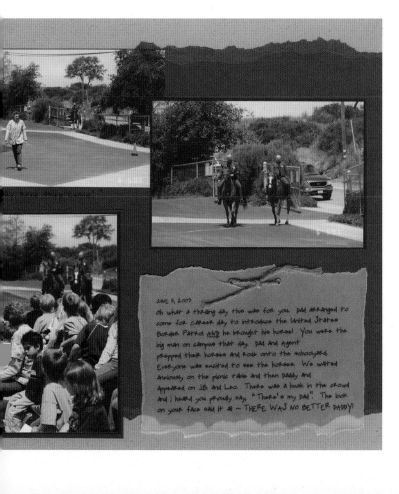

CAREER DAY

• create background by adhering torn brown cardstock to tan cardstock • attach gold eyelets to brown cardstock and lace twine over gap • single and double mat some photos • cut out title using template, mat and adhere to background • print journaling onto vellum • tear and chalk edges • attach to background with eyelets and twine • handwrite journaling next to photos •

Supplies – Letter Template: Provo Craft; Font: Janelleshand

191

Designer: Tami Botwinski

THINK, STUDY, LEARN
• create background by adhering scanned and lightened worksheet of child's homework to black cardstock • triple mat photo and adhere to layout • reverse print title and cut out letters • adhere to background • print journaling onto cardstock, cut out and attach to layout with eyelets • attach eyelets to layout • string fiber and wire through eyelets • embellish layout with star buttons threaded with wire •
Supplies — Cardstock: Bazzill; Fiber: Making Memories; Buttons: Dress It Up; Eyelets: Making Memories; Wire: Fiber Creations; Font: Marydale, Beach

Homework

Designer: Tracy A. Weinzapfel Burges

I had the special privilege to be Room Mom this year. I coordinated parties, carnivals, etc. all helped Mrs. Snyder any way I could. I also had the pleasure of **volunteering** in the classroom every Friday. With the twins in tow I would assist Mrs. Snyder with lessons, recess, and daily activities.

I learned a lot on those Fridays. First I learned that teaching is exhausting but **rewarding**. enjoyed watching the bond Mrs. Snyder had with the kids and their parents. I too formed a **bond** with her and the kids. I got to work with the "Red Bears" group that included Tyler, Emma, Carter, Vincent, and Lauren. It was fun to sit there and "teach" them during the various activities Mrs. Snyder had laid out for us. Then we would do a class art project, which was my **favorite**. Kindergarten crafts are so much **fun**! Finally I would help supervise reces which the twins **LOVED**. This gave me the chance to talk to Mrs. Snyder. It was my chan to always stay on top of Tyler's progress and behavior.

Being Room Mom is an unpaid job but very **rewarding** in so many ways. I got to see Tyl **interacting** with his friends. When there was a bruised knee that required a Mommy's touch or a trip to the nurse I was there. When there were disagreements I got to play referee. Other moms would ask how I did it with the twins and all but I saw that making Tyler a **priority** meant a lot to him. I also got to know Mrs. Snyder as a teacher and **friend**.

Overall, I would say my first year as Room Mom was **successful** and fun. Being a home allotted me this opportunity and I am so **thankful** for it. I once had a friend tell m that no paycheck can beat that and she was so right. I center my world around my kids an hope they **benefit** from it.

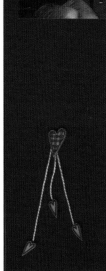

ASSESSMENT REPORT

• create background by adhering piece of textured cardstock to green patterned paper forming a pocket • adhere photo to background • reverse print title and cut out • adhere to vellum with window cut to show photo • handwrite school name and year onto vellum for journaling • embellish layout with fibers attached with gold brads • place report card in pocket •
Supplies – Patterned Paper: Provo Craft; Cardstock: Bazzill; Punch: Paper Shapers; Font: LD Chicken Scratch

Mt. Woodson ~ Kindergarten ~ '02-03

Designer: Tracy A. Weinzapfel Burgos

VOLUNTEER EXTRAORDINAIRE

• begin with black cardstock for background • print journaling onto piece of white paper and adhere to background • attach swirl stickers for title • adhere photo to layout • create pocket from school award attached to background with black brads • put party-coordinating information into pocket • remove shanks from heart buttons and hang with floss • adhere hearts and floss to layout •
Supplies – Stickers: David Walker; Floss: DMC; Buttons: Dress it Up; Alphawear: Creative Imaginations; Font: LD Cool

Designer: Susan Stringfellow

CLASSIC ALEX

• create background by adhering trimmed brown cardstock and strip of black and white checked paper to black cardstock • double mat photo and adhere to background • reverse print title onto black cardstock and cut out • adhere title to layout • print journaling, date and border words onto clear vellum • attach journaling to layout with mini silver brads • scan and reduce sheet music and print onto white cardstock • create border squares by matting four punched squares of sheet music paper with black cardstock • mat four white circles with black cardstock • attach border words and circles to squares with silver eyelets • adhere completed squares to checked border • attach date to layout with black eyelet •

Supplies – Vellum: Paper Adventures; Brads: Making Memories; Eyelets: Making Memories; Font: Harlow

CLIMB HIGH, CLIMB FAR

• create background by adhering blocks of vellum, mesh and patterned paper to blue cardstock • tear one edge of each photo, color with watercolor crayons and adhere to background • attach sticker letters to background for title • adhere vellum quotes to layout • color leaves onto vellum with watercolor crayons • crackle center block of vellum and paint with acrylic paint • blend colors with a watercolor crayon • print words onto twill tape and attach to layout with black brads • adhere beads to layout • embellish layout with stickers, keys, fiber, circle clips and bookplates •

Supplies – Patterned Paper: Creative Imaginations, My Mind's Eye; Vellum: Autumn Leaves; Mesh: Magenta; Stamps: Hero Arts; Brads: American Tag Company; Bookplates: Two Peas in a Bucket; Quotes: Memories Complete; Beads: Magic Scraps; Title: Making Memories; Stickers: EK Success; Swirl Clips: Boxer Productions; Acrylic Paint: Delta; Font: Two Peas in a Bucket Flea Market

NOBODY KNOWS

- create background by adhering strips of cardstock to green cardstock • mat one photo with cardstock and square punch other photos • frame one small photo with a metal frame • print title and journaling directly onto background cardstock • print quote onto tan cardstock, tear bottom edge and double mat • adhere to background over torn circle of cardstock • adhere photos to layout with three small photos over a torn oval of cardstock • embellish layout with metal snaps and jute •

Supplies – Metal Frame: Making Memories; Metal Snaps: Making Memories; Metal Letter: Making Memories

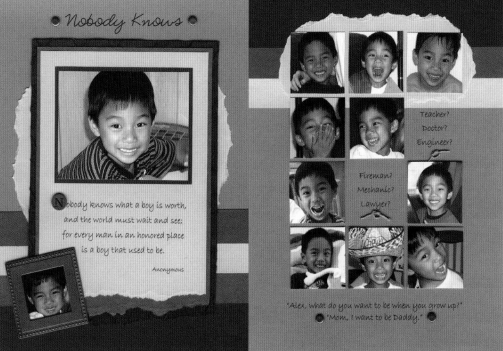

Designer: Leah Fung

Designer: Marsha Musselman

SCANNING

Scanning photos and images into a computer opens up a world of possibilities for the scrapbooker. Once a photo has been scanned, photos can be altered in a photo software program or sent to family and friends over the Internet. Scanning is not a difficult process:

1. Place item to be scanned face down on glass.

2. Select the area you want to be scanned.

3. Check the settings.

    a. Keep the resolution at a minimum of 300 DPI (Dots Per Inch).

    b. Scan the image size larger or equivalent to the size you want to print.

4. Scan the item.

5. Save the file.

    a. JPEG files are the most common for emailing since they are the most Internet compatible.

    b. TIFF files are the best option for altering images in design programs and printing high quality prints.

Enjoy altering your photos and images on the computer; just remember that it takes some patience and work to get the same color tones you see on your screen to appear on the printed photo.

Designer: Jayne Hanback

WORDS COULD NOT EXPRESS

• create background by adhering inked dictionary paper to cursive patterned paper • ink edges of large photo, stamp name and year to photo and adhere to background • tear edges of small photo, mod-podge and mat with sheet of used fabric softener and black cardstock • adhere photo to layout • mod-podge word stickers for title and adhere to layout • stamp letters to finish title • punch square of dictionary patterned paper, mat with black paper and attach to large photo with red heart eyelet • embellish layout with matted metal heart •

Supplies – Patterned Paper: Mustard Moon, 7 Gypsies; Ink: Staz-on; Metal Heart: Making Memories

Designer: Leah Fung

WHERE HAS THE TIME GONE?

• begin with patterned paper for background • double mat large photo with cardstock and frame small photo with a metal frame • adhere photos to background • print title and journaling onto transparency and adhere to background • embellish layout with fibers, metal hearts, Chinese coins and a clock piece adhered to a black slide •

Supplies – Patterned Paper: Club Scrap; Chinese Coins: All the Extras; Fiber: Fibers by the Yard; Charm: All the Extras; Watch: All the Extras; Metal Slide: Making Memories; Fonts: Two Peas in a Bucket Stamp Act, Two Peas in a Bucket Hot Chocolate

Designer: Martha Crowther

MEN OF CHARACTER

• create background by adhering trimmed patterned paper to black cardstock • mat large photo with cardstock, corrugated paper and pleated suede • adhere all photos to layout • print journaling onto red patterned paper and tear one edge • sew small journaling block to patterned and corrugated paper • adhere journaling blocks to layout • adhere die cuts to large journaling block for title • embellish journaling blocks with strips of checked paper, snaps and an alphabet eyelet •

Supplies – Patterned Paper: K & Company, Making Memories; Snaps: Making Memories; Title: Quickutz

Creating a great scrapbook page can become a whole lot easier if you have the right tools and equipment. We asked some of our best designers to give us a list of the scrapbooking tools they could not live without. Here is their list:

1. BUTTONS
2. CARDSTOCK
3. EYELET TOOL
4. FIBERS
5. METAL ACCENTS
6. PAPER TRIMMER
7. WALNUT INK
8. WIRE
9. MESH

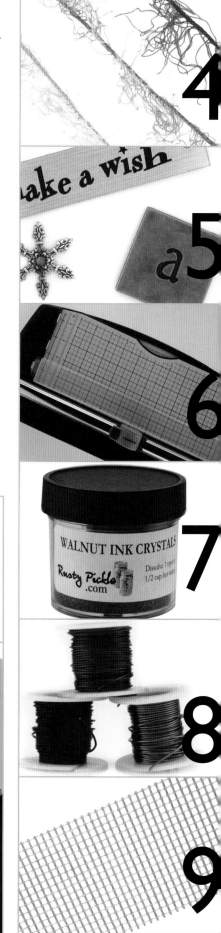

198

SOURCES

The following companies manufacture products featured in this section. Please check with your local retail store for these materials. We have made every attempt to identify and give proper credit for the materials used in this section. If by chance we have missed giving the appropriate credit, we would appreciate hearing from you.

3L Corp.
(800) 828-3130 3lcorp.com

3M Stationary
(800) 364-3577 3m.com

7-Gypsies
(800) 588 6707 7gypsies.com

Accu-Cut Systems
(800) 288-1670 accucut.com

American Tag Company
(800) 223-3956 americantag.net

Amscan
(800) 284-4333 amscan.com

Artistic Wire
(630) 530-7567 artisticwire.com

Bazzill
(480) 558-8557 bazzillbasics.com

Bo-Bunny Press
(801) 771-4010 bobunny.com

Boxer Scrapbook Productions, LLC
(888) 625-6255 or (503) 625-0455
boxerscrapbooks.com

Canson, Inc.
(800) 628-9283 canson-us.com

Carl Mfg. USA, Inc.
(800) 257-4771 carl-products.com

Chatterbox, Inc.
(888) 416-6260 chatterboxinc.com

Close to My Heart
Closetomyheart.com

Coats & Clark
coatsandclark.com

Cock-A-Doodle Design, Inc.
(800) 262-9727
cockadoodledesign.com

Colorbok
(800) 366-4660 colorbok.com

Craf-T Products
(800) 530-3410 craf-tproducts.com

Crafter's Workshop, The
(877) CRAFTER thecrafterswork-
shop.com

Creative Imaginations
(800) 942-6487 cigift.com

Creative Memories
(800) 341-5275
creativememories.com

Cut-It-Up
(530) 389-2233 cut-it-up.com

Darice
(800) 426-4659 darice.com

DCWV
(801) 224-6766 diecutswithaview.com

Decoart
(606) 365-3193 decoart.com

Delta Crafts
(800) 423-4135 deltacrafts.com

Deluxe Cuts
(480) 497-9005 deluxecuts.com

Design Originals
d-originals.com

DJ Inkers
Djinkers.com

DMC
(973) 589-0606 dmc-usa.com

Dress It Up
dressitup.com

DYMO
(800) 426-7827 dymo.com

EK Success
(800) 524-1349 eksuccess.com

Fibers by the Yard
fibersbytheyard.com

Fiber Creations
(770) 965-0018 bjsfibercreations.com

FiberScraps
(215) 230-4905 fiberscraps.com

FoofaLa
(402) 758-0863 foofala.com

Frances Meyer
francesmeyer.com

Herma Fix
Herma.co.uk.com

Hero Art Rubber Stamps, Inc.
(800) 822-4376 heroarts.com

Hobby Lobby
Hobbylobby.com

HyGlo Crafts
(480) 968-6475 hyglocrafts.com

Imaginations, Inc.
(801) 225-6015 imaginations-inc.com

Jest Charming
(702) 564-5101 jestcharming.com

Karen Foster Design
(801) 451-9779
karenfosterdesign.com

Keeping Memories Alive
(800) 419-4949 scrapbooks.com

KI Memories
(469) 633-9665 kimemories.com

Leave Memories
Leavememories.com

Leisure Arts
(888) 257-7548
business.leisurearts.com

Li'l Davis Designs
(949) 838-0344 lildavisdesigns.com

Magenta Rubber Stamps
Magentarubberstamps.com

Magic Mesh
(651) 345-6374 magicmesh.com

Magic Scraps
(972) 238-1838 magicscraps.com

Making Memories
(800) 286-5263 makingmemories.com

Me and My Big Ideas
(949) 589-4607 meandmybigideas.com

Memories Complete
(888)966-6365
memoriescomplete.com

Michael's
(800) 642-4235 michaels.com

Mrs. Grossman's
(800) 429-4549 mrsgrossmans.com

Mustard Moon
(408) 229-8542 mustardmoon.com

My Minds Eye
Frame-ups.com

Offray & Son, Inc.
Offray.com

On the Surface
(847) 675-2520

Paper Adventures
(800) 727-0699 paperadventures.com

Paper Bliss
Paperbliss.com

Paper Garden
papergarden.com

Paper Patch
Paperpatch.com

Provo Craft
(888) 577-3545 provocraft.com

PSX
(800) 782-6748 psxdesign.com

Quickutz
(888) 702-1146 quickutz.com

Scrapworks, LLC
scrapworksllc.com

SEI, Inc.
(800) 333-3279 shopsei.com

Serendipity Stamps
(816) 532-0740
serendipitystamps.com

Stampabilities
(800) 888-0321 stampabilities.com

Stamp Craft
(08) 8941 1066 stampcraft.com

Sticker Studio
Stickerstudio.com

The Robin's Nest
(435) 789-5387 robinsnest-scrap-
book.com

Two Peas In A Bucket
twopeasinabucket.com

Un-Du
Un-du.com

Westrim Crafts
(800) 727-2727 westrimcrafts.com

Xyron
(800) 793-3523 xyron.com

IT'S ALL ABOUT

ravel & acation

e travel & vacation memories with these creative scrapbooking ideas

Our trip to France

SUNRISE til SUNSET

202

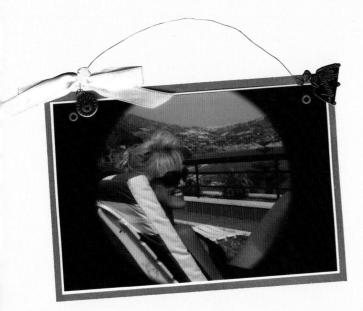

Dear Scrapbooker,

Although this section is All About Travel and Vacation, I, personally, like vacationing much more than I do traveling. My favorite place is a quiet, secluded beach where the wind doesn't blow, the sun always shines and cell phones and pagers don't work! But even that, I imagine, could get tiring after a year or two, and I might be interested in rolling over in my lounge chair to look at some of the habitat around me.

They say that half the fun of traveling is the 'anticipation' of going somewhere exciting and the other half may well be the bragging right of having 'been-there-and-done-that!' Whatever the case may be, we have greatly anticipated bringing this fun collection to press and only wish we had traveled to all the enchanting places that are photographed on these scrapbook pages. We are delighted with the variety of techniques showcased and know that you will find numerous ideas to "scrap-lift" onto your pages.

A new feature in this section is our focus on COLOR. We have provided color guidelines and color palette suggestions to enhance your travel scrapbook pages.

Our design staff and submitters continue to amaze us with their creativity and expertise. From world travel to theme parks to camping in the great outdoors, documenting these great times with family and friends will make memories last even longer.

Happy trails to you as you incorporate some of these great techniques and ideas in your travel pages,

Nancy

Nancy M. Hill

TRAVEL & VACATION 20 04

Table of Contents

SPLASH MOUNTAIN

Zip-a-dee-doo-dah
Zip-adee-ay
My oh my what a
wonderful day
Plenty of sunshine
headed our way
Zip-a-dee-doo-dah
Zip-a-dee-ay

Mr. Blue Bird on my
shoulder
It's the truth, it's actual!
Everything is satisfactory
Zip-a-dee-doo-dah
Zip-a-dee-ay

Color

COLOR IS VITAL IN SCRAPBOOKING and can create a mood for your page that is reminiscent of the event you are capturing. Color can stimulate a full range of emotions from happiness to sadness to laughter and tranquility. Good color choice helps create pages that are not only pleasing to the eye, but that promote emotion. Throughout this book you will find color palettes perfect for scrapbooking specific places and themes. Use the colors from the palettes exactly as they are, a variation to meet your needs, or just use the palettes as a guide to what colors go well together.

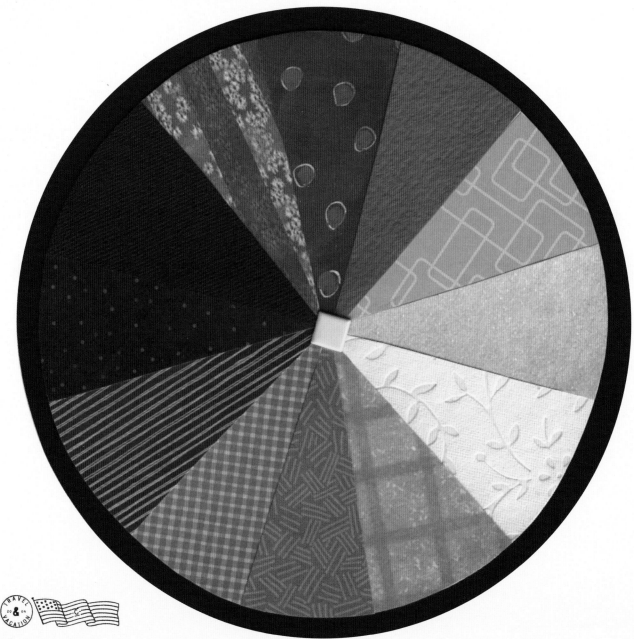

The COLOR WHEEL

The color wheel (see left) is a valuable tool for understanding color, not only does it show the relationship between colors, but it also aids in understanding the following:

Hue: color and hue are equivalent. Red, yellow and blue are primary colors. Orange, green and purple are secondary colors. Tertiary colors are a combination of two secondary colors.

Saturation: the intensity of color. A fully saturated color is considered to be pure; a less saturated, or grayer, color is muted.

Value: the darkness of color. Light colors are referred to as tints, mid-value colors as mid-tones, and dark colors as shades.

Temperature: the warmth or coolness of color. Red, orange and yellow are warm colors recalling fire and the sun. Green, blue and purple are cool colors recalling water and grass.

Monochromatic: a color scheme based on one color. The color variation comes from different saturations and values of that one color.

Analogous: a color scheme based on colors adjacent to each other on the color wheel. These colors work well together because they share the same undertones.

Complimentary: a color scheme based on colors opposite each other on the color wheel. These colors balance and contrast each other, enhancing both colors, making them appear more vibrant.

COLOR AND EMOTIONS

Color evokes emotion. The eye transmits signals to the brain and pituitary gland based on the color it sees creating an emotional reaction. Individuals have unique emotional reactions to color based on their memories, experiences and culture. The following are some common emotional reactions to color:

Red – *exciting, striking, stimulating*
Orange – *energizing, friendly, loud*
Yellow – *sunny, cheerful, warming*
Green – *refreshing, natural, soothing*
Blue – *cool, tranquil, serene, carefree*
Purple – *elegant, valiant, sensual*
Pink – *sweet, youthful, romantic*
Brown – *rustic, rich, earthy, masculine*
Neutrals – *timeless, natural, calming*
White – *pure, innocent, clean, crisp*
Black – *strong, classic, elegant*

All color palettes can be found together on page 263.

Getting There

BREAD BASKET

PACK YOUR BAGS
Page design | Jennifer Parrnelli
Supplies | Cardstock: Bazzill; Patterned Paper: K & Company; Tag: Rebecca Sower; Stickers: All The Extras, Doodlebug Designs Inc., Nostalgiques by EK Success; Rub-ons: Making Memories; Twill Tape: Wrights Ribbon Accent; Acrylic Paint: Plaid Enterprises, Inc.; Labels: Dymo; Font: Two Peas in a Bucket Jack Frost

SEA OF CORTEZ

FUTURE WORLD TRAVELERS
Page design | Sam Cousins
Supplies | Patterned Paper: Sonnets by Creative Imaginations; Fiber: Fibers by the Yard; Brads: Making Memories; Stickers: David Walker; Watch Crystal: Altered Pages; Compass: Altered Pages; Tiles: Us Art Quest; Stamps: PSX Design, Making Memories

MONTEREY

TO BOLDLY GO
Page design | Ann Gunkel
Supplies | Software: Adobe Photoshop; Font: Weltron Urban

◄GETTING THERE►

Water & Sand

On the scrapbook layout:

See Chelle
by the
SEASHORE

(handwritten on tag) Again we took to the beach for another day —Thoreau

(along right edge, vertical) Smelt Sands State Park OREGON COAST Nov 2003

210

SEE CHELLE BY THE SEASHORE
Page design | Jeanne Wynhoff
Supplies | Cardstock: Bazzill; Patterned Paper: Sonnets by Creative Imaginations; Tags: My Mind's Eye, Inc.; Fiber: Fibers by the Yard; Brads: Making Memories; Nail Heads: Jest Charming Embellishments; Stickers: Provo Craft; Mesh: PaperPhernalia; Font: Two Peas in a Bucket Sonnets Script Light

by the sea

OCEANSIDE

the beach

THE LIFE GIVEN US BY NATURE IS SHORT, BUT THE MEMORY OF A *well-spent life* IS ETERNAL
cicero

sea · wind

beach

COSTA DEL SOL

BY THE OCEANSIDE

Page design | Martha Crowther

Supplies | Patterned Paper: Wordsworth Stamps; Fibers: Fibers by the Yard; Pewter Shell: Magenta Rubber Stamps; Stickers: Shotz by Creative Imaginations, Wordsworth Stamps; Bamboo Clip: Magic Mesh; Transparency: Hewlett-Packard; Adhesives: Therm O Web, Inc.

The Ocean

The ocean is so very big and I'm so very small.
Isn't it a wonder that God knows us one and all?

The sky is oh so big and blue and seems to never end.
Isn't it a special thing that God gives us good friends?

The sand is soft between my toes and squishy when it's wet.
Isn't it just way too neat that God gave us dogs for pets?

If my mind seems to wander remember that I'm young
And in God's mighty plan for things I've only just begun!

For here I stand so all alone upon God's mighty shore
and even though I'm just a babe he could not love me more!
August 27, 2003   Written by: Thena Smith

stroll

just add
WATER

◄ WATER & SAND ►

211

FROM SEA TO SHINING SEA
Page design | Carrie O'Donnell
Supplies | Cardstock: Bazzill; Vellum: Strathmore Papers;
Page Pebbles: Making Memories; Photo Border: The Print
Shop by Broderbund; Fonts: Dearest Script, Century Gothic

From sea to shining sea.

Pride

Freedom

Peace

PACIFIC SPRAY

SOMEBODY STOP HER! SHE'S TRYING TO STEAL THE BOAT!

ALL ABOARD
Page design | NanC and Company Design
Supplies | Cardstock: DCWV; Patterned Paper: Memories in the Making; Vellum: DCWV; Stamps: Hero Arts Rubber Stamps, Inc

Oct. 97

Summer 2003

Corey– Ludington State Park

waves

ocean

COREY LUDINGTON STATE PARK
Page design | Tammy Gauck
Supplies | Patterned Paper: KI Memories; Tag: Avery Dennison; Fiber: Fibers by the Yard; Button: Dress It Up!; Brads: Doodlebug Designs Inc.; Diecut: KI Memories

◄WATER & SAND►

THE LAKE
Page design | Milissa Howes
Supplies | Cardstock: Bazzill; Patterned Paper: NRN Designs; Stickers: Sonnets by Creative Imaginations; Punch: Emagination Crafts, Inc.; Chalk: EK Success

SUMMER CAMP

BEACH BABE
Page design | Tammy Olson
Supplies | Patterned Paper: Provo Craft; Template: Deluxe Designs; Feathers: Zucker Feather Products; Chalk: EK Success; Circle Clip: Making Memories; Beads: Mill Hill

PLAYING IN THE SAND
Page design | Mendy Mitrani
Supplies | Patterned Paper: Memories in the Making; Stickers: DCWV; Chalk: ColorBox by Clearsnap, Inc.; Font: Brady Bunch

Max and Noelle have been friends since kindergarten. They had a great time playing in the sand at the Hill Country Hyatt in San Antonio last summer.

May '03

Gulf Shores

Alabama

Sun

SAND CASTLE

hot

Madeline
Chace
Mallory

July
2002

GULF SHORES
Page design | Lisa Anderson
Supplies | Cardstock: Bazzill; Patterned Paper: NRN Designs; Ribbon Charm: Making Memories; Page Pebble: Leave Memories; Rub-ons: Making Memories; Slide Mount: Leave Memories; Transparency: Magic Scraps

Watch The Wind Blow By

And all I wanna do is let it be and be with you
And watch the wind blow by
And all I wanna see is you and me go on forever
Like the clear blue sky -Tim McGraw

WATCH THE WIND BLOW BY
Page design | Ginger McSwain
Supplies | Fibers: Scrapgoods;
Charm: All The Extras; Font: Van Dijk

◄WATER & SAND►

SUNRISE TO SUNSET
Page design | NanC and Company Design
Supplies | Cardstock: DCWV; Patterned Paper: Memories in the Making; Fibers: Fibers by the Yard; Page Pebbles: Making Memories

Sunrise to Sunset

Cabo San Lucas Fall '03

MAKING WAVES
Page design | Linda Beeson
Supplies | Cardstock: Making Memories; Patterned Paper: Pebbles, Inc.; Brads: Karen Foster Design; Stickers: Pebbles, Inc., Doodlebug Designs Inc., Wordsworth Stamps

HONEYMOONERS
Page design | Jessica Williams
Supplies | Cardstock: DCWV; Patterned Paper: Memories in the Making; Charms: Memories in the Making

enjoy life

waves

bubbles

ocean

paradise

leave it all behind

refresh

escape

ENJOY LIFE
Page design | NanC and Company Design
Supplies | Cardstock: DCWV; Patterned Paper: Memories in the Making, DCWV; Metal Frame: Making Memories; Metal Hinges: Making Memories; Stickers: SEI; Rub-ons: Making Memories

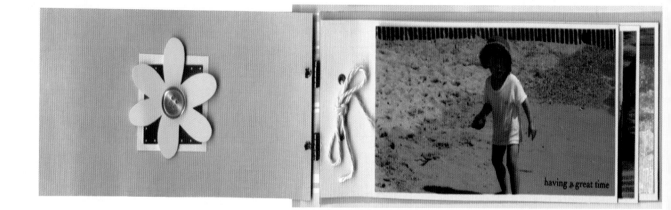

having a great time

SUMMER FUN
Page design | Tammy Olson
Supplies | Cardstock: Bazzill;
Craft Foam: Darice, Inc.; Stickers:
Provo Craft; Pen: ZIG by EK Success

Summer Fun

~The Olson Family~

We had a wonderful time at the vacation
home that we stayed at in Yachats, Oregon.
We stayed 4 nights at this home that was
so beautifully furnished and was ocean-
front. We took Keisha with us and she
loved it.
~ May 2002

SIESTA TIME

Page design | Sam Cousins

Supplies | Patterned Paper: SEI, Memories in the Making; Stickers: Sonnets by Creative Imaginations, Making Memories, SEI; Watch Crystal: Altered Pages; Walnut Ink: Altered Pages

KYLE

Page design | Becky Dezarn

Supplies | Tag: Making Memories; Metal Quote: Making Memories; Stamp: Making Memories, Stampin' Up; Ink: Close To My Heart, Tsukineko; Embossing Powder: Ranger Industries; Font: Carpenter

222

FORT WORDEN BEACH

Page design | Tonya Doughty
Supplies | Software: Adobe Photoshop CS

Fort Worden
(Washington)
beach

Our view of June 2003

‹WATER & SAND›

South of the Border

SAFARI

MOMENTS IN GHANA

Page design | Camille Jensen

Supplies | Cardstock: DCWV; Patterned Paper: DCWV, Memories in the Making; Silver Leaf: Magenta Rubber Stamps; Stickers: Memories in the Making; Mesh: Magenta Rubber Stamps; Stamp: Making Memories

The good Life

scenery · sunset · serene · fun · solitude

picturesque · vacation · stroll

horizon · discover · caribe

ambience · breeze · paradise · beauty

as GOOD as it GETS!

THE GOOD LIFE

Page design | Sam Cousins

Supplies | Patterned Paper: Chatterbox, Inc.; Vellum: Chatterbox, Inc.; Tags: Making Memories; Brads: Making Memories; Stickers: Doodlebug Designs Inc., Creative Imaginations

◄SOUTH OF THE BORDER►

225

HAKUNA MATATA
Page design | Linda De Los Reyes

Supplies | Cardstock: Making Memories; Textured Paper: Artistic Scrapper; Conchos: Scrapworks; Shell Charms: Fancifuls, Inc.; Wire: Wild Wire by NSI Innovations; Stamps: Stampin' Up; Embossing Powder: Suze Weinberg; Ink: Versamark by Tsukineko

REMEMBER THIS
Page design | Sam Cousins

Supplies | Patterned Paper: Club Scrap, Inc.; Fibers: Fibers by the Yard; Letters: Foofala; Sticker: Jolee's Boutique, Rebecca Sower; Rub-ons: Making Memories; Stamps: PSX Design

GULF OF
GUINEA

IN EVERLASTING MEMORY
OF THE ANGUISH OF OUR ANCESTORS
MAY THOSE WHO DIED REST IN PEACE
MAY THOSE WHO RETURN FIND THEIR ROOTS
MAY HUMANITY NEVER AGAIN PERPETRATE
SUCH INJUSTICE AGAINST HUMANITY.
WE, THE LIVING VOW TO UPHOLD THIS

CAPE COAST

eLMino

SLAVE
CASTLE

GULF OF GUINEA
Page design | Camille Jensen
Supplies | Cardstock: DCWV;
Patterned Paper: Memories in the
Making; Snaps: Making Memories;
Stickers: Memories in the Making;
Mesh: Magenta Rubber Stamps;
Stamps: Making Memories

KASTOM VILLAGE
Page design | Missy Partridge
Supplies | Patterned Paper: Fiskars, Inc.;
Textured Paper: Provo Craft; Vellum: The
Paper Company; Snaps: Making Memories;
Sticker: Nostalgiques by EK Success; Grass
Diecuts: Jolee's Boutique; Pen: ZIG by EK
Success; Adhesive: ZIG by EK Success; Font:
Times New Roman

INDIANA WHO?
Page design | Sam Cousins
Supplies | Cardstock: Club Scrap, Inc.; Fibers:
Fibers by the Yard; Brads: Making Memories

◄SOUTH OF THE BORDER►

HAWAII

Page design | Jessica Williams

Supplies | Cardstock: DCWV; Patterned Paper: Memories in the Making, Provo Craft

VERACRUZ

IT'S NOT A DREAM

Page design | Sue Kelemen

Supplies | Cardstock: Bazzill; Patterned Paper: Two Busy Moms by Deluxe Designs; Fibers: Fibers by the Yard; Metallic Words: DCWV; Brads: Boxer Scrapbooks; Diecuts: QuicKutz; Punch: Emaginations Crafts, Inc.

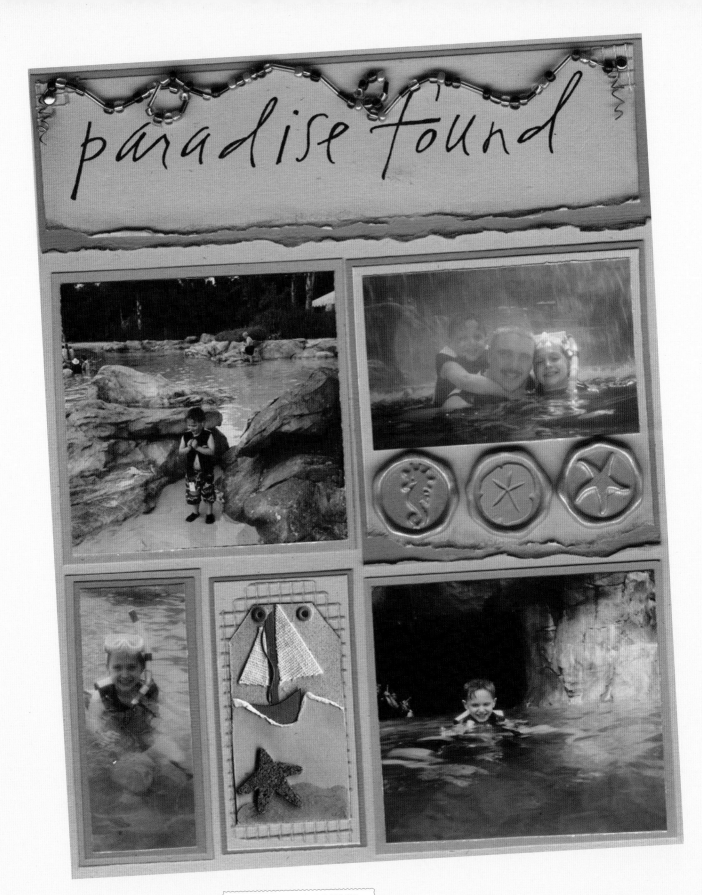

PARADISE FOUND
Page design | Angela Green
Supplies | Vellum: Stampin' Up;
Diecuts: EK Success; Rub-ons: Making
Memories; Mesh: Magic Mesh; Wax
Seals: Sonnets by Creative Imagina-
tions; Chalk: Stampin' Up; Template:
Deluxe Designs

◂SOUTH OF THE BORDER▸

Park Destinations

We went to the Rose & Crown for a bit of a snack. Perry and I had their Traditional Sherry Trifle and the boys had the Rose & Crown Chocolate Mousse Parfait. It was lovely.

ENGLAND
Page design | Susan Stringfellow
Supplies | Cardstock: Bazzill; Patterned Paper: Daisy D's Paper Company; Vellum: Making Memories; Fibers: Fibers by the Yard; Metallic Tags: DCWV; Brads: Making Memories; Maps: Jolee's Boutique; Photo Corners: Making Memories; Punch: Disney; Stamp: Stampabilities, Stamp Craft; Ink: Stampin' Up; Walnut Ink: Altered Pages; Transparency: Altered Pages; Fonts: CAC Valiant, Kelly Ann Gothic

DISCOVERY

Page design | Susan Stringfellow

Supplies | Cardstock: Making Memories; Patterned Paper: Sonnets by Creative Imaginations; Fibers: Fibers by the Yard; Brads: ScrapLovers; Charm: All The Extras; Stickers: NRN Designs; Beads: Crafts Etc.; Chalk: Craf-T Products; Adhesive: JudiKins; Fonts: Atlantix, Atlantean

GUM BALLS

HOGLE ZOO

Page design | Camille Jensen

Supplies | Patterned Paper: Memories in the Making; Textured Paper: Magenta Rubber Stamps; Brads: Lasting Impressions; Floss: DMC; Stamp: Magenta Rubber Stamps, Making Memories, Hero Arts Rubber Stamps, Inc., Wordsworth Stamps

◄PARK DESTINATIONS►

Deutschland

EPCOT

FESTWEIN

Germany ~ Epcot

We really enjoyed Germany. We did a little shopping, posed with some German Cast Members, and ate dinner at the Biergarten while listening to the Oktoberfest Musikanten.

Germany

Shop for unique gifts, crystal and collectibles here. You'll also find German wines, wine tasting, authentic dining and lederhosen, of course.

Riesling

DEUTSCHLAND

Page design | Susan Stringfellow

Supplies | Cardstock: Bazzill; Patterned Paper: Memories in the Making; Brads: Making Memories; Paper Clip: Boxer Scrapbooks; Diecut: Memories in the Making; Label Image: Altered Pages; Stickers: Magenta Rubber Stamps; Walnut Ink: Altered Pages; Transparency: 3M Stationary

COASTER

LEGOLAND

Page design | Camille Jensen

Supplies | Cardstock: DCWV; Patterned Paper: Memories in the Making; Metallic Frames: DCWV; Overlay: DCWV; Stamps: Making Memories

AFRICA

Page design | Susan Stringfellow

Supplies | Cardstock: Bazzill; Patterned Paper: Memories in the Making; Patterned Vellum: EK Success; Fibers: Fibers by the Yard; Buttons: Dress It Up!; Sticker: Altered Pages; Beads: Crafts Etc!; Bamboo Clips: Altered Pages; Trim: Altered Pages; Mesh: ScrapLovers; Chalk: ColorBox by Clearsnap, Inc.; Stamps: Dollar Tree; Ink: Tsukineko; Transparency: Altered Pages; Font: African

236

SPLASH MOUNTAIN

Page design | Susan Stringfellow

Supplies | Cardstock: Bazzill; Patterned Paper: Memories in the Making; Fibers: Fibers by the Yard; Diecut: Memories in the Making; Chalk: ColorBox by Clearsnap, Inc.; Stamps: Making Memories; Ink: Stampin' Up; Transparency: 3M Stationary; Adhesive: JudiKins; Font: Antique Type

Entrance →

SPLASH MOUNTAIN

Cooling off and Splashing Down!!!

July '02 W.D.W.

Zip-a-dee-doo-dah
Zip-adee-ay
My oh my what a
wonderful day
Plenty of sunshine
headed our way
Zip-a-dee-doo-dah
Zip-a-dee-ay

Mr. Blue Bird on my
shoulder
It's the truth, it's actual
Everything is satisfactual
Zip-a-dee-doo-dah
Zip-a-dee-ay
Wonderful feeling,
Wonderful Day!

briar patch!

The Great Outdoors

YELLOWSTONE

JENNY LAKE

GEYSERS

HOT POTS

JACKSON HOLE

WHITNEY

ZACHARY

JAKE

BUCHANAN FAMILY REUNION
AT MAMMOTH, YELLOWSTONE
AUGUST 1-5, 1996
THIS WAS SUCH A FUN TRIP.
BRYAN COULDN'T GO BUT I JUST
PILED THE KIDS IN THE CAR AND
WE HAD A BLAST!
A LOT OF DRIVING THOUGH!!!
THE KIDS WERE GREAT AND SO
FUN TO BE WITH-WILD AS THEY
WERE...

MOOSE

YELLOWSTONE FALLS

BUFFALO

BEARS

YELLOWSTONE
Page design | Camille Jensen
Supplies | Patterned Paper: Memories in the Making; Vellum: DCWV;
Tags: Darice, Inc.; Metal Embellishments: Making Memories

MORNING GLORY

THE SNAKE

Page design | NanC and Company Design
Supplies | Cardstock: DCWV; Patterned Paper: Memories in the Making; Metallic Frame: DCWV

A scene of *beauty*

A SCENE OF BEAUTY

Page design | NanC and Company Design
Supplies | Cardstock: DCWV; Patterned Paper: Memories in the Making; Brads: Making Memories; Stickers: Memories in the Making, Making Memories

LODGEPOLE PINE

DAN

Page design | NanC and Company Design
Supplies | Cardstock: DCWV; Metal Frame:
Making Memories; Metal Clip: Making Memories;
Brads: Making Memories; Page Pebbles: Making
Memories; Vellum Quote: DCWV; Sticker: Paper Bliss
by Westrim Crafts

The best and most beautiful things in the world cannot be seen or even touched... they must be felt with the heart.

–Helen Keller

◄THE GREAT OUTDOORS►

Nature's Inspirations

TREE OF LIFE

Page design | Lisa Anderson

Supplies | Cardstock: Bazzill; Patterned Paper: Hot Off The Press; Tag: Avery Dennison; Page Pebble: Making Memories; Beads: Blue Moon Beads; Stamp: Inkadinkado; Ink: Versamark by Tsukineko; Embossing Powder: Stamps 'n' Stuff

TULIPS

MOSS GARDEN

ORDINARY TREE

Page design | Briana Fisher

Supplies | Cardstock : DCWV

242

FIRST FROST
Page design | NanC and Company Design
Supplies | Cardstock: DCWV; Patterned Paper:
Memories in the Making; Tag: Making Memories;
Metallic Frame: DCWV; Metallic Letters: DCWV

WATERFALLS OF WONDER
Page design | NanC and Company Design
Supplies | Cardstock: DCWV; Patterned Paper:
Memories in the Making; Floss: Making Memories; Ribbon: Offray & Son, Inc.

◄NATURE'S INSPIRATIONS►

Sight Seeing

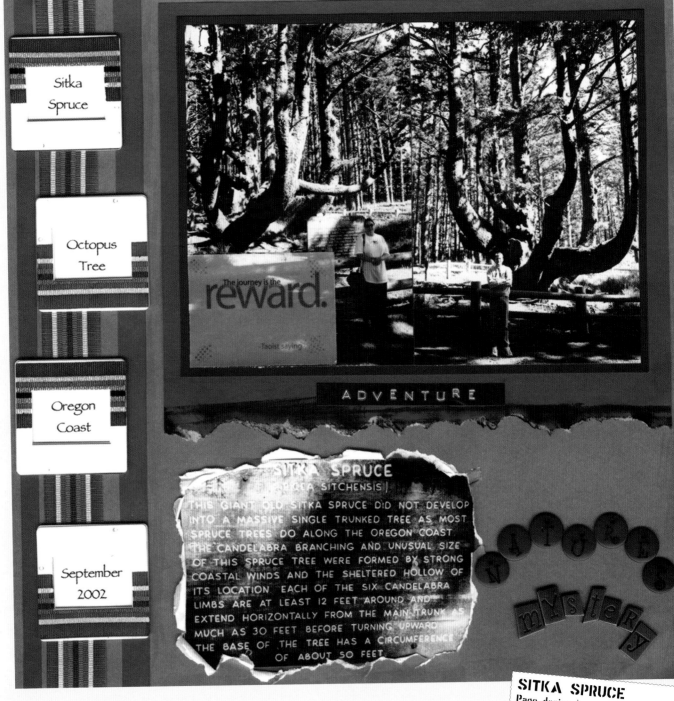

Sitka Spruce

Octopus Tree

Oregon Coast

September 2002

The journey is the **reward.**

-Taoist saying

A D V E N T U R E

SITKA SPRUCE
[PICEA SITCHENSIS]
THIS GIANT OLD SITKA SPRUCE DID NOT DEVELOP INTO A MASSIVE SINGLE TRUNKED TREE AS MOST SPRUCE TREES DO ALONG THE OREGON COAST. THE CANDELABRA BRANCHING AND UNUSUAL SIZE OF THIS SPRUCE TREE WERE FORMED BY STRONG COASTAL WINDS AND THE SHELTERED HOLLOW OF ITS LOCATION. EACH OF THE SIX CANDELABRA LIMBS ARE AT LEAST 12 FEET AROUND AND EXTEND HORIZONTALLY FROM THE MAIN TRUNK AS MUCH AS 30 FEET BEFORE TURNING UPWARD. THE BASE OF THE TREE HAS A CIRCUMFERENCE OF ABOUT 50 FEET

NATURE

mystery

SITKA SPRUCE
Page design | Briana Fisher
Supplies | Patterned Paper: Memories Complete; Button Letters: Junkitz; Metal Letters: Making Memories; Sticker: Pebbles, Inc.

DUSK

WYOMING
Page design | Catherine Lucas
Supplies | Cardstock: The Rusty Pickle;
Stickers: Karen Foster Design; Slide Frame:
Club Scrap, Inc.; Font: Textile

DEEP WEST
Page design | Catherine Lucas
Supplies | Cardstock: The Rusty
Pickle; Tag: Making Memories; Fiber:
Fibers by the Yard; Eyelets: Making
Memories

be an explorer
the universe is filled with
wonder and magical things

- flavia

WHERE IN THE WORLD

Page design | Christine Johnson

Supplies | Cardstock: Bazzill; Patterned Paper: Anna Griffin, Mustard Moon Paper Co.; Rub-ons: Making Memories; Font: Two Peas in a Bucket Falling Leaves

FREEDOM
Page design | Pam Rawn
Supplies | Tag: Making Memories; Dog Tag: Li'l Davis Designs; Flag Tag: The Paper Loft; Metal Words: Making Memories; Metal Mesh: Making Memories; Screw Eyelets: Making Memories; Rub-ons: Making Memories; Ribbon: Making Memories; Photo Clips: Making Memories; Twistel: Making Memories; Bookplate: Li'l Davis Designs; Safety Pins: Li'l Davis Designs; Mesh: Magic Scraps; Stamp: Hero Arts Rubber Stamps, Inc.; Ink: Versamark by Tsukineko, Stampin' Up; Font: Daniel

MOJAVE

FARMERS MARKET
Page design | Susan Stringfellow
Supplies | Patterned Paper: Memories Complete; Button Letters: Cardstock: Making Memories; Patterned Paper: Memories in the Making; Fibers: Fibers by the Yard; Thread: Coats & Clark; Brads: Making Memories; Stickers: Memories in the Making; Rivet: Chatterbox, Inc.; Ink: Stampin' Up; Walnut Ink: Altered Pages; Embossing Powder: Stamps 'n' Stuff; Labels: Altered Pages; Transparency: 3M Stationary; Foam Tape: Magic Mounts

◄SIGHT SEEING►

247

NINA

Page design | Carla Jacobsen

Supplies | Patterned Paper: Colorbok, Hot Off The Press; Fibers: Adornments by EK Success; Eyelets: Making Memories; Snaps: Making Memories; Stickers: Sonnets by Creative Imaginations; Rub-ons: Craf-T Products; Chalk: EK Success

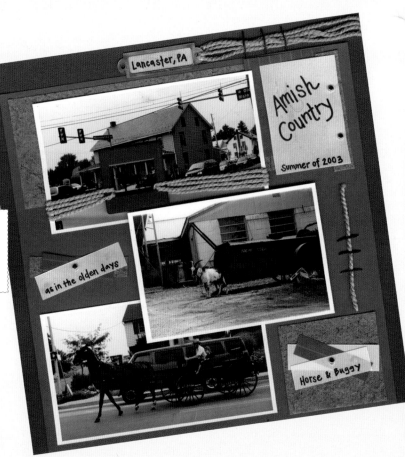

AMISH COUNTRY

Page design | NanC and Company Design

Supplies | Cardstock: DCWV; Patterned Paper: Memories in the Making; Metallic Frame: DCWV; Brads: Making Memories; Slide Mount: Magic Scraps; Floss: Making Memories

MIDGET MAN MARCH

Page design | Ann Gunkel
Supplies | Software: Adobe Photoshop; Font: Weltron Urban

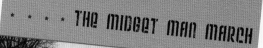

THE MIDGET MAN MARCH

NEW YORK

Page design | Jessica Williams
Supplies | Cardstock: DCWV; Patterned Paper: Memories in the Making; Sticker: Memories in the Making

WALL ST

I ♥ NY

DEAR FAMILY,
    NEW YORK IS SO
EXCITING. WE VISITED THE
STATUE OF LIBERTY & THE EMPIRE
STATE BUILDING YESTERDAY!
MISS YOU GUYS, SEE YOU SOON.
    LOVE, DAD

◄SIGHT SEEING►

Foreign Lands

JAPAN
Page design | Camille Jensen
Supplies | Cardstock: DCWV; Metallic Tags:
DCWV; Photo Overlay: DCWV; Charms: Memories
in the Making

LONDON
Page design | Camille Jensen
Supplies | Cardstock: DCWV; Patterned Paper: Memories in the Making; Metallic Frame: DCWV; Metallic Tag: DCWV; Stickers: Pebbles, Inc.; Page Pebbles: Making Memories; Slide Mount: Magic Scraps; Acrylic Paints: Making Memories; Stamps: Making Memories, Hero Arts Rubber Stamps, Inc.

STAINED GLASS

TOWER OF LONDON
Page design | Camille Jensen
Supplies | Cardstock: DCWV; Patterned Paper: Memories in the Making; Metallic Frame: DCWV; Metallic Tag: DCWV; Stickers: Pebbles, Inc.; Page Pebbles: Making Memories; Slide Mount: Magic Scraps; Acrylic Paints: Making Memories; Stamps: Making Memories, Hero Arts Rubber Stamps, Inc.

◄FOREIGN LANDS►

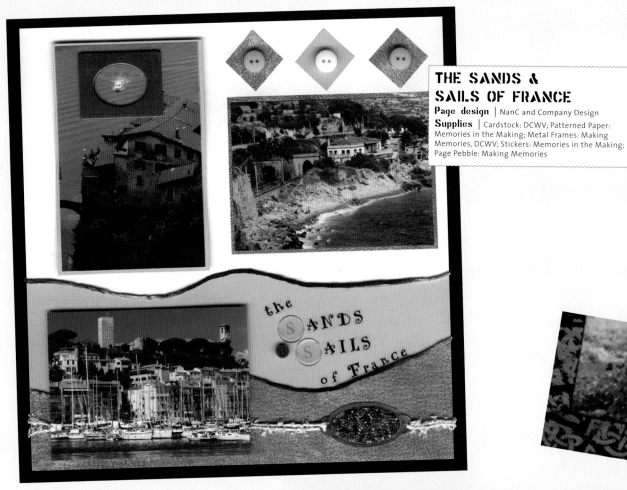

THE SANDS & SAILS OF FRANCE

Page design | NanC and Company Design
Supplies | Cardstock: DCWV; Patterned Paper: Memories in the Making; Metal Frames: Making Memories, DCWV; Stickers: Memories in the Making; Page Pebble: Making Memories

the
S ANDS
S AILS
of France

THE EMPEROR'S SUMMER PALACE

Page design | NanC and Company Design
Supplies | Cardstock: DCWV; Patterned Paper: Memories in the Making; Metal Frame: DCWV; Photo Corners: Memories in the Making; Tiles: EK Success

Fall 1999
China

MONGOLIAN GRASSLANDS

the
Emperor's Summer Palace
was a magnificent sight. Even though it was not very far from the Forbidden City, it must have felt nice to be able to escape to the river bank. The architecture was magnificent & we enjoyed the day exploring.

TRAVEL TAG
Design | Tammy Gauck
Supplies | Patterned Paper: 7 Gypsies; Fibers: Fibers by the Yard; Buttons: Dress It Up!; Stamp: Stampin' Up

SWISS ALPS
Page design | NanC and Company Design
Supplies | Cardstock: DCWV; Patterned Paper: Memories in the Making; Metal Frame: DCWV; Brads: Making Memories

The moment is unexplainable, as one stands beside something as extraordinary as the Swiss Alps. I felt so small and trivial that it was hard to take in the magnificent beauty of one of God's most incredible creations. Until you see it with your own eyes, it is hard to imagine a place like this actually exists!

Swiss Alps 2002

ANDALUSIA

THE STREETS OF FRANCE BY FOOT

Page design | NanC and Company Design
Supplies | Cardstock: DCWV; Patterned Paper:
Memories in the Making; Stickers: Nostalgiques
by EK Success

Some of the most beautiful sights of France can only be seen by getting out of the car and off of the train and walking down the back roads of the beautiful city. The architecture and beautiful flowers are simply a part of daily life for the people who live there, but for us, it is a new magical world of endless possibilities.

european

G e t **A** **W** **A** **Y**

memories

EUROPEAN GETAWAY
Page design │ NanC and Company Design
Supplies │ Cardstock: DCWV; Patterned Paper: Memories in the Making; Tag: DCWV; Metal Letters: Making Memories; Button: DCWV

These scenes of the French Riviera were taken on our trip to France in 1998. The water makes a beautiful background for the city.

vacation

remember

ROME IN RUINS

Page design | Camille Jensen
Supplies | Cardstock: DCWV; Patterned Paper: Memories in the Making; Stamps: Making Memories

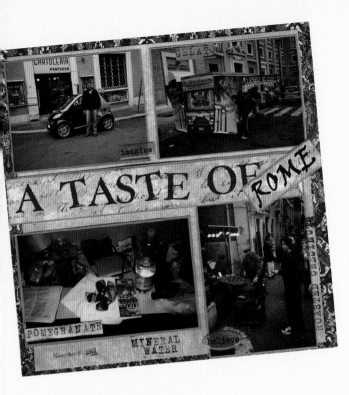

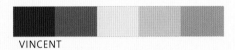

VINCENT

FRESH FLOWERS OF FRANCE
Page design | NanC and Company Design
Supplies | Cardstock: DCWV; Patterned Paper:
Memories in the Making; Metal Hinge: Making
Memories

Fresh
Flowers
of
France

PEN PALS

Page design | Misty Posey

Supplies | Cardstock: Bazzill; Vellum: Paper Garden; Fibers: Fibers by the Yard; Mesh: Jest Charming Embellishments, Magic Scraps; Slide Mount: All The Extras; Stamps: A Stamp in the Hand Co.; Ink: Rubber Stampede; Embossing Powder: Stamps 'n' Stuff; Font: Two Peas in a Bucket Stained Glass

There is nothing on this earth to be more prized than

True Friendship

An Afternoon at the Chinese Market

One of my mom's favorite things to do in a foreign country is to go to the market. She loves to see how other people shop and what foods are available. This market was very unique, lining the streets in Beijing. They sold everything from baked goods and spices to fresh meat and produce. It was an enjoyable experience except when getting a whiff of the fish!

CHINESE MARKET

Page design | NanC and Company Design

Supplies | Cardstock: DCWV; Patterned Vellum: Memories in the Making; Button: Making Memories

SUNRISE 'TIL SUNSET
Page design | NanC and Company Design
Supplies | Cardstock: DCWV; Patterned Paper: Memories in the Making; Tags: Making Memories; Rub-ons: Making Memories; Floss: Making Memories; Charm: Making Memories; Ribbon: Offray & Son, Inc.

Our trip to France

SUNRISE til SUNSET

TRAVEL TAG
Page design | Tammy Gauck
Supplies | Patterned Paper: Mustard Moon Paper Co., 7 Gypsies; Fibers: Fibers by the Yard; Stamps: Stampington & Company, Stampin' Up

◄FOREIGN LANDS►

Coming Home

ALMOST HOME
Page design | Thena Smith
Supplies | Software: Digital Image Pro; Background Papers: Cottage Arts; Mats: Cottage Arts; Embellishments: Cottage Arts

BIG SPRINGS

THE END
Page design | Sam Cousins
Supplies | Patterned Paper: 7 Gypsies, DCWV; Fibers: Fibers by the Yard; Brad: Making Memories; Stickers: All My Memories, Wordsworth Stamps; Money Embellishments: Jolee's Boutique

Stas visted the Carousel in Bryant Park. This lovely mid-town park has an old-fashioned carousel that Stasiu loves! He even rode it twice--once on the Rabbit with Mommy & once on the Frog with Daddy!

Nothing is more fun than FOOD in New York. Uncle Paulie joined us for a super dinner at Chef Mario Batali's Lupa. Two hours later, Stas was still a great boy--loving the boutique prosciutto, eating gnocchi alla romana and inhaling chocolate tartuffo gelato for dessert!

NEW YORK
Page design | Ann Gunkel
Supplies | Software: Adobe Photoshop; Font: Wendy Medium

To commemorate our spectacular Autumn in New York, I wrote a book, starring our son, Stas. Designed in glossy magazine style, the book traces our steps, highlighting the sights, sounds & tastes of New York. The book was then laminated and bound for my son's Christmas present. We love reading it and reliving the fun again & again. Its the best vacation souvenier I can think of!

The "Stas Loves New York" Project

Stas Loves New York!

ALOHA

Sources

It's All About Travel & Vacation

3M Stationary
(800) 364-3577
3m.com

A Stamp in the Hand Co.
(310) 884-9700
astampinthehand.com

Adobe
(800) 833-6687
adobe.com

All My Memories
(888) 553-1998
allmymemories.com

All The Extras
(425) 868-6628
alltheextras.com

Altered Pages
alteredpages.com

Anna Griff
(888) 817-8170
annagriffin.com

Artistic Scrapper
(818) 786-8304
artisticscrapper.com

Avery Dennison
averydennison.com

Bazzill
(480) 558-8557
bazzillbasics.com

Blue Moon Beads
(800) 377-6715
beads.net

Boxer Scrapbooks
(888) 625-6255
boxerscrapbooks.com

Broderbund
(415) 382-4400
broderbund.com

Chatterbox, Inc.
(888) 416-6260
chatterboxinc.com

Clearsnap, Inc.
(800) 448-4862
clearsnap.com

Close To My Heart
(888) 655-6552
closetomyheart.com

Club Scrap, Inc.
(888) 634-9100
clubscrap.com

Coats & Clark
coatsandclark.com

Colorbok
(800) 366-4660
colorbok.com

Cottage Arts
cottagearts.net

Craf-T Products
(800) 530-3410
craf-tproducts.com

Crafts Etc!
(800) 888-0321
craftsetc.com

Creative Imaginations
(800) 942-6487
cigift.com

Daisy D's Paper Company
(888) 601-8955
daisydspaper.com

Darice, Inc.
(800) 321-1494
darice.com

DCWV
(801) 224-6766
diecutswithaview.com

Deluxe Designs
(480) 497-9005
deluxecuts.com

Disney
go.disney.com

DMC
(973) 589-9890
dmc-usa.com

Dollar Tree
757-321-5000
dollartree.com

Doodlebug Designs Inc.
801-966-9952
timelessmemories.ca

Dress It Up!
dressitup.com

Dymo
dymo.com

EK Success
(800) 524-1349
eksuccess.com

Emagination Crafts, Inc.
(630) 833-9521
emaginationcrafts.com

Fancifuls, Inc.
(607) 849-6870
fancifulsinc.com

Fibers by the Yard
fibersbytheyard.com

Fiskars, Inc.
(715) 842-2091
fiskars.com

Foofala
(402) 758-0863
foofala.com

Hero Arts Rubber Stamps, Inc.
(800) 822-4376
heroarts.com

Hewlett-Packard
hp.com

Hot Off The Press
(800) 227-9595
paperpizazz.com

Inkadinkado
(781) 938-6100
inkadinkado.com

Jest Charming Embellishments
(702) 564-5101
jestcharming.com

Jolee's Boutique
joleesbyyou.com

JudiKins
(310) 515-1115
judikins.com

Junkitz
junkitz.com

K & Company
(888) 244-2083
kandcompany.com

Karen Foster Design
(801) 451-9779
karenfosterdesign.com

KI Memories
kimemories.com

Leave Memories
leavememories.com

Li'l Davis Designs
(949) 838-0344
lildavisdesigns.com

Magenta Rubber Stamps
magentarubberstamps.com

Magic Mesh
magicmesh.com

Magic Mounts
(800) 332-0050
magicmounts.com

Magic Scraps
(972) 238-1838
magicscraps.com

Making Memories
(800) 286-5263
makingmemories.com

Memories Complete
(866) 966-6365
memoriescomplete.com

Memories in the Making
(800) 643-8030
leisurearts.com

Mill Hill
millhill.com

Mustard Moon Paper Co.
(408) 229-8542
mustardmoon.com

My Mind's Eye, Inc.
(801) 298-3709
frame-ups.com

NRN Designs
nrndesigns.com

NSI Innovations
nsiinnovations.com

Paper Company, The
(800) 426-8989
thepaperco.com

Paper Garden
(210) 494-9602
papergarden.com

PaperPhernalia
paperphernalia.com

Pebbles, Inc.
pebblesinc.com

Plaid Enterprises, Inc.
(800) 842-4197
plaidonline.com

Provo Craft
(888) 577-3545
provocraft.com

PSX Design
(800) 782-6748
psxdesign.com

QuicKutz
(888) 702-1146
quickutz.com

Ranger Industries
(800) 244-2211
rangerink.com

Rebecca Sower
mississippipaperarts.com

Rubber Stampede
(800) 423-4135
rubberstampede.com

Rusty Pickle, The
(801) 274-9588
rustypickle.com

Scrapgoods
scrapgoods.com

ScrapLovers
scraplovers.com

Scrapworks
scrapworksllc.com

SEI
(800) 333-3279
shopsei.com

Stamp Craft
stampcraft.com.au

Stampabilities
stampabilities.com

Stampin' Up
(800) 782-6787
stampinup.com

Stampington & Company
(949) 380-7318

Stamps 'n' Stuff
(515) 331-4307
stampsnstuff.com

Strathmore Papers
(800) 628-8816
strathmore.com

Suze Weinberg
(732) 761-2400
schmoozewithsuze.com

Therm O Web, Inc.
(800) 323-0799
thermoweb.com

Tsukineko
(800) 769-6633
tsukineko.com

Two Peas in a Bucket
twopeasinabucket.com

Us Art Quest
(517) 522-6225
usartquest.com

Westrim Crafts
(800) 727-2727
westrimcrafts.com

Wordsworth Stamps
(719) 282-3495
wordsworthstamps.com

Wrights Ribbon Accents
(877) 597-4448

Zucker Feather Products
(573) 796-2183
zuckerfeathers.com

COLOR PALETTES

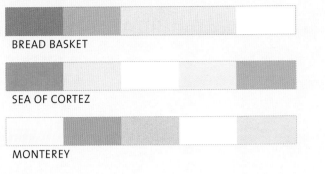

GETTING THERE

BREAD BASKET

SEA OF CORTEZ

MONTEREY

WATER & SAND

SUMMER CAMP

COSTA DEL SOL

NANTUCKET

PACIFIC SPRAY

SAND CASTLE

SOUTH OF THE BORDER

SAFARI

PATAGONIA

VERACRUZ

PARK DESTINATIONS

GUM BALLS

COASTER

THE GREAT OUTDOORS

MORNING GLORY

LODGEPOLE PINE

NATURE'S INSPIRATIONS

TULIPS

MOSS GARDEN

SIGHT SEEING

DUSK

MOJAVE

FOREIGN LANDS

STAINED GLASS

MONGOLIAN GRASSLANDS

ANDALUSIA

VINCENT

LAVENDER FIELDS

COMING HOME

ALOHA

BIG SPRINGS

LONDON

hawaii

SUMMER VACATION

It is good to have an end to journey towards,
but it is the *j o u r n e y* that matters in the end.
Ursula LeGuin

NEW YORK

ARE

WE

THERE

YET?

Two roads diverged in a wood, and I—
I took the one less traveled by,
And that has made all the difference.
Robert Frost

The perfect trip is a circle—getting there and coming home.

camping

scenic route

road trip

IT DOESN'T MATTER IF IT

TAKES A LONG TIME GETTING

THERE; THE POINT IS TO

HAVE A DESTINATION.

EUDORA WELTY

who said you can't take it with you?

seashells
by the seashore

JOURNEY

The longest journey is the journey inward.

DAG HAMMARSKJOLD

sightseeing

Europe

going places

weekend getaway

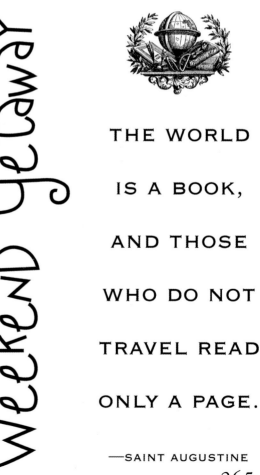

THE WORLD

IS A BOOK,

AND THOSE

WHO DO NOT

TRAVEL READ

ONLY A PAGE.

—SAINT AUGUSTINE

JOY

BLACK CURRANT

sweetness

AMERIC

OLLIE

The eyes are the window of the soul.

pets & animals

with these great ideas and quotes for scrapbooking pets & animals

268

Dear Scrapbooker,

Is this the most beautiful, sweetest, smartest, loyal dog you have ever seen? His name is Mr. Beau Jangles, he is mine, and I love him to death!! He has recently acquired a little brother, named Lazlo, who is also a miniature German Schnauzer and looks just like him. Ironically, I never considered myself an animal lover until after my children left home and the pleas for having pets ceased. Since then, I have benefited from the joy and companionship of Beau and Lazlo. With my newfound love of animals you can imagine what a pleasure it has been to be involved with the creation of this idea collection.

It has been so much fun sharing our designers' happy animal memories and experiences through their scrapbook pages. Whether in the wild or at home these pages show a special appreciation and love for pets and animals.

I hope you enjoy the many ideas these pages have to offer. "Lift" the ideas directly onto your own scrapbook pages or just use them to spark your creativity. Pets and animal quotes have been sprinkled throughout to help when you are simply at a loss for words. Enjoy!

Happy Scrappin',

Nancy M. Hill

it's all about **Pets & Animals**
table of contents

270

Small Animals 310

Zoo & Animal Parks 320

In the Wild 326

Farm Animals 316

Dogs

Socks

Supplies - Cardstock: DMD Industries; Patterned Paper: Laura Ashley by EK Success, K & Company, Keeping Memories Alive; Metals: Making Memories; Floss: DMC; Stickers: Creative Imaginations; Template: Deja Views by The C-Thru Ruler Company; Ribbon: Offray & Son, Inc.; Font: Bookman Old Style

Designer - Sherry Laffoon

My **goal** in life is to be as **good** of a person my **dog** already thinks I am.   Author Unknown

Dawson Loves Wubby

Supplies - Cardstock: Bazzill; Patterned Paper: K & Company; Corrugated Paper: DMD Industries; Tag: Making Memories; Buttons: Dress It Up!; Stickers: Sonnets by Creative Imaginations, Rebecca Sower; Ribbon: Offray & Son, Inc.; Ink: Hero Arts Rubber Stamps, Inc.; Fonts: Two Peas in a Bucket Flea Market, Menagerie, P22 Garamouche

Designer - Wendy Malichio

Dogs are not our whole **life**, but they make our lives **whole.** ~Roger Caras

A Boy and His Dog

Supplies - Cardstock: Paper Garden; Patterned Paper: Laura Ashley by EK Success; Bookplate: Making Memories; Stickers: Laura Ashley by EK Success; Rub-ons: Making Memories; Ribbon: Making Memories; Photo Corners: Canson, Inc.; Ink: Close To My Heart

Designer - Darlynn Kaso

True Friends

Supplies - Software: Adobe Photoshop;
Fonts: Weltron Urban, Hamburger Menu

Designer - Ann Gunkel

No **matter** how little money and how **few possesions** you own, having a **dog** makes you **rich**.

~Louis Sabin

My Dog

If I could choose
just one friend th
would be foreve
at my side and
love me
unconditionally
it would be
my dog.
He accepts me a
I am and never
fails to make
me smile.

There is not
quite a more
comfortable
thought as
knowing he's
my loya
companion.

The world could
take lessons fr
my dog.

Casey Party Animal

Supplies - Cardstock: Bazzill; Patterned Paper:
Memories in the Making; Metallic Letters: DCWV;
Fibers: Fibers by the Yard; Brads: ScrapLovers;
Buttons: Dress It Up!; Stickers: Memories in the
Making; Stamps: Dollar Tree; Ink: Stampin' Up;
Chalk: Stampa Rosa; Adhesive: Magic Mounts;
Font: Two Peas in a Bucket Well Behaved

Designer - Susan Stringfellow

My little dog - a heartbeat at my feet. ~Edith Wharton

Pals

Supplies - Cardstock: Bazzill; Tags: Avery
Dennison; Metal Letters: Making Memories;
Fiber: Fibers by the Yard; Heart Eyelet: Making
Memories; Vellum Quote: Quick Quotes; Chalk:
Craf-T Products; Fonts: Texas Hero, Pristina

Designer - Maureen Spell

Nature at Its Best

Supplies - Cardstock: Bazzill; Patterned Paper: Club Scrap, Inc.; Handmade Paper: Artistic Scrapper; Fibers: Adornments by EK Success; Button: Sticko by EK Success; Date Stamp: Making Memories; Stamp: Penny Black; Ink: Close To My Heart; Font: Times New Roman

Designer - Suzanne Webb

To sit with a dog on a hillside on a glorious afternoon is to be back in Eden, where doing nothing was not boring - it was peace.

~Milan Kundera

Taking a Sunday Stroll

Supplies - Cardstock: DCWV; Patterned Paper: Memories in the Making; Metallic Letters: DCWV; Mesh: Making Memories

Designer - NanC and Company Design

A Boy's Best Friends

Supplies - Cardstock: Bazzill, SEI; Patterned Paper: SEI; Metal Words: Making Memories; Fonts: Yippy Skippy, Type Wrong

Designer - Wendy Bickford

What Do You Dream

Supplies - Cardstock: Bazzill; Fiber: Fibers by the Yard; Brads: Doodlebug Designs Inc.; Wordfetti: Making Memories; Clip: Paper Pizazz by Hot Off The Press; Stickers: Karen Foster Design, Pebbles in my Pocket, Creative Imaginations; Ink: ColorBox by Clearsnap, Inc.

Designer - Kim Musgrove

Loyal Friend

Supplies - Cardstock: Bazzill; Patterned Paper: K & Company, 7 Gypsies, Rebecca Sower; Stickers: Sticker Studio, Making Memories, David Walker; Labels: Dymo; Ink: Stampin' Up; Stamps: Ma Vinici's Reliquary

Designer - Elizabeth Cuzzacrea

Cherish

Supplies - Patterned Paper: 7 Gypsies; Metallic Hearts: Anima Designs; Definition: Making Memories; Netting: Loose Ends

Designer - Sherrill Ghilardi Pierre

Dogs are miracles with paws. ~Author Unknown

Casey Dog

Supplies – Cardstock: Bazzill; Patterned Paper: Memories in the Making, Karen Foster Design; Fibers: Fibers by the Yard; Brads: Making Memories; Buttons: Dress It Up!; Cork Pieces: Lazerletterz, Altered Pages; Stamps: Wordsworth Stamps; Font: Riverside

Designer - Susan Stringfellow

The Greatest Gift of Life

Supplies - Patterned Paper: NRN Designs, Sarah Lugg; Specialty Paper: Magenta Rubber Stamps; Definition: Making Memories; Stickers: Magenta Rubber Stamps, Doodlebug Designs Inc.; Transparency: 7 Gypsies
Designer - Sherrill Ghilardi Pierre

Old dogs, like old shoes, are comfortable. They might be a bit out of shape and a little worn around the edges, but they fit well. ~Bonnie Wilcox

Kinship with All Animals

Supplies - Cardstock: Bazzill; Patterned Paper: KI Memories; Corrugated Paper: Paper Reflections by DMD Industries; Stickers: Doodlebug Designs Inc., Shotz by Creative Imaginations, Sonnets by Creative Imaginations; Labels: Dymo; Ink: ColorBox by Clearsnap, Inc.; Pen: ZIG by EK Success

Designer - Lindsay Teague

One Simple Life

Supplies - Patterned Paper: KI Memories; Staples: Making Memories; Buttons: Making Memories; Stickers: Wordsworth Stamps; Twill Tape: Wrights; Artist Pastels: EK Success; Stamps: PSX Design; Ink: Tsukineko; Fonts: CK Elusive, CK Fresh Fonts

Designer - Teri Anderson

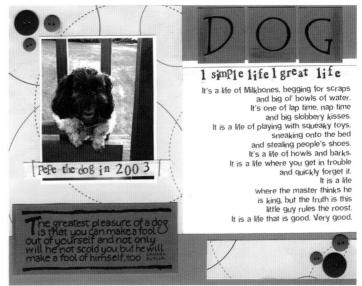

Taffy

Supplies - Software: Adobe Photoshop CS

Designer - Tonya Doughty

Dreaming in Black n' White

Supplies - Cardstock: Bazzill; Patterned Paper: Memories in the Making; Eyelets: Making Memories

Designer - NanC and Company Design

Do You Remember

Supplies - Patterned Papers: Chatterbox, Inc.; Clip: Clipola; Ribbons: Offray & Son, Inc.; Stamps: Rubber Stampede, Stamps by Judith, Hero Arts Rubber Stamps, Inc.; Ink: Tsukineko; Adhesive: Therm O Web, Inc.; Font: Angelia

Designer - Laura Stewart

Hayden & Cowboy

Supplies - Cardstock: DCWV; Patterned Paper: Memories in the Making; Font: Tempus Sans

Designer - Laura Olsen

There is no psychiatrist in the world like a puppy licking your face. ~Bern Williams

Binky 2004

Supplies - Cardstock: DCWV; Patterned Paper: Memories in the Making, DCWV; Charm: Making Memories; Wooden Tiles: DCWV; Rub-ons: Creative Imaginations; Fonts: Hannibal Lector, Century Gothic

Designer - Anna Estrada Davison

Joy is Not in Things

Supplies - Patterned Paper: DCWV; Fiber: Fibers by the Yard; Metallic Frame: DCWV; Brads: Making Memories; Vellum Quote: DCWV

Designer - Sam Cousins

Sweet Goofy

Supplies - Patterned Paper: DCWV; Bookplate: DCWV; Brads: Lasting Impressions; Font: CK Thick Brush

Designer - Miranda Isenberg

Scratch a dog and you'll find a permanent job.

~ Franklin P. Jones

The Dog Days of Summer

Supplies - Cardstock: DCWV; Patterned Paper: Memories in the Making; Stamp: Rubber Stampede

Designer - NanC and Company Design

The pug is living proof that God has a sense of humor.

Margo Kaufman

Boy's Best Friend

Supplies - Patterned Paper: Memories in the Making; Cardstock: DCWV; Buttons: Making Memories

Designer - Camie Lloyd

Be Mine

Supplies - Patterned Paper: Memories in the Making; Stickers: Memories in the Making; Vellum Quote: DCWV; Ribbon: Offray & Son, Inc.; Chalk: ColorBox by Clearsnap, Inc.

Designer - Mendy Mitrani

285

Meet Pete

Supplies - Cardstock: Bazzill; Patterned Papers: Chatterbox, Inc.; Vellum: Chatterbox, Inc.; Fibers: Fibers by the Yard; Brads: Making Memories; Stickers: Flavia; Font: Two Peas in a Bucket Angel

Designer - Sam Cousins

Dogs laugh, but they laugh with their tails.

~Max Eastman

The great pleasure of a dog is that you may make a fool of yourself with him and not only will he not scold you, but he will make a fool of himself too. ~Samuel Butler

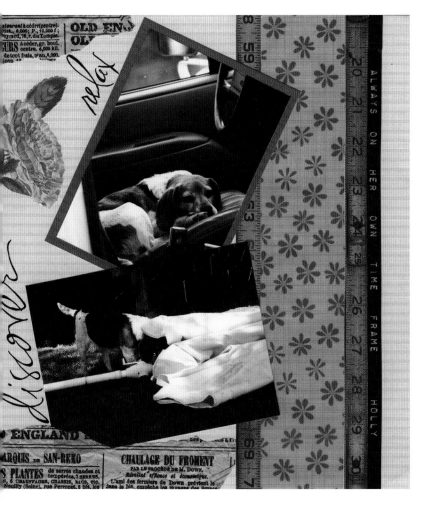

Holly

Supplies - Patterned Papers: Chatterbox, Inc., K & Company; Fiber: Adornments by EK Success; Stickers: Sticker Studio, Nostalgiques by EK Success; Rub-ons: Making Memories; Flower Postage Stamp: Art Accents by Provo Craft; Date Stamp: Making Memories; Labels: Dymo; Stamp: Close To My Heart; Ink: Close To My Heart

Designer - Suzanne Webb

Bad Santa

Supplies - Software: Adobe Photoshop;
Background Paper: Scrapbook-Bytes; TV Frame:
Scrapbook-Bytes; Font: Space Toaster

Designer - Ann Gunkel

Puppy Love

Supplies - Metal Letters: Making Memories; Bookplate: Making Memories; Brads:
Creative Impressions; Safety Pins: Li'l Davis Designs; Stickers: Creative Imaginations

Designer - Pamela Rawn

Whoever said you can't buy happiness forgot little puppies. ~Gene Hill

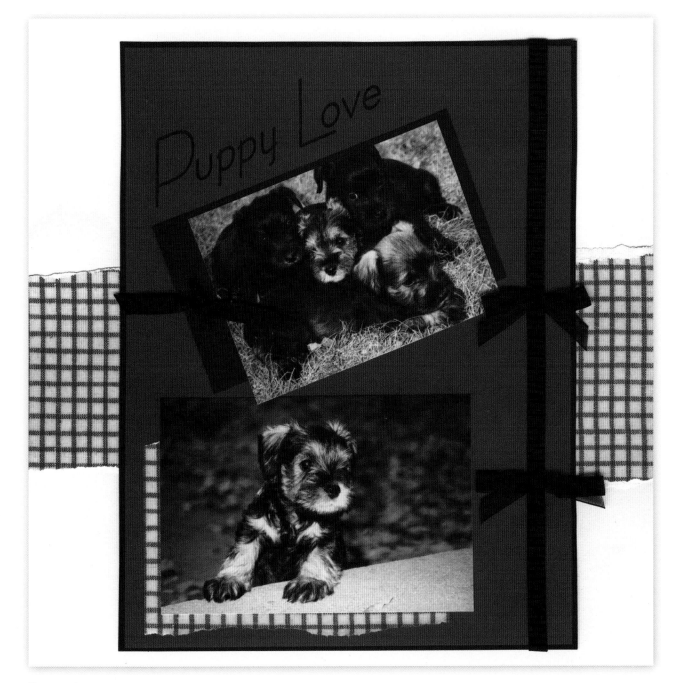

Puppy Love

Supplies - Cardstock: DCWV; Patterned Paper: Memories in the Making; Ribbon: Offray & Son, Inc.

Designer - NanC and Company Design

Just Another Reason to Own a Dog

Supplies - Alphabet Charms: Making Memories; Letter Tiles: Westrim Crafts; Shaker Box: EK Success; Font: Typewriter

Designer - Elsa Duff

A **dog** is the only thing on **earth** that **loves** you **more** than you love **yourself.** ~Josh Billings

Dog Daze

Supplies - Cardstock: Bazzill; Patterned Paper: Paper House Productions; Tags: Paper House Productions; Circle Letters: Paper House Productions; Brads: Making Memories; Labels: Dymo; Photo Corners: Canson, Inc.; Stamps: Ma Vinici's Reliquary; Ink: ColorBox by Clearsnap, Inc.; Transparency: Apollo; Fonts: Adler, Two Peas in a Bucket Burlap, Two Peas in a Bucket Flea Market, Two Peas in a Bucket Quirky

Designer - Wendy Malichio

A Dog and His Boy

Supplies - Cardstock: Bazzill; Patterned Paper: K & Company; Charm: Marcella by K & Company; Bamboo Clips: Magic Scraps; Puzzle Pieces: The Gifted Note; Tiles: Paper Reflections by DMD Industries; Mini Folder: Paper Bliss by Westrim Crafts; Definitions: Making Memories; Labels: Dymo; Acrylic Paint: Anita's Craft Paint; Stamps: Ma Vinici's Reliquary, Hero Arts Rubber Stamps, Inc.; Ink: Hero Arts Rubber Stamps, Inc.

Designer - Wendy Malichio

Heaven Through Our Binky's Eyes

Supplies- Patterned Paper: The Rusty Pickle, Memories in the Making, Creative Imaginations; Wooden Tiles: DCWV; Denim Tag: Memories in the Making; Labels: Dymo; Stickers: Memories in the Making; Rub-ons: Making Memories, Creative Imaginations

Designer - Anna Estrada Davison

Purrfect Pals

Supplies - Cardstock: DMD Industries; Patterned Paper: Paper Adventures, The Paper Patch; Vellum: Provo Craft; Tags: DMD Industries; Buttons: Making Memories; Floss: DMD Industries; Stickers: Doodlebug Designs Inc.; Ribbon: Offray & Son, Inc.; Font: Kristen ITC

Designer - Sherry Laffoon

We Love Panther

Supplies - Cardstock: Bazzill; Patterned Paper: Karen Foster Design; Vellum: Making Memories; Metallic Tag: DCWV; Brads: ScrapLovers; Word: Dress It Up!; Stickers: NRN Designs; Ribbon: Offray & Son, Inc.; Stamps: Close To My Heart; Ink: Stampin' Up, ColorBox by Clearsnap, Inc.; Embossing Powder: Ranger Industries; Font: Two Peas in a Bucket Scrumptious

Designer - Susan Stringfellow

One cat just leads to another.

Ernest Hemingway

This is My Ball

Supplies - Cardstock: Making Memories; Patterned Papers: Memories in the Making, Karen Foster Design; Patterned Vellum: Visions by American Crafts; Silver Letters: ScrapYard 329; Fibers: Fibers by the Yard; Thread: Coats & Clark; Eyelets: Gotta Notion; Brads: Making Memories; Button: Dress It Up!; Stickers: Memories in the Making; Wire: Artistic Wire Ltd; Transparency: 3M Stationary; Font: Crafty

Designer - Susan Stringfellow

293

Fierce!

Supplies - Cardstock: Bazzill;
Patterned Paper: Memories
in the Making; Buttons: Dress
It Up!; Mesh: Magic Mesh;
Ribbon: Michaels; Chalk:
ColorBox by Clearsnap, Inc.;
Stamps: Stamp Craft; Ink:
Stampin' Up; Font: Pepita MT

Designer - Susan Stringfellow

As every cat owner
knows,
nobody
owns a cat.

~Ellen Perry Berkeley

Kittens Don't Need Beauty Products

Supplies - Cardstock: Bazzill;
Patterned Paper: Colorbok;
Conchos: ScrapLovers; Fibers:
Fibers by the Yard; Fabric: Hobby
Lobby; Stamp: Hero Arts Rubber
Stamps, Inc.; Gold Leaf: Mona
Lisa Products; Stickers: Magenta
Rubber Stamps; Embossing
Powder: Scrap 'n Stuff; Adhesive:
JudiKins; Font: Create a Card
Shishone

Designer - Susan Stringfellow

It's **really** the cat's **house** - we just
pay the **mortgage**. ~Author Unknown

The Wonderful Thing About Tiggers

Supplies - Cardstock: Bazzill; Patterned Papers: Mustard Moon Paper Co., NRN Designs, Hot Off The Press; Fibers: Fibers by the Yard; Brads: Making Memories; Stickers: Memories in the Making; Wire: Artistic Wire Ltd; Ink: Stampin' Up; Embossing Powder: Stamps 'n' Stuff; Adhesives: Magic Mounts, JudiKins; Fonts: Pooh, Tigger

Designer - Susan Stringfellow

Flea Market

Supplies - Patterned Paper:
DMD Industries; Mulberry
Paper: The Paper Company;
Brads: Coffee Break Design;
Font: Modern #20

Designer - Julie K. Eickmeier

Jonah

Supplies - Patterned Paper:
Memories Complete; Page Pebble:
Making Memories; Vellum Tag:
Making Memories

Designer - Shannon Logan

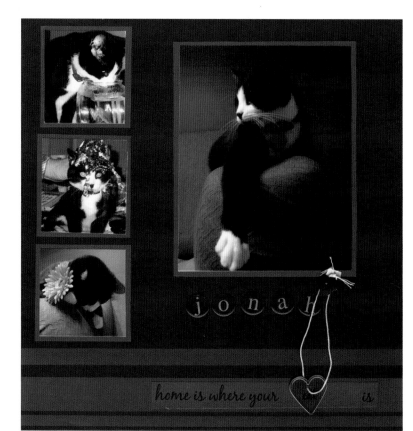

Our Most Fun Tradition

Supplies - Cardstock: Chatterbox, Inc.; Patterned Paper: Chatterbox, Inc.; Tags: Chatterbox, Inc.; Nail Heads: Chatterbox, Inc.; Tacks: Chatterbox, Inc.; Frames: Chatterbox, Inc.; Font: P22 Garamouche

Designer - Tarri Botwinski

Cats sleep **anywhere**, any table, any chair. Top of **piano**, window-ledge, in the middle, on the **edge**. Open draw, empty **shoe**, anybody's **lap** will do. **Fitted** in a cardboard box, in the **cupboard** with your frocks. Anywhere! They don't **care**! Cats **sleep** anywhere.

Eleanor Farjeon

Caught Green Handed!

Supplies - Cardstock: Bazzill; Patterned Papers: Bo-Bunny Press, EK Success; Eyelets: ScrapLovers; Font: Grinched

Designer - Susan Stringfellow

What?

Supplies - Cardstock: Bazzill; Vellum: Making Memories; Floss: DMC; Stamp: Hero Arts Rubber Stamps, Inc.; Ink: Tsukineko; Font: Yippy Skippy

Designer - Susan Stringfellow

Stripes

Supplies - Cardstock: Bazzill; Patterned Paper: Memories in the Making; Brads: Making Memories; Heart Charm: Memories in the Making; Cork Embellishments: LazerLetterz; Thread: Coats & Clark; Ribbon: Offray & Son, Inc.; Stamp: Close To My Heart; Ink: Stampin' Up; Transparency: 3M Stationary; Fonts: Two Peas in a Bucket Prose, Create a Card One Seventy

Designer - Susan Stringfellow

Who among us hasn't envied a cat's ability to ignore the cares of daily life and to relax completely? ~Karen Brademeyer

Sleepy Tiger

Supplies - Cardstock: Bazzill; Patterned Paper: Memories in the Making;
Fibers: Fibers by the Yard; Brads: ScrapLovers; Mica Pieces: Altered Pages;
Stamps: Making Memories, Close To My Heart; Ink: Tsukineko

Designer - Susan Stringfellow

I had been **told** that the **training** procedure with **cats** was difficult. It's not. **Mine** had **me** trained in **two** days. ~Bill Dana

Sterling

Supplies - Cardstock: Bazzill; Patterned Paper: Chatterbox, Inc.; Snap: Making Memories; Stickers: Sonnets by Creative Imaginations

Designer - Donna Manning

Eight Things

Supplies - Patterned Paper: Chatterbox, Inc.; Metal Letters: Making Memories; Metal Heart: Making Memories; Bookplate: Making Memories; Ribbon: Making Memories; Ink: Ranger Industries; Font: Two Peas in a Bucket Jack Frost

Designer - Angelia Wigginton

Mommy's Little Him

Supplies - Cardstock: Bazzill; Patterned Paper: Rebecca Sower; Sticker: Tag Along by Deluxe Designs; Chalk: EK Success

Designer - Lori Bowders

Horses

Enjoy the Journey

Supplies - Cardstock: Bazzill; Patterned Papers: The Rusty Pickle, K & Company; Vellum Tags: Making Memories; Envelope: Laura Ashley by EK Success; Buttons: Making Memories; Stickers: K & Company, Pebbles in my Pocket, Rebecca Sower, Creative Imaginations, Sticker Studio; Page Pebble: Making Memories; Photo Anchor: Making Memories; Washer Words: Making Memories; Watch Part: 7 Gypsies; Stamps: Magenta Rubber Stamps

Designer - Kathlene Clark

Lacee & Kip

Supplies - Patterned Paper: Pixie Press; Textured Paper: Aitoh Company; Clips: Making Memories; Stickers: PixiePress

Designer - Wendy Malichio

No hour of life is wasted that is spent in the saddle. ~Winston Churchill

MMM Ranch

Supplies - Patterned Papers: Memories in the Making; Letter Tiles: DCWV; Photo Overlay: DCWV; Sticker: Memories in the Making; Ink: ColorBox by Clearsnap Inc.

Designer - Mendy Mitrani

Grandma Jakes Farm

Supplies - Patterned Paper: Karen Foster Design; Stickers: Karen Foster Design

Designer - Cindy Ballagh

Horse sense, n.: Stable thinking. ~Author Unknown

A horse gallops with his lungs, Perseveres with his heart, And wins with his character. ~Tesio

My Dream Horse

Supplies - Cardstock: Bazzill; Patterned Papers: Chatterbox, Inc., Provo Craft; Alphabet Eyelets: Making Memories; Bookplate: Magic Scraps; Fibers: Fibers by the Yard; Leather Tag: 7 Gypsies; Vellum Tag: Making Memories; Nail Heads: Chatterbox, Inc.; Mesh: Magic Mesh; Rub-ons: Making Memories; Stamps: Hero Arts Rubber Stamps, Inc.; Walnut Ink: 7 Gypsies; Fonts: Dearest Script, Provo Craft Jen Pen, Bickley Script, Schindler Small Caps

Designer - Kathlene Clark

Birds

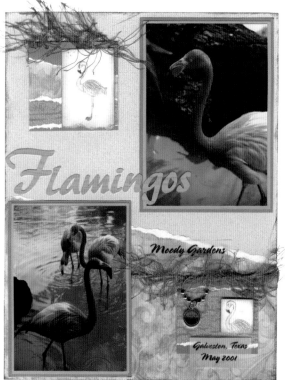

Flamingos

Supplies - Cardstock: Making Memories; Patterned Papers: Memories in the Making, Sonnets by Creative Imaginations; Vellum: Making Memories; Fibers: Fibers by the Yard; Charm: Gotta Notion; Stamp: The Uptown Design Company; Ink: Tsukineko, Stampin' Up; Chalks: Craf-T Products

Designer - Susan Stringfellow

It is not only fine feathers that make fine birds. ~Aesop

While at Xel-Ha we saw these macaws. They were absolutely beautiful!

Just as we were coming into the park, there were two macaws perched in a little sitting area near two venders. You could sit down and enjoy a coke with a macaw perched by your side.

Further into the park there was a center island with several trees. There were several macaws just preening for the cameras.

It was so neat to be able to get that close to these beautiful birds!

The Macaws

Up, Up & Away

Supplies - Cardstock: DCWV;
Patterned Paper: Memories in the
Making; Metallic Letters: DCWV;
Ribbon: DCWV

Designer - NanC and Company Design

Hope is the thing
with feathers
That perches in the
soul, And sings
the tune without
the words, And
never stops at all.

Emily Dickenson

The Macaws

Supplies - Patterned Paper:
KI Memories; Tag: Making
Memories; Stickers: Doodlebug
Designs Inc.; Font: Two Peas in
a Bucket Typo

Designer - Amy Alvis

A **bird** does not **sing** because it has
an **answer**. It sings because it has a
song. ~Chinese Proverb

Sneaky Parrots

Supplies - Cardstock: Bazzill; Patterned Papers: Memories in the Making, Karen Foster Design; Vellum: Paper
Adventures; Fibers: Fibers by the Yard; Brads: ScrapLovers; Jump Rings: Making Memories; Beads: Crafts Etc!;
Mesh: Magic Mesh; Punch: EK Success; Rub-ons: Craf-T Products; Stamps: Dollar Tree; Ink: Stampin' Up

Designer - Susan Stringfellow

Robin

Rufous Hummingbird

Canadian Geese

Hummingbird

Flying High in New Hope

Supplies - Cardstock: DCWV; Patterned Paper: Memories in the Making; Vellum Quote: DCWV

Designer - NanC and Company Design

Bald Eagle

Quail Family

Hummingbird

Pleasant Pheasant

Supplies - Cardstock: Club Scrap, Inc.; Patterned Paper: Club Scrap, Inc.; Metal Clip: Making Memories; Tags: Making Memories; Ribbon: Club Scrap, Inc.; Font: Club Scrap, Inc.

Designer - Catherine Lucas

Small Animals

Grasshopper Hunter

This is my littler grasshopper hunter. He runs through the grass watching grasshoppers hop and land. He then busily combs the grass looking for them. When he finds one, he runs around trying to so hard to catch them. Some of them are faster than he is but somehow he does manage to catch one or two of them. Sometimes he calls them crickets and sometimes he calls them friends. Mostly he calls them "his friends". He puts them in his motorized car and takes them on a ride with him. It is fun watching his sense of adventure when it comes to hunting down his "friends". I hope he never loses his curiosity of the world around him so that he will always be "My Grasshopper Hunter"!

Grasshopper Hunter

Supplies - Patterned Paper: Stampin' Up; Stamps: The Angel Company; Ink: Staz-on by Tsukineko; Font: Barbara Hand Scribble

Designer - Wanda Troupe

There are two lasting **bequests** we can give our children: one is **roots**. The other is **wings**. ~Hodding Carter, Jr

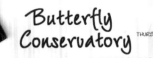

Butterfly Conservatory

TO DEMONSTRATE HOW FLEXIBLE WE ARE, AFTER THROWING SOME OPTIONS AROUND WE DECIDED TO GO TO THE BUTTERFLY CONSERVATORY AND THEN START THE LONG DRIVE HOME. THE IDEA OF BREAKING THE DRIVE UP INTO DAYS, PLUS GETTING HOME FRIDAY AFTERNOON WAS APPEALING. AFTER ALL WE'D ABOUT DONE EVERYTHING WE WANTED OR NEEDED TO IN THE AREA, SO WE PACKED UP, CHECKED OUT AND DROVE TO FORTINOS FOR OUR MORNING FIX. BELIEVE IT OR NOT, I REALLY WASN'T IMPRESSED WITH THE BOTANICAL GARDENS. I GUESS ONE REASON WAS BECAUSE WE DIDN'T TAKE THE TIME TO GO VERY DEEP INTO IT - BUT TO BE HONEST, WE DIDN'T SEE ANY REASON TO. IT WAS ONE OF THE HOTTEST DAYS OF THE YEAR AND WE WERE READY TO GO HOME, SO ...

BUT THE BUTTERFLY CONSERVATORY WAS A DIFFERENT STORY! WHEN I WALKED THROUGH THAT DOOR, IT TOOK MY BREATH AWAY. I HAVE NEVER SEEN SO MANY GORGEOUS AND DIFFERENT BUTTERFLIES IN ONE PLACE IN MY LIFE! THEY WERE FLUTTERING ALL OVER THE PLACE. I WENT THROUGH A ROLL OF FILM PRETTY QUICKLY. CARI WAS USING THE MANUAL CAMERA AND WAS SNAPPING AWAY TOO. THIS WAS ONE OF MY TOP THREE PICKS OF THE WEEK. I COULD JUST CAMP OUT IN THERE ALL DAY WAITING FOR THAT PERFECT PICTURE.

AFTER STOPPING AT A FEW MORE SOUVENIR STORES, WE SETTLED IN TO DRIVE FOR A WHILE. WE ENDED UP GOING THROUGH CUSTOMS SEVERAL TIMES BECAUSE WE DIDN'T REALIZE WE NEEDED TO GET OUR RECEIPTS VALIDATED AT THE CANADIAN DUTY FREE PLACE - UNTIL WE WENT THROUGH U.S. CUSTOMS SO WE TURNED AROUND AND WENT BACK THROUGH CANADA AGAIN - UGH!! AFTER ALL THAT, WE ONLY ENDED UP GETTING $17 BACK IN ALL THE TAXES WE PAID - UNREAL! BY THE TIME WE WERE REALLY ON THE ROAD GOOD, IT WAS AROUND 6PM. CARI AND I HAD QUITE A COMPETITION DECIPHERING DIFFERENT SHAPE S IN THE CLOUDS. OF COURSE SHE WON - HER IMAGINATION IS SO MUCH MORE VIVID THAN MINE. SINCE WE COULDN'T FIND A CRACKER BARREL FOR DINNER, WE SETTLED FOR WENDY'S - HEY WE WERE HUNGRY! WE STOPPED AT A HOLIDAY INN IN SOMERSET, PA FOR THE NIGHT. BY 9:30AM WE WERE BACK ON THE ROAD AND HOME!

Krystal and Ollie

Supplies - Patterned Paper: Pebbles in my Pocket, Creative Imaginations, Doodlebug Designs Inc.; Concho: Scrapworks, LLC; Oval: Scrapbook Essentials; Rub-ons: Making Memories; Vellum Quote: Memories Complete; Ribbon: Close To My Heart

Designer - Sherrill Ghilardi Pierre

Butterfly Conservatory

Supplies - Patterned Paper: Stampin' Up; Stamps: The Angel Company; Ink: Staz-on by Tsukineko; Font: Barbara Hand Scribble

Designer - Wanda Troupe

I **identify** most strongly with the turtle: I patiently plod along till I **reach** my **destination**--and occasionally I **stick** out my neck. ~Paulette Peltan

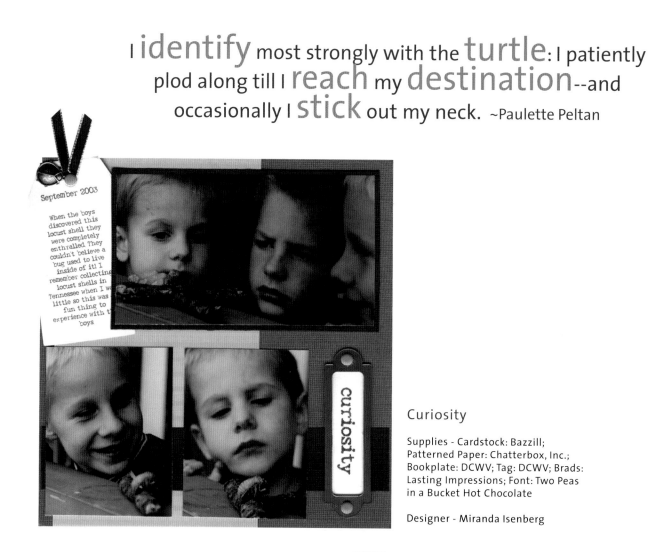

September 2003

When the boys discovered this locust shell they were completely enthralled. They couldn't believe a bug used to live inside of it! I remember collecting locust shells in Tennessee when I was little so this was fun thing to experience with the boys.

curiosity

Curiosity

Supplies - Cardstock: Bazzill; Patterned Paper: Chatterbox, Inc.; Bookplate: DCWV; Tag: DCWV; Brads: Lasting Impressions; Font: Two Peas in a Bucket Hot Chocolate

Designer - Miranda Isenberg

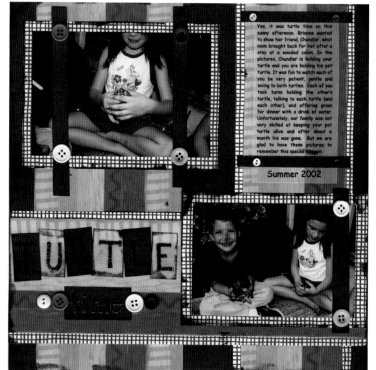

Turtle Time

Supplies - Cardstock: DCWV; Patterned Paper: Memories in the Making; Stickers: Memories in the Making; Font: Comic Sans MS

Designer - Toni Boucha

Nanny and Pappy bought Mr. Krabby for Max on his 10th Birthday. Max got to pick out his container and decorate it with lots of cool crabby-like things. Mr. Krabby needs to be bathed, given hermit crab food and lots of exercise each day. He also needs a bigger empty shell inside his house to crawl into after he grows out of his older shell. Max picked a bigger ladybug shell and put it in the corner. After this picture was taken, Mr. Krabby already moved into his new shell!

Mr. Krabby

Supplies - Patterned Paper: Memories in the Making; Stamps: Inkadinkado; Chalk: ColorBox by Clearsnap, Inc.; Adhesive: Magic Scraps; Font: William's Light

Designer - Mendy Mitrani

Animals are such agreeable friends - they ask no questions, they pass no criticisms. ~George Eliot

Hold

Supplies - Patterned Paper: Memories in the Making; Stickers: Memories in the Making; Chalk: ColorBox by Clearsnap, Inc.; Font: Adler Typed

Designer - Mendy Mitrani

313

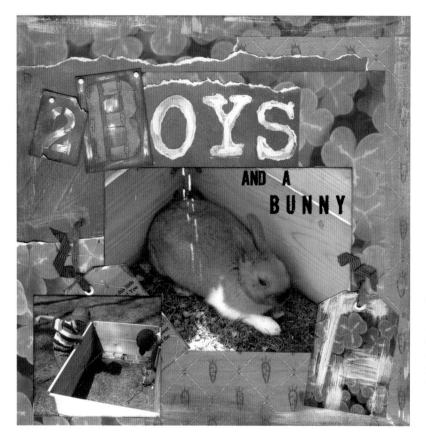

Two Boys and a Bunny

Supplies - Patterned Paper:
The Paper Loft, Daisy D's Paper
Company; Tag: The Paper Loft;
Stamps: Ma Vinici's Reliquary;
Chalk: ColorBox by Clearsnap,
Inc.; Font: Dirty Ego

Designer - Melodee Langworthy

It's not easy being green. ~Kermit the Frog

Toadally Frogs

Supplies - Cardstock: Making Memories; Patterned Paper:
Scrap-Ease; Mulberry Paper: DCWV; Fibers: Fibers by the
Yard; Brads: ScrapLovers; Rub-ons: Craf-T Products; Punches:
EK Succes, McGill, Inc.; Gold Leaf: Mona Lisa Products;
Embossing Powder: Scrap 'n Stuff; Pen: ZIG by EK Success;
Adhesive: Magic Mounts; Fonts: Basic Font, Horatio D Light

Designer - Susan Stringfellow

Give love like your pet does.
Unconditionally and
without questions. ~Author Unknown

Ollie

Supplies - Patterned Paper: The
Rusty Pickle; Copper Words: K &
Company; Pins: 7 Gypsies; Ribbon:
Me & My Big Ideas; Netting:
Loose Ends; Stickers: Rebecca
Sower; Walnut Ink: Anima
Designs

Designer - Sherrill Ghilardi Pierre

Time

Supplies - Patterned Paper: 7 Gypsies, Mustard Moon Paper Co.; Brads: Magic
Scraps; Chain: Li'l Davis Designs; Photo Corners: Canson, Inc.; Font: Two Peas in a
Bucket Hot Chocolate

Designer - Angelia Wigginton

Farm Animals

Baby Chicks

Supplies - Patterned Paper:
Memories in the Making;
Mulberry Paper: DCWV; Wire:
Artistic Wire Ltd; Beads:
Mustard Moon Paper Co.

Designer - Jessica Williams

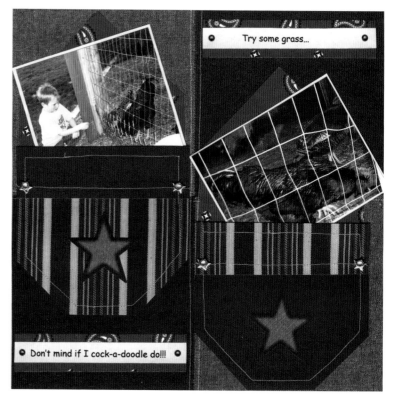

Try Some Grass

Supplies - Patterned Paper:
Memories in the Making; Stickers:
Memories in the Making; Eyelets:
Making Memories

Designer - Camie Lloyd

Until one has loved an animal, a part of one's soul remains unawakened. ~Anatole France

Great Day at the Farm

Supplies - Patterned Paper: Memories in the Making; Stickers: Memories in the Making; Eyelets: Making Memories

Designer - Camie Lloyd

Goats & Giggles

Supplies - Patterned Paper: Chatterbox, Inc.; Metal Circles: Li'l Davis Designs; Metal Letters: Making Memories; Metal Mesh: ScrapYard 329; Stickers: Nostalgiques by EK Success; Stamps: Wordsworth Stamps

Designer - Angelia Wigginton

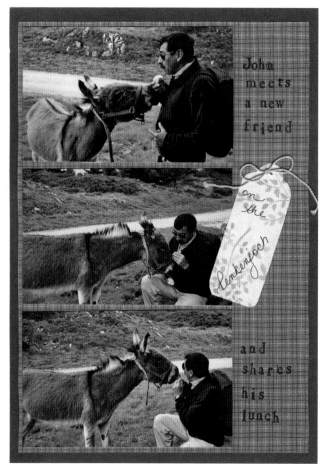

We can judge the heart of a man by his treatment of animals. ~Immanual Kant

A New Friend

Supplies - Patterned Paper: Keeping Memories Alive; Template: PSX Design; Stamps: PSX Design; Ink: ColorBox by Clearsnap, Inc.

Designer - Charity Alva

Chickens & Watermelon

Supplies – Cardstock: The Paper Garden; Patterned Paper: The Paper Loft;
Aluminum Studs: ScrapYard 329; Wire Mesh: ScrapYard 329; Template: ScrapPagerz

Designer - MaryLea Boatwaglit

Zoo & Animal Parks

Zoo: An excellent place to study the habits of human beings. ~Evan Esar

Come Out and Play at the Zoo

Supplies - Cardstock: Bazzill, DMD Industries; Patterned Paper: Daisy D's Paper Company; Letter Charms: Making Memories; Vellum Tag: Making Memories; Eyelets: Making Memories; Staples: Making Memories; Stickers: PSX Design; Rub-ons: Making Memories; Mesh: Magic Mesh; Marker: Tsukineko; Font: Problem Secretary

Designer - Dawn Burden

Louisville Zoo

Supplies - Cardstock: Bazzill;
Patterned Paper: NRN Designs,
Magenta Rubber Stamps; Floss: DMC;
Stickers: Me & My Big Ideas, Magenta
Rubber Stamps; Acrylic Slide: Heidi
Grace Designs; Stamp: A Stamp in
the Hand Company, All Night Media,
Stampendous!; Ink: Tsukineko,
ColorBox by Clearsnap, Inc.

Designer - Mendy Douglass

Elephants

Supplies - Clear Vellum: Paper
Adventures; Fibers: Fibers by the
Yard; Brads: American Tag Co.;
Font: Malagua

Designer - Susan Stringfellow

When you have got an elephant by the hind leg, and he is trying to run away, it's best to let him run. ~Abraham Lincoln

Elephant Swim

Supplies - Patterned Paper: Provo Craft; Stamps: Hero Arts Rubber Stamps, Inc.; Ink: The Angel Company; Charms: Embellish It!

Designer - Wanda Troupe

Pandas at Play

Supplies - Cardstock: DCWV; Patterned Paper: Memories in the Making; Wooden Tiles: DCWV; Ribbon: DCWV

Designer - NanC and Company Design

Beijing's Prized Panda Bears

Splash and Spray

Supplies - Patterned Paper:
DCWV; Metallic Tag: DCWV;
Fibers: Fibers by the Yard; Brads:
Making Memories; Stamp: Hero
Arts Rubber Stamps, Inc.

Designer - Susan Stringfellow

Dolphins

Supplies - Fibers: Fibers by
the Yard; Wire: JewelCraft,
LLC; Beads: Beadazzled; Tags:
Manto Fev; Font: Aquiline

Designer - Sam Cousins

Giraffe

Supplies - Cardstock: Bazzill; Patterned Paper: Memories in the Making; Fibers: Fibers by the Yard; Brads: ScrapLovers; Buttons: Dress It Up!, Chatterbox, Inc.; Stickers: NRN Designs; Stamp: Stampin' Up; Ink: Stampin' Up, Tsukineko; Font: Adler

Designer - Susan Stringfellow

An animal's eyes have the power to speak a great language.

~Martin Buber

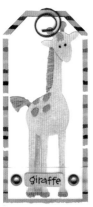

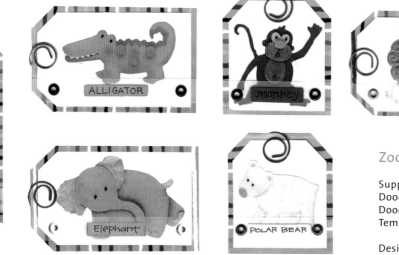

Zoo Tags

Supplies - Patterned Paper: Doodlebug Designs Inc.; Stickers: Doodlebug Designs Inc.; Template: Deluxe Cuts

Designer - Miranda Isenberg

Swimming Tigers

Supplies - Cardstock: Bazzill; Patterned Paper: Magenta Rubber Stamps; Fibers: Fibers by the Yard; Eyelets: Making Memories; Ribbon: All The Extras; Punch: EK Success; Stamp: Stampabilities; Ink: Stampin' Up; Templates: Deluxe Cuts; Font: Morocco

Designer - Susan Stringfellow

Elephant Tag

Supplies - Cardstock: Bazzill; Patterned Paper: Memories in the Making; Stamps: Stamp Craft, Hero Arts Rubber Stamps, Inc.; Ink: Stampin' Up; Netting: All The Extras; Brads: All The Extras; Eyelets: BagWorks Inc.; Button: Dress It Up!; Fibers: Fibers by the Yard; Beads: All The Extras, Crafts Etc!

Designer - Susan Stringfellow

Wild Animals

Supplies - Cardstock: DCWV; Patterned Paper: Memories in the Making; Leather Letters: Alphawear by Creative Imaginations; Rub-ons: Making Memories

Designer - NanC and Company Design

in the wild

Black Bear

Supplies - Cardstock: Stampin' Up; Patterned Paper: Provo Craft; Punches: Marvy Uchida; Stamps: PSX Design, Stampin' Up; Ink: Stampin' Up

Designer - Wanda Troupe

The Woods

Supplies – Cardstock: DMD Industries; Patterned Paper: Outdoors and More; Vellum: DMD Industries; Brads: Boxer Scrapbooks; Quick Cropper Cuts: Outdoors and More; Font: Times New Roman

Designer - Laura Nicholas

Tiger Tales

Supplies - Cardstock: Canson, Inc., Bazzill; Vellum: Strathmore Papers; Specialty Paper: Provo Craft; Micro Beads: Art Accentz by Provo Craft; Punch: EK Success; Ink: Close To My Heart; Font: BoysRGross

Designer - Pam Canavan

Life is like a camel; you can make it do anything except back up.
~Marcelene Cox

Conversation with a Camel

Supplies - Cardstock: Bazzill; Clips: Scrapworks, LLC; Stickers: Creative Imaginations; Fonts: Two Peas in a Bucket Jana Banana, Two Peas in a Bucket Champagne

Designer - Miranda Isenberg

3M Stationary
(800) 364-3577
3m.com

7 Gypsies
(800) 588-6707
7gypsies.com

A Stamp in the Hand Company
(310) 884-9700
astampinthehand.com

Adobe
(800) 833-6687
adobe.com

Aitoh Company
(800) 681-5533
aitoh.com

All Night Media
(800) 842-4197
allnightmedia.com

All The Extras
(425) 868-6628
alltheextras.com

Altered Pages
alteredpages.com

American Crafts
(800) 879-5185
americancrafts.com

American Tag Co.
(800) 642-4314
americantag.net

Anima Designs
(800) 570-6847
animadesigns.com

Anita's Craft Paint
(404) 373-7284
synta.com

Apollo
(800) 777-3750
apolloavproducts.com

Artistic Scrapper
(818) 786-8304
artisticscrapper.com

Artistic Wire Ltd.
(630) 530-7567
artisticwire.com

Avery Dennison
averydennison.com

BagWorks Inc.
(817) 446-8080
bagworks.com

Bazzill
(480) 558-8557
bazzillbasics.com

Beadazzled
(703) 848-2323
beadazzled.net

Bo-Bunny Press
(801) 770-4010
bobunny.com

Boxer Scrapbooks
(888) 625-6255
boxerscrapbooks.com

Camscan
camscan.com

Canson, Inc.
(800) 628-9283
canson-us.com

Chatterbox, Inc.
(888) 416-6260
chatterboxinc.com

Clearsnap, Inc.
(800) 448-4862
clearsnap.com

Clipola
clipola.com

Close To My Heart
(888) 655-6552
closetomyheart.com

Club Scrap, Inc.
(888) 634-9100
clubscrap.com

Coats & Clark
coatsandclark.com

Colorbok, Inc.
(800) 366-4660
colorbok.com

Craf-T Products
(800) 530-3410
craf-tproducts.com

Crafts Etc!
(800) 888-0321
craftsetc.com

Creating Keepsakes
(888)-247-5282
creatingkeepsakes.com

Creative Imaginations
(800) 942-6487
cigift.com

C-Thru Ruler Company, The
(800) 243-8419
cthruruler.com

Daisy D's Paper Company
(888) 601-8955
daisydspaper.com

Darice, Inc.
(800) 321-1494
darice.com

DCWV
(801) 224-6766
diecutswithaview.com

Deluxe Designs
(480) 497-9005
deluxecuts.com

DMC
(973) 589-9890
dmc-usa.com

DMD Industries
(800) 805-9890
dmdind.com

Dollar Tree
757-321-5000
dollartree.com

Doodlebug Designs Inc.
801-966-9952
timelessmemories.ca

Dress It Up!
dressitup.com

Dymo
dymo.com

EK Success
(800) 524-1349
eksuccess.com

Embellish It!
(720) 312-1628
embellishit.com

Fibers by the Yard
fibersbytheyard.com

Flavia
(805) 882-2466
flavia.com

Heidi Grace Designs
(253) 973-5542
heidigrace.com

Herma Fix
herma.co.uk.com

Hero Arts Rubber Stamps, Inc.
(800) 822-4376
heroarts.com

Hot Off The Press
(800) 227-9595
paperpizazz.com

Inkadinkado
(781) 938-6100
inkadinkado.com

JewelCraft, LLC
(201) 223-0804
jewelcraft.biz

JudiKins
(310) 515-1115
judikins.com

K & Company
(888) 244-2083
kandcompany.com

Karen Foster Design
(801) 451-9779
karenfosterdesign.com

Keeping Memories Alive
(800) 419-4949
keepingmemoriesalive.com

KI Memories
(972) 243-5595
kimemories.com

Lasting Impressions
lastingimpressions.
safeshopper.com

azerLetterz
azerletterz.com

'l Davis Designs
949) 838-0344
davisdesigns.com

oose Ends
503) 390-2348
oseends.com

a Vinici's Reliquary
rafts.dm.net/mall/reliquary/

agenta Rubber Stamps
agentarubberstamps.com

agic Mesh
agicmesh.com

agic Mounts
800) 332-0050
agicmounts.com

agic Scraps
972) 238-1838
agicscraps.com

aking Memories
800) 286-5263
akingmemories.com

anto Fev
402) 689-2569
antofev.com

arvy Uchida
800) 541-5877
chida.com

McGill, Inc.
cgillinc.com

Me & My Big Ideas
949) 589-4607
eandmybigideas.com

Memories Complete
866) 966-6365
emoriescomplete.com

Memories in the Making
800) 643-8030
isurearts.com

Mona Lisa Products
800) 272-3804

Mustard Moon Paper Co.
(408) 229-8542
mustardmoon.com

NRN Designs
nrndesigns.com

Offray & Son, Inc.
offray.com

Outdoors & More Scrapbook
Décor
outdoorsandmore.com

Paper Adventures
(800) 727-0699
paperadventures.com

Paper Company, The
(800) 426-8989
thepaperco.com

Paper Garden
(210) 494-9602
papergarden.com

Paper House Productions
(800) 255-7316
paperhouseproductions.com

Paper Loft, The
(801) 254-1961
paperloft.com

Paper Patch, The
(801) 253-3018
paperpatch.com

Pebbles in my Pocket
pebblesinc.com

Pixie Press
(702) 646-1156
pixiepress.com

Provo Craft
(888) 577-3545
provocraft.com

PSX Design
(800) 782-6748
psxdesign.com

Quick Quotes
stickersgalore.com

Ranger Industries
(800) 244-2211
rangerink.com

Rebecca Sower
mississippipaperarts.com

Rubber Stampede
(800) 423-4135
rubberstampede.com

Rusty Pickle, The
(801) 274-9588
rustypickle.com

Sarah Lugg
sarahlugg.com

Scrap Ease
(800) 272-3874
scrap-ease.com

Scrap 'n Stuff
scrapnstuff.com

Scrap Pagerz
(435) 645-0696
scrappagerz.com

Scrapbook Essentials
scrapbookessentials.com

Scrapbook-Bytes
scrapbook-bytes.com

ScrapLovers
scraplovers.com

Scrapworks, LLC
scrapworksllc.com

ScrapYard 329
(775) 829-1227
scrapyard329.com

Stamp Craft
stampcraft.com.au

Stampa Rosa
stamparosa.com

Stampabilities
stampabilities.com

Stampendous!
(800) 869-0474
stampendous.com

Stampin' Up
(800) 782-6787
stampinup.com

Stamps by Judith
stampsbyjudith.com

Stamps 'n' Stuff
(515) 331-4307
stampsnstuff.com

Sticker Studio
stickerstudio.com

Strathmore Papers
(800) 628-8816
strathmore.com

The Angel Company
(785) 820-9181
theangelcompany.net

The Gifted Note
thegiftednote.com

Therm O Web, Inc.
(800) 323-0799
thermoweb.com

Tsukineko
(800) 769-6633
tsukineko.com

Two Peas in a Bucket
twopeasinabucket.com

Uptown Design Company, The
(253) 925-1234
uptowndesign.com

Westrim Crafts
(800) 727-2727
westrimcrafts.com

Wordsworth Stamps
(719) 282-3495
wordsworthstamps.com

Wrights
(877) 597-4448
wrights.com

Friends are people who help you be more yourself...more the person you are intended to be.
—Nadia Shain

it's all about

mini albums

twins

friends

laughter

enjoy

happiness

truction tips and ideas for creating mini albums from start to finish

When g r a n d m a

was little like me!

The Early Days

wish dream

PHOTOS

Dear Scrapbooker,

I simply cherish this mini album to the left that a daughter-in-law gave me at Christmas time. Receiving it was one of the great joys of my holiday season! I enjoy not only receiving mini albums as gifts, but also making them and sharing them with friends. Hopefully, with ideas from this collection, you too will experience how to create fun mini albums.

Mini albums are the perfect gift! They are quick to make, are ideal for capturing a special event or subject in a few pages and will be treasured by those who receive them. Mini albums are also a great addition to your personal scrapbook collection. They are just the right size to capture memorable moments, trips, or focus on a loved one or hobby.

Don't be intimidated or think you need to purchase a lot of new products to create mini albums. They use the same skills and many of the same products as regular sized pages, but are just made on a smaller scale. The page dimensions featured here are 8 x 8, 6 x 6, 5 x 7 and other irregular sized mini pages.

This section is full of fantastic ideas and examples to spark your imagination. "Lift" the ideas exactly as they are or copy the basic design and add your own creative touches. NanC and Company designs offer a wide range of options to choose from with helpful hints and ideas along the way.

Enjoy trying these great ideas and, remember, the best part is sharing your finished mini album with someone else!

Nancy

Nancy M. Hill

it's all about mini albums

table of contents

you are always in my heart

CONSTRUCTION TIPS

1. A posterity mini album is one of the greatest gifts you can make for yourself or a loved one. Family and friends will treasure the pages for generations.

2. Cut a piece of burlap to cover a portion of a page. Cut holes in the burlap and then put into a clothes dryer to fray the edges.

3. How to make a paper quilt:
   a. Crumple patterned papers and spray with walnut ink.
   b. Iron to flatten and dry the paper.
   c. Punch out squares of the patterned paper.
   d. Adhere squares to cardstock.
   e. Machine or hand stitch around each square.

4. Print journaling directly onto linen fabric by trimming and adhering a piece of thin linen fabric to a sheet of copy paper with spray adhesive. Run sheet of fabric and paper through printer.

5. Embellish a mini page with a tiny mini album of photos.

SUPPLIES - 5 x 7 Album

Cardstock: Bazzill; Patterned Paper: Chatterbox, Inc.; Corrugated Paper: DMD Industries; Metallic Embellishments: K & Company, 7 Gypsies, Making Memories, Darice; Fibers: Darice; Nail Heads: American Tag Co., Chatterbox, Inc.; Moldings: Chatterbox; Eyelets: Making Memories; Snaps: Making Memories; Safety Pin: Making Memories; Halos: Cloud 9 Designs; Stickers: NRN Designs, K & Company, Pixie Press; Cut Out: Karen Foster Design; Label: 7 Gypsies; Floss: DMC; Ribbon: Making Memories; Envelope Template: Deluxe Designs; Punch: Family Treasures; Stamps: Hero Arts Rubber Stamps, Inc.; Ink: Tsukineko; Paint: Delta; Photo Corners: 3M Stationary; Font: CK Nostalgia

Designer: Marsha Musselman

posterity gift album

SUPPLIES - 6 x 6 Album

Cardstock: Bazzill; Patterned Paper: Memories in the Making, 7 Gypsies; Metallic Embellishments: 7 Gypsies, DCWV; Fibers: Adornments by EK Success; Stamps: Making Memories; Ribbon: Offray & Son, Inc.; Fonts: Lucinda Calligraphy, Gigi, Arial Rounded MT Bold, Times New Roman, Abadi MT Condensed

Designer: Tracy Weinzapfel Burgos

CONSTRUCTION TIPS

1. How to create a bronze coating on metallics:
   a. Rub metallic accents with embossing pad.
   b. Sprinkle with bronze Ultra Thick Embossing Enamel (UTEE).
   c. Shake off excess UTEE and heat with an embossing gun (use caution with heat in order to prevent metallic accents from bending or becoming deformed).
   d. While still hot apply a second coat and heat.
   e. Repeat with additional coats until desired look is achieved.
2. Alter ribbon by soaking in walnut ink. Dry ribbon completely and stamp with stamps and ink (make sure the ribbon is completely dry to ensure the ink won't bleed).

family
photo shoot

CONSTRUCTION TIPS

1. Create a slide show by framing photos with slide mounts and adhering them to a strip of cardstock.

SUPPLIES - 7 x 7.5 Album

Cardstock: DCWV; Slide Mounts: Magic Scraps; Ribbon: Making Memories; Stamps: Stampin' Up

Designer: Ashley Smith

friends

SUPPLIES - 6 x 6 Album

Patterned Paper: Chatterbox, Inc., Anna Griffin, Karen Foster Design, Frances Meyer, Inc., Magenta Rubber Stamps, SEI; Envelope: Foofala; Letters: Foofala; Definition: Foofala; Tag: Foofala; Flower Brad: Making Memories; Ribbon: Michaels; Ribbon Charm: Making Memories

Designer: Melissa Chapman

SUPPLIES (RIGHT) - 6 x 6 Album

Cardstock: Making Memories, Bazzill; Patterned Paper: Memories in the Making; Patterned Vellum: Paper Adventures, Chatterbox, Inc.; Metallic Embellishments: DCWV, Making Memories, Altered Pages; Fibers: Fibers by the Yard; Thread: Coats & Clark; Flower Brad: Making Memories; Silver Brads: ScrapLovers; Round Buttons: Doodlebug Designs Inc.; Heart Buttons: Dress It Up!; Stickers: Altered Pages; Beads: Two Mom's Scrap n Stamp; Scrapbook Nails: Chatterbox, Inc.; Square Conchos: ScrapLovers; Ink: Stampin' Up, ColorBox by Clearsnap, Inc.; Ribbon: Michaels; Transparency: 3M Stationary; Adhesive: Magic Mounts, JudiKins, Magic Scraps; Fonts: Black Jack Regular, Bauer Bodini BT, Cricket

Designer: Susan Stringfellow

Amy, Caroline, & Ashley

Since we live so far apart, Amy and I have always sent each other holiday packages. For Easter many years ago, she started giving me handpainted glass egg ornaments. Now I have a beautiful collection. She also hand paints character eggs for Easter and Halloween.

Magic is when two friends walk in opposite directions but still stay side by side.

Mexico '03

CONSTRUCTION TIPS

1. Print journaling and photos onto a printable transparency to allow the background to show through. Use brads, eyelets or stitching to attach the transparency to a page, or for an adhesive, vellum spray works very well. Be sure to follow the directions on the vellum spray in order to get optimal results.

2. Adhere beads to conchos with the use of diamond glaze adhesive. Double-sided tape can be used as an easy alternative.

FINGERS & TOES

Pretty fingers & toes
for pretty girls!
1st day of summer 2003

AUDREY AND WHITNEY

friends much lo

WHIT

TURNING 13

342

book of friends

CONSTRUCTION TIPS

1. Jump rings are a great way to hang embellishments from key chains, fibers and frames. The jump rings allow the embellishment to jingle.

2. Combine different colors of embroidery floss to embellish layouts, write names and weave in and out of mesh.

SUPPLIES - 6 x 6 Album

Cardstock: DCWV; Patterned Paper: Memories in the Making, Making Memories, Close To My Heart; Vellum: Making Memories; Tag: Making Memories; Metallic Embellishments: DCWV; Brads: Making Memories, Lasting Impressions; Page Pebble: Making Memories; Rings: Making Memories; Acrylic Flower: KI Memories; Tiles: Tiles Play by EK Success; Rub-ons: Making Memories; Vellum Quote: DCWV; Floss: DMC; Date Stamp: Making Memories

Designer: Camille Jensen

animals are family too

SUPPLIES - 8 x 8 Album

Cardstock: Bazzill; Patterned Paper: Memories in the Making; Metallic Embellishments: Making Memories; Fibers: Fibers by the Yard; Mini Brads: ScrapLovers; Square Brads: Making Memories; Buttons: Dress It Up!, Junkits; Wire: Artistic Wire Ltd.; Mesh: Magenta Rubber Stamps; Glass Embellishments: Altered Pages, Halcraft; Cork Embellishments: Lazerletterz; Bamboo Clip: Altered Pages; Burlap Fabric: Hobby Lobby; Stamps: Dollar Tree, Close To My Heart, Stamp Craft, Disney; Ink: ColorBox by Clearsnap, Inc., Stampin' Up; Embossing Powder: Ranger Industries; Transparencies: 3M Stationary, Altered Pages; Adhesive: JudiKins; Fonts: Cricket, DC Recess Journal, Benderville, P22 Oh Ley, Two Peas in a Bucket Renaissance

Designer: Susan Stringfellow

344

CONSTRUCTION TIPS

1. Alter wire embellishments and words by flattening portions of the wire with a hammer.

2. Alter cork embellishments by stamping with a rubber stamp and inkpad, and inking the edges.

3. Create the look of a wax seal by heating several layers of Ultra Thick Embossing Enamel (UTEE) and while still warm, pressing a rubber stamp into the UTEE. Hold stamp in place until set (approximately 2 minutes).

the little book about me

CONSTRUCTION TIPS

1. Give an expectant mother a gift she will treasure: a baby gift book. Prepare the pages so the new mother only needs to add photos and facts.

2. Use snaps or brads instead of eyelets to hold down tags for journaling. This way the new mother can remove the tags to add journaling and reattach them without ruining the page.

SUPPLIES - 6 x 6 Album

Patterned Paper: Chatterbox, Inc., Memories in the Making; Tags: Chatterbox, Inc.; Jewelry Tags: Avery Dennison; Tacks: Chatterbox, Inc.

Designer: Leah Fung

school book

SUPPLIES - 6 x 6 Album

Patterned Paper: Chatterbox, Inc., Memories in the Making; Metallic Embellishments: DCWV, Memories in the Making, Making Memories; Tags: Chatterbox, Inc.; Snaps: Chatterbox, Inc.; Ribbon: Offray & Son, Inc.

Designer: Jlyne Hanback

348

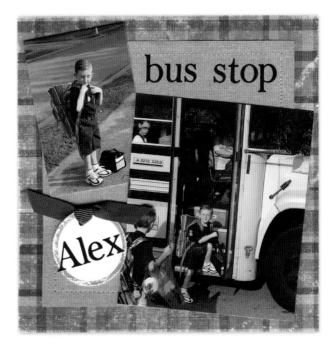

CONSTRUCTION TIPS

1. Sand paper to give it a used look.
2. Don't be afraid to use the same photo on a page twice. Enlarge or shrink one of the photos to be an accent.

character quiet book

SUPPLIES - 8 x 8 Album

Cardstock: Bazzill; Tags: DCWV, Making Memories; Fiber: Fibers by the Yard; Brads: Making Memories; Staples: Making Memories; Stickers: Sticker Studio, Phrase Café by EK Success, Me & My Big Ideas, Chatterbox, Inc., Shotz by Creative Imaginations; Mesh: Magic Scraps; Photo Flips: Provo Craft, Making Memories; Envelope: EK Success; Pen: ZIG by EK Success

Designer: Sam Cousins

CONSTRUCTION TIPS

1. A quiet book is a great way to keep children (and many adults) entertained. Create your own quiet book with interactive pages that teach about color, the alphabet and texture. Choose elements that can be removed or flipped through to keep a child looking for more.

2. Create a unique background by adhering square photos directly next to one another on a piece of cardstock. Cover the photos with vellum and use as a background for your scrapbook page.

3. Add another dimension to your scrapbook pages by having envelopes, pockets and flip charts reveal hidden journaling and photos. Not only is it fun to remove an object from its holding place or lift a portion of a page to reveal what's underneath, but it's also a great way to add more journaling and photos to a mini page.

4. Gather inspiration and ideas from many different sources. The inspiration for this cover came from a daily newspaper.

a year in the life of twins

CONSTRUCTION TIPS

1. Use the lines of a patterned paper to mat a photo without cutting extra paper.
2. Finish off a page by inking and distressing the edges of the paper. Simply brush an inkpad over the edges and, occasionally, across the inside of the pages.
3. Torn paper adds a nice texture to any layout.

SUPPLIES - 8 x 8 Album

Cardstock: Bazzill; Patterned Paper: Memories in the Making; Metallic Mesh: Making Memories; Stickers: Memories in the Making; Ribbon Charm: Making Memories; Ribbon: Making Memories; Font: Adler

Designer: Tracy Weinzapfel Burgos

CONSTRUCTION TIPS (RIGHT)

1. Simple pages really put the focus on great photos.

SUPPLIES (RIGHT) - 6 x 6 Album

Cardstock: Bazzill; Patterned Paper: DCWV; Metal Tags: Making Memories; Brads: Making Memories

Designer: Miranda Isenberg

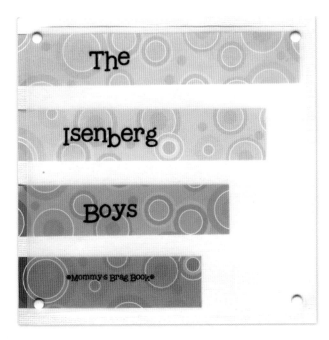

The

Isenberg

Boys

●Mommy's Brag Book●

Connor

Carter

Cameron

the isenberg boys

tin of photos

CONSTRUCTION TIPS

1. Make a two-sided mini accordion book. One side can document your childhood and the other your adult life. Tie both sides together with the same color palette and black and white or sepia photos.

SUPPLIES - 3.5 x 4 Album

Patterned Paper: K & Company, Karen Foster Design, 7 Gypsies; Tags: The Rusty Pickle; Metallic Embellishments: K & Company, Making Memories; Fibers: Adornments by EK Success; Eyelets: Making Memories; Stickers: K & Company, Karen Foster Design; Ribbon: Offray & Son, Inc.; Stamps: PSX Design; Felt: Offray & Son, Inc.

Designer: Melissa Fortenberry

CONSTRUCTION TIPS

1. How to make a tin of photos:
   a. Adorn the outside of the tin.
   b. Punch out cardstock circles, just smaller than the diameter of the tin, with a circle punch.
   c. Trim a ribbon to 20 inches long.
   d. Sandwich the ribbon in-between two cardstock circles. Repeat, spacing the circles 2 inches apart from each other.
   e. Adorn circles with photos and other embellishments.
   f. Wrap ribbon around all of the circles and place inside the decorated tin.

SUPPLIES - 2.75 Diameter Album

Cardstock: Bazzill; Die Cut: Paper House Productions; Stickers: Paper House Productions; Ribbon: Jo-Ann; Stamps: Stampa Rosa, PSX Design; Ink: ColorBox by Clearsnap, Inc.; Embossing Powder: Stampendous!; Fonts: Two Peas in a Bucket Ditzy, Garamouche

Designer: Wendy Malichio

a girl's dream

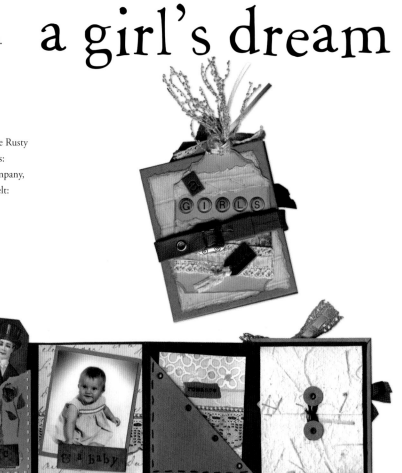

all star

CONSTRUCTION TIPS

1. Emphasize a portion of a photo by encircling that area with a metallic accent. This can also be accomplished by tearing a window in vellum.

SUPPLIES - 6 x 6 Album

Cardstock: Bazzill; Patterned Paper: Ever After Scrapbook Co., Frances Meyer, Inc.; Metallic Embellishments: DCWV; Eyelets: Making Memories; Stickers: Chatterbox, Inc., Shotz by Creative Imaginations, Doodlebug Designs Inc.; Rub-ons: Making Memories; Soccer Balls: Card Connection

Designer: Tarri Botwinski

lily's book of fun

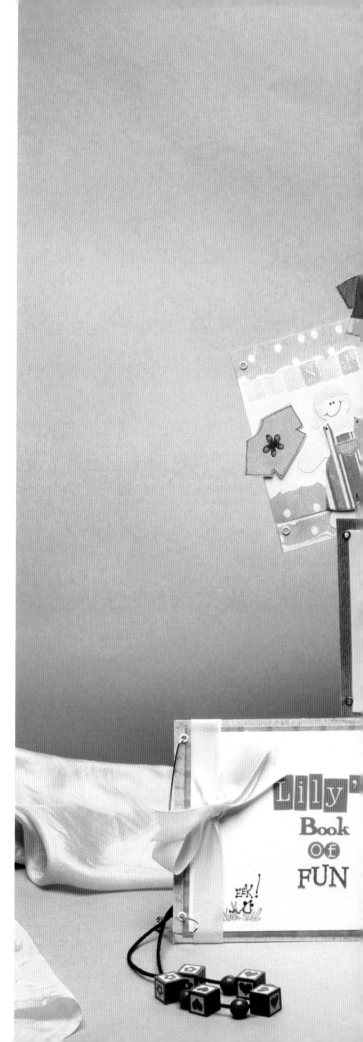

CONSTRUCTION TIPS

1. Assemble a book of fun for children. Make the book interactive with games and challenges on each page. Create a doll to be dressed with clothes made from patterned paper. Attach felt flowers to buttons to create a garden and even learn about animals by flipping up hinges.

2. Laminate pages that will last through the years and that will clean up easily with spills.

3. Place a magnetic piece of white erase board for an interactive page (magnetic because it is thicker and will hold up better). Cut the board the same size as the other pages in the book and attach border stickers around the edges.

SUPPLIES - 5 x 7 Album

Cardstock: DCWV, Making Memories; Patterned Paper: Memories in the Making; Pockets: Xyron, Inc., 3L Corp.; Concho: Scrapworks; Brads: Lasting Impressions; Stickers: Making Memories; Paper Doll and Clothes Template: EK Success; Stamps: Hero Arts Rubber Stamps, Inc., Simply Stamped; Fonts: CK Eight Ball, CK Constitution, CK Blackout, CK Academia

Designer: Camille Jensen

357

the top 10
reasons i love you

CONSTRUCTION TIPS

1. Use colors from your photos to create color schemes for your layouts.
2. Use a sewing machine to stitch pieces of paper together. Be sure to check the tension on a scrap piece of paper before sewing directly onto your background.

358

SUPPLIES - 8 x 8 Album

Patterned Paper: KI Memories, Chatterbox, Inc., Memories in the Making, Paperfever Inc.; Brads: Lasting Impressions; Token: Doodlebug Designs Inc.; Bookplate: KI Memories; Alphabet Charm: Making Memories; Acrylic Frame: Heidi Grace Designs; Stamps: Hero Arts Rubber Stamps, Inc.; Ink: Stampin' Up; Fonts: Two Peas in a Bucket Hot Chocolate, Two Peas in a Bucket Grandpa, Two Peas in a Bucket Kipper, Two Peas in a Bucket Loose Curls, Two Peas in a Bucket Ragtag

Designer: Miranda Isenberg

359

abc scripture
album

CONSTRUCTION TIPS

1. Generate a continuous feel throughout a book by using the same background paper, border strip and title format on each page.

2. Make an ABC scripture album with leftover photos and your favorite scriptures.

SUPPLIES - 8 x 8 Album

Cardstock: Paper Garden; Patterned Paper: Anna Griffin; Beads: Bead Heaven; Wire: Making Memories; Stickers: Mrs. Grossmans; Woodchips: Scrapfindings; Fresh Cuts: Rebecca Sower

Designer: Maegan Hall

my book
of firsts

CONSTRUCTION TIPS

1. Create background by applying ink to make-up sponges and sponging white cardstock. Sprinkle clear embossing powder over sponged background and heat with an embossing gun. Repeat embossing steps until desired shine is achieved.

SUPPLIES - 8 x 8 Album

Patterned Paper: Memories in the Making; Metallic Embellishments: Scrap-Ease; Stickers: Wordsworth Stamps; Punches: Marvy Uchida; Ribbon: Making Memories; Stamps: Making Memories; Ink: Tsukineko; Pens: Pentel

Designer: Tracy Weinzapfel Burgos

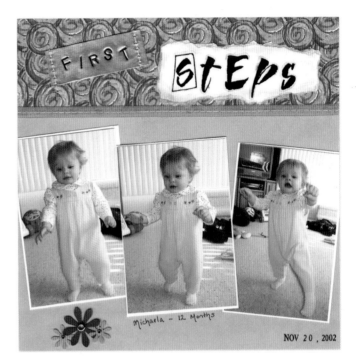

the bride

The Bride

A Selection of Candid Photographs

SUPPLIES - 5 x 7 Album

Cardstock: Chatterbox, Inc.; Patterned Paper: Chatterbox, Inc.; Tag: Chatterbox, Inc.; Snaps: Chatterbox, Inc.; Stickers: Chatterbox, Inc.; Ribbon: 7 Gypsies

Designer: Tarri Botwinski

CONSTRUCTION TIPS

1. How to tear and curl paper:
   a. Dampen area of paper to be torn with water and tear.
   b. Make sure the tear is still damp and curl paper back. Continue rolling paper with your fingertips until desired curl is achieved.
   c. When the paper dries the curl will remain.
2. Make delicate titles and letters by reverse printing (in a photo manipulation program) onto a sheet of paper. Cut out the letters with an exacto knife.

bryan & camille

SUPPLIES - 8 x 8 Album

Patterned Paper: DCWV, Memories in the Making, Susan Branch; Vellum: Memories in the Making, DCWV; Metallic Embellishments: DCWV; Silver Bug: American Crafts; Love Charm: Magenta Rubber Stamps; Brads: Lasting Impressions; Mesh: Magenta Rubber Stamps; Slide Mounts: Magic Scraps; Stamps: Hero Arts Rubber Stamps, Inc.; Date Stamp: Making Memories; Ribbon: Making Memories; Embossing Powder: Suze Weinberg

Designer: Camille Jensen

CONSTRUCTION TIPS

1. Create a fold out flap:

    a. Adhere a trimmed sheet protector or pre-made flap to the outer edge of the original sheet protector with double sided tape as if you were extending the page. Overlap the trimmed sheet protector three quarters of an inch.

    b. Slide a narrow page into the sheet protector with personal journaling on the inside when folded in.

2. How to paint a page:

    a. Use chipboard for the background instead of paper (so the background will not buckle from the paint).

    b. Mix two shades of green acrylic paint.

    c. Dry brush the background with the mixed paint and let dry.

    d. Brush a pearlizing acrylic medium over the dried paint for shine.

the great outdoors

CONSTRUCTION TIPS

1. Weave fibers through a background page to add texture and interest. Punch holes in the paper and thread fibers through to create a weaving pattern. You can use thick or multiple fibers by making a larger hole in the background.

2. Invite your children to write the journaling for a scrapbook page. It is fun to see children's handwriting and learn their perspective on the experience you are scrapping.

3. Create a microscope glass slide embellishment:

    a. Cut a piece of patterned paper the same size as a slide.

    b. Place dried flowers between the cut paper and the slide and adhere together.

    c. Heat emboss the edges of the slide with gold embossing powder.

    d. Finish by tying a ribbon around the microscope glass slide embellishment.

SUPPLIES - 6 x 7.5 Album

Cardstock: Bazzill; Patterned Paper: Memories in the Making, Chatterbox, Inc., Autumn Leaves; Vellum: Making Memories; Metallic Embellishments: ScrapLovers, Making Memories; Fibers: Fibers by the Yard; Brads: ScrapLovers, American Crafts; Stickers: Memories in the Making, Autumn Leaves; Cork: Lazerletterz; Chalk: Craf-T Products; Stamps: Dollar Tree, PSX Design, Stampin' Up; Ink: Altered Pages, Stampin' Up, Tsukineko; Embossing Powder: Stamps 'n' Stuff; Slide: Altered Pages; Leather Strips: Two Mom's Scrap n Stamp; Transparency: 3M Stationary; Adhesive: JudiKins; Font: Ancient Script

Designer: Susan Stringfellow

THE **great outdoors**

This is the best Campout. We went on a LONG Wild Hike, we took the wrong trail and ended up hiking 8 miles. We saw lots of alligators, birds, squirrels, and flowers everywhere. Before we left the park, Dad wanted to do a bit of fishing, but the boys just wanted to take a rest in the shade.

MARCH 2001

DO YOUR BEST

CAMP april '02

spring Camp out

FALL CAMP OUT

Our First Cub Scout family Campout. Perry, Chris and Alex had never been camping before, so it was real adventure! Dad bought Alex a walking stick at the Ranger station. He had so much fun with that thing!
~ October 2000 ~

sandcastles in the sun

starfish

surfboard

sand castles

summer

seagulls

scallop shells

sand dollars

1. Add texture and interest by gluing sand and seashells directly onto a tag or page.

2. How to make a gathered ribbon and button embellishment:

   a. Place gingham ribbon onto page.

   b. Plan placement of buttons.

   c. Gather ribbon where buttons will be adhered and tie with a piece of thread.

   d. Adhere buttons atop gathered ribbon with glue dots.

SUPPLIES - 8 x 8 Album

Cardstock: DCWV; Patterned Paper: DCWV; Mulberry Paper: DCWV; Tags: Sizzix; Metallic Embellishment: DCWV; Eyelets: Making Memories; Buttons: Dress It Up!; Stickers: RA Lang Card Company; Vellum Quote: DCWV; Stamps: Stamp Craft; Ink: Stampin' Up; Chalk: Craf-T Products; Adhesive: Therm O Web, Inc., Herma Fix; Fonts: Amazon BT, Synchronous

Designer: Brenda Nakandakari

cancun 2003

CONSTRUCTION TIPS

1. How to bind a mini book with fiber:
   a. Punch holes along the side of each page (create a template so the holes will line up).
   b. Sandwich the pages in-between the front and back covers.
   c. Line up the holes and weave the fiber through the book.
   d. Finish the book by tying the fiber off at the ends.
2. Print a photo onto a transparency to allow the background to show through and give the illusion that the photo is etched into the sandpaper.

SUPPLIES - 5 x 7 Album

Patterned Paper: NRN Designs, Bisous, Pixie Press, Making Memories; Metallic Embellishments: DCWV; Fibers: Fibers by the Yard; Brads: Making Memories; Stickers: Creative Imaginations, NRN Designs, Sticker Studio, Shotz by Creative Imaginations, Me & My Big Ideas; Vellum Quote: DCWV; Wax Seal: Sonnets by Creative Imaginations Stamps: PSX Design; Pen: ZIG by EK Success; Transparency: Magic Scraps; Adhesive: Creative Imaginations

Designer: Sam Cousins

autograph book

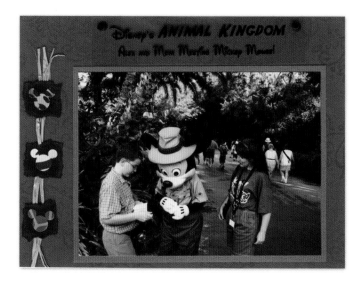

CONSTRUCTION TIPS

1. Create an autograph mini book to capture childhood memories from a family vacation. Leave a place for the children to journal their thoughts and memories as well as space for the 'celebrity' autographs.

Alex & Terk from Tarzan

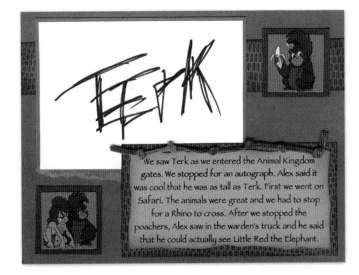

We saw Terk as we entered the Animal Kingdom gates. We stopped for an autograph. Alex said it was cool that he was as tall as Terk. First we went on Safari. The animals were great and we had to stop for a Rhino to cross. After we stopped the poachers, Alex saw in the warden's truck and he said that he could actually see Little Red the Elephant.

We Scare Because We Care

MGM

Sulley and Mike were really cool! Sulley was really big and he kept leaning on me! -Alex

SULLEY AND MIKE COULDN'T SIGN AUTOGRAPHS BUT THEY WERE REALLY COOL!

MIKE

alex and SULLEY

SUPPLIES - 5 x 7 Album

Cardstock: Making Memories; Patterned Papers: Memories in the Making, Hot Off The Press, Frances Meyer, Inc.; Vellum: Making Memories; Metallic Embellishments: ScrapYard 329; Fibers: Fibers by the Yard; Thread: Coats & Clark; Brads: Making Memories, ScrapLovers; Stickers: Memories in the Making, NRN Designs, Stickopotomus by EK Success, Sandylion; Beads: Crafts Etc!; Bamboo

Clip: Altered Pages; Mesh: Magic Mesh; Punch: EK Success; Chalk: Craf-T Products; Embossing Ink: Stampin' Up; Embossing Powder: Ranger Industries; Ink: Tsukineko; Transparency: 3M Stationary; Adhesive: JudiKins; Fonts: Beach Type, Walt Disney, Adventure

Designer: Susan Stringfellow

christmas at our house

SUPPLIES - 6 x 6 Album

Cardstock: Chatterbox, Inc.; Patterned Paper: Chatterbox, Inc.; Fibers: Fibers by the Yard; Tacks: Chatterbox, Inc.; Nails: Chatterbox, Inc.; Rivets: Chatterbox, Inc.; Moldings: Chatterbox, Inc.; Frames: Chatterbox, Inc.; Stickers: Chatterbox, Inc.;

Ribbon: Offray & Son, Inc.; Ink: ColorBox by Clearsnap, Inc.; Pen: Marvy Uchida; Labels: Dymo

Designer: Tarri Botwinski

374

CONSTRUCTION TIPS

1. How to make an accordion book:

    a. Cut background cardstock large enough to be folded in half to create two facing pages.

    b. Overlap the latter half of the first page to the first half of the second page and glue together. Then, overlap the latter half of the second page to the first half of the third page and glue together. Continue this process until you have as many accordion pages as desired.

    c. Make sure the folds alternate pointing forward and backward so the book can be folded properly.

    d. Finish the book by adhering ribbon horizontally to the back cover of the book. Leave extra ribbon on both sides to wrap around to the front of the book and tie in a bow on top.

2. Use a label maker for journaling.

holidays through the year

SUPPLIES - 6 x 6 Album

Cardstock: Bazzill; Patterned Paper: Carolee's Creations; Tag: DCWV, Making Memories; Metallic Embellishments: Making Memories, DCWV; Fibers: Fibers by the Yard; Brads: ScrapLovers; Eyelets: Making Memories; Stickers: The Scrapbook Wizard, Shotz by Creative Imaginations, Terri Martin by Creative Imaginations, Jolee's Boutique, Bo-Bunny Press; Rub-ons: Making Memories; Stamp: Making Memories; Ribbon: Making Memories, Impress Rubber Stamps

Designer: Sam Cousins

CONSTRUCTION TIPS

1. Manipulate photos with the use of a computer software program. Convert a photo to black and white and then add color back to certain portions of the photo.

2. Tissue paper comes in a variety of colors and patterns and can be used as a background for scrapbook pages. Attach the tissue paper to the background cardstock with a glue stick or other adhesive. Choose whether to make it smooth or crumpled.

3. How to paint metals and brads:

   a. Paint metals and brads with acrylic paint.

   b. Set with matte spray or clear embossing powder.

easter album

SUPPLIES - 6 x 6 Album

Snaps: Chatterbox, Inc.; Ribbon: Offray & Son, Inc.

Designer: Jlyne Hanback

CONSTRUCTION TIPS

1. Use paint swatches for journaling and as an accent on a page.

halloween album

CONSTRUCTION TIPS

1. Mat a photo with torn mulberry paper. Fold the top portion of the mulberry paper over the top of the photo. Stitch the flap of mulberry paper to the top of the photo. The stitching will hold the photo in place and provide a flap that can be flipped up to reveal journaling or other photos.

SUPPLIES - 6 x 6 Album

Cardstock: DCWV; Patterned Paper: Memories in the Making, The Paper Patch; Mulberry: DCWV; Metallic Embellishment: DCWV; Thread: DMC; Eyelets: Making Memories; Stickers: Memories in the Making; Adhesive: Herma Fix

Designer: Brenda Nakandakari

boo

CONSTRUCTION TIPS

1. Create your own sheet-protected 6 x 6 mini book:
   a. Fold 12 x 12 cardstock or other heavy paper in half horizontally and adhere insides together for the cover.
   b. Trim the tops of 12 x 12 sheet protectors to 6 inches tall. Cut the desired amount of sheet protectors (each trimmed sheet protector will hold 4 pages).
   c. Open the cover with the front faced down and place trimmed sheet protectors one upon the other with all the openings at the top. With a sewing machine, stitch straight down the center of the book to create the binding.
   d. Fold the pages and cover at the seam.
   e. Slide pages, just shy of 6 inches, into the sheet protectors.
2. Age metal embellishments by rubbing the metal with an inkpad. With a rubber stamp, stamp letters and images onto the weathered looking metal.

SUPPLIES - 6 x 6 Album

Cardstock: DCWV; Patterned Papers: Memories in the Making, PSX Design, Making Memories, Frances Meyer, Inc.; Vellum: DCWV; Metallic Embellishments: DCWV; Buttons: Doodlebug Designs Inc.; Slide Mount: Magic Scraps; Vellum Quotes: DCWV; Floss: DMC; Date Stamp: Making Memories; Ink: Staz-On by Tsukineko

Designer: Camille Jensen

the many reasons i love you

CONSTRUCTION TIPS

1. Run faux suede paper through a printer to create an embossed leather look. Choose a font color a few shades darker than the color of the faux suede or leather to achieve the desired effect.

2. Hinges are a great way to add metallic accents to a page and also to allow a flap to be flipped up to reveal journaling or another surprise.

SUPPLIES - 5 x 7 Album

Patterned Paper: Memories in the Making; Metallic Embellishments: Making Memories; Snaps: Making Memories; Eyelets: Making Memories; Jump Rings: Making Memories; Buttons: Junkitz; Stickers: K & Company, Sticko by EK Success; Pen: Sanford Uni-ball; Font: Felix Titling

Designer: Leah Fung

The Many Reasons I Love You

My dear husband, I love you very much. After 10 years of marriage, you still can surprise me. There are so many reasons why I love you, and no book could ever capture all of those reasons. But, I want you to know some of things that I love most about you. You're a very special person, and I thank God for you and our family. Love you.

A Man of Character

Values You Uphold

Faith in God
Integrity
Family
Hard Work
Wisdom
Compassion
Honor

A Loving Husband

I can't remember a day when you didn't say "I love you"

You take care of me whenever I'm sick

You wash the dishes and do the laundry without me having to ask

You know when I need a hug even before I do

A Caring Father

You read books with your children and you pray with them too

You care enough to discipline, and you discipline with love

The kids and I mean more to you than anything else in this world, and it shows

383

super dad

CONSTRUCTION TIPS

1. Make a superhero book as a gift for a loving parent. Journal why the parent is like each superhero.

SUPPLIES - 6 x 6 Album

Cardstock: National Cardstock; Patterned Paper: Westrim Crafts; Eyelets: Making Memories; Buttons: Paper Bliss by Westrim Crafts; Stickers: Paper Bliss by Westrim Crafts; Die Cuts: Sizzix; Ribbon: Offray & Son, Inc.; Fonts: Comic Sans, Alor Narrow Condensed, Impact, Arial Black, Copperplate Gothic, Times New Roman

Designer: Mary Walby

Just in case my Dad doesn't know, Mom and I decided to show him how cool we both think he is. Mom says that we don't always celebrate the great stuff that Dad does and how much fun we have with him. This book was created for Father's Day in 2004, as told to Mom by Dad's little groupie. . .

My Dad is a SUPERHERO

. . . I Just Don't Know Which One!?*

THE HULK

The Hulk is another pick for my Dad's secret identity. Whenever I get tired and don't want to walk any further, Dad puts me on his shoulders without complaining -- even when Mom says I'm too big for her to carry any more.

EXHAUSTED, THE CHILD CLUNG TO OUR SUPERHERO AS THEY HEADED FOR HOME.

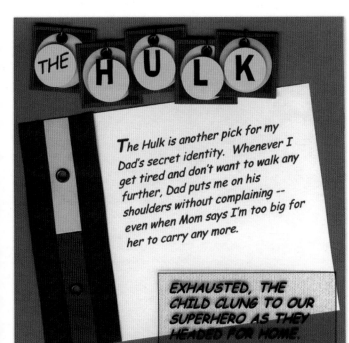

AUTHOR'S NOTE: My dad is a superhero, and I love him very much.

Even though my Dad reminds me of all these super heroes -- he is still smarter, faster, stronger and braver than any of them. I'm sure his powers will last forever, and I'll always stay his biggest fan. Maybe, when I grow up, I'll write a comic book about Super Dad, and everyone will want to be like him.

385

if flowers
could talk

CONSTRUCTION TIPS

1. Create a mini book of your hobby. It is fun to imagine what each flower would say, if it could talk and journal these sayings.

2. Make a shaker box from slide mounts:

    a. Use two slide mounts of the same size and color.

    b. Trim and adhere a transparency to the backside of the front slide mount.

    c. Adhere the front side of the back slide mount to the page. Adhere foam tape atop that slide.

    d. Place buttons or other embellishments into the middle of the slide mount.

    e. Remove the protective covering to reveal the second sticky side of the foam tape and adhere the top slide mount with the transparency onto the bottom slide mount.

SUPPLIES - 8 x 8 Album

Album: Paper Pulp Products Inc.; Cardstock: Bazzill, Canson Mi-Teintes; Patterned Paper: KI Memories; Thread: DMC; Buttons: Making Memories; Slide Holder: Scrapvillage; Font: Two Peas in a Bucket Unforgettable

Designer: Betsy Sammarco

a year of recipes

Back To School Pencil Cake

1 pkg. cake mix (any flavor)
2 containers vanilla frosting, divided
red and yellow food color
chocolate sprinkles

Preheat oven to 350. Grease and flour 13x9 inch pan. Prepare, bake and cool cake following package directions for basic recipe. For frosting tint one cup vanilla frosting pink with red food coloring. Tint remaining frosting with yellow food coloring. To assemble cut cooled cake (cut in half length wise and cut one of the 2 resulting rectangles to give the look of a sharpened pencil) and arrange end to end on large baking sheet or piece of sturdy cardboard. Spread pink frosting on cake for eraser at one end and for wood at other end. Spread yellow frosting over remaining cake. Decorate with chocolate sprinkles for pencil tip and eraser band (directly under eraser, separating it from yellow).

SUPPLIES - 5 x 7 Album

Patterned Paper: Chatterbox, Inc., Karen Foster Design, Doodlebug Designs Inc., Memories in the Making; Brads: Lasting Impressions; 3-D Stickers: Jolee's Boutique; Fonts: Two Peas in a Bucket Lasagna, Two Peas in a Bucket Jack Frost, Chatterbox, Inc. Armymen, Two Peas in a Bucket Picnic Basket, BH Playful, Two Peas in a Bucket Renaissance, Two Peas in a Bucket Princess

Designer: Miranda Isenberg

patriotic pie

1 refrigerator pie crust
1 quart fresh strawberries, divided
1 8 oz. pkg. of cream cheese
3/4 cup cold milk
1 8.3 oz. pkg. of white chocolate instant pudding and pie filling
1 1/2 cups fresh blueberries
1 cup frozen whipped topping, thawed

Preheat oven to 425. Allow pie crust to warm to room temperature (about 15 minutes). Unroll piecrust onto floured surface. Roll to 11 1/2 inch circle and then place in a deep dish pie plate. Prick bottom and sides of piecrust. Bake for 10 minutes or until brown. Cool completely. Wash and dry strawberries. Choose 8 uniformly sized and shaped strawberries and cut in half through the stem, set aside. Hull and slice remaining strawberries. Layer sliced strawberries over the bottom of the cooled pie crust. Beat cream cheese until smooth. Add milk gradually and mix until well blended. Add pudding mix and beat until mixture begins to thicken. Spread evenly over strawberries. Arrange blueberries evenly over top of pie filling. Dot whipped cream around edge of pie using a cake decorator or a sandwich bag with a hole in one corner. Place halved strawberries on whipped topping border. Keep refrigerated until ready to serve.

directions

line baking sheet with waxed paper. Pour popcorn into large bowl. combine sugar syrup in medium saucepan bring to a boil over medium heat stirring constantly. boil remove from heat add peanut butter and green food color. stir until peanut butter completely melted pour over popcorn stir to coat well. lightly butter hands popcorn mixture into trees while trees are still warm, press red cinnamon candies place on prepared baking sheet let stand until firm. about 30 minutes

festive POPCORN trees

ingredients
6 cups popped popcorn
1/2 cup sugar
1/2 cup light corn syrup
1/4 cup peanut butter
1/4 cup red cinnamon candies
green food coloring

CONSTRUCTION TIPS

1. Create a mini book of your favorite recipes so friends and
    family can share your traditions, as well as your great meals.

Father's Day Fix-It

Ingredients

-1 pkg. (about 18 oz) refrigerated chocolate cookie dough
-flour
-white decorator frosting
-assorted colored sprinkles and colored frostings
-cardboard
white decorator frosting:
-1 pound powdered sugar
-1/2 cup vegetable shortening or unsalted butter
-1 Tbsp corn syrup
-6 to 8 Tbsp milk
-assorted paste food colorings
Beat sugar, shortening, corn syrup and milk in medium bowl at high speed of electric mixer 2 minutes or until fluffy. Add food colorings to achieve desired colors.

Draw patterns for tools on cardboard, cut out patterns. Preheat oven to 350. Remove dough from wrapper according to pkg. directions. Divide dough into 2 equal sections. Reserve one section; cover and refrigerate remaining section. Roll reserved dough on lightly floured surface to 1/8 inch thickness. Sprinkle with flour to minimize sticking if necessary. Lay sheet of waxed paper over dough. Place patterns over waxed paper. Cut dough around patterns with sharp knife; remove patterns and waxed paper. Place cookies 2 inches apart on ungreased cookie sheets. Repeat with remaining dough and any scraps. Bake 8 to 10 minutes or until firm, but not browned. Cool on cookie sheets 2 minutes. Remove to wire rack; cool completely. Spread frosting evenly over top of each cookie. Decorate with sprinkles and frostings.

when grandma was little like me

SUPPLIES - 5 x 7 Album

Cardstock: DCWV; Patterned Paper: Memories in the Making; Metallic
Embellishments: DCWV; Brads: Memories in the Making; Photo Corners:
3M Stationary

Designer: NanC and Company Design

CONSTRUCTION TIPS

1. How to make a horizontal mini album:

   a. Cut cardstock to 5 x 7 inches for inside and cover pages.

   b. Adhere a strip of brown paper to the binding side of each page (both front and back).

   c. With an exacto knife cut two slits at the left seam of the brown strip of paper on each page leaving an inch on the top and bottom of the page (use a template to make sure the slits all line up).

   d. Cut two pieces of ribbon and slide a piece through the top slits of all the pages. Tie the ribbon into a knot on the side of the book. Follow the same steps with the second ribbon through the bottom slits of the pages.

   e. Cut two more pieces of ribbon to tie the book closed. Adhere one ribbon horizontally along the midline of the inside cover of the book. Cut a vertical slit 3/8 of an inch in from the opening side of the cover. Thread the ribbon through the slit so the tail of the ribbon comes out the front of the cover. Cover the inside cover with a black piece of cardstock to hide your steps. Repeat this process for the back cover.

   f. Tie the two pieces of ribbon together in a bow to close the mini book.

christmas album

SUPPLIES - 5.5 x 7.5 Album

Patterned Paper: Memories in the Making; Charms: Memories in the Making;
Micro Beads: Provo Craft; Foil: AMACO

Designer: Camille Jensen

CONSTRUCTION TIPS

1. How to make a vertical mini album:
   a. Cut a piece of corrugated cardboard to 6 x 12 inches, 6 x 7 inches and 2.5 x 6 inches. Make sure the lines of the cardboard are always horizontal with the 6-inch cut.
   b. Trim sheet protectors to 5.5 x 7.5 inches with the openings on the side. The reinforced edges of the sheet protectors should be at the top.
   c. Sandwich the corrugated cardboard and sheet protectors as follows: The long piece of corrugated cardboard right side down, sheet protectors with a thin strip (0.75 x 5.5 inches) of cardboard in-between each reinforced edge of the sheet protector, and the shorter piece of cardboard right side up. Make sure all elements are lined up along the top.
   d. Fold the 2.5 x 6 inch piece of cardstock to cap the top of the book and overlap onto the back and front covers.
   e. Punch two holes through the cardboard cap, covers, sheet protectors and cardboard strips. Make sure the punches are an inch in from the sides of the book and centered from top to bottom on the cardboard cap.
   f. String many threads of raffia through all the holes and tie in a bow on the front cover to bind the book together.
   g. Fold the bottom cover of corrugated cardboard forward creating two creases to allow room for the sheet protectors to be filled with pages. Make sure the top cover overlaps the bottom cover.
   h. Sew two buttons onto the book. Sew the first button, centered, a half-inch above where the front cover overlaps the back cover. Sew the second button, centered, a half-inch below where the covers meet. Tie a piece of string 12 inches long to the top button to be used to wrap around both buttons to close the book.
   i. Decorate the cover of the book and fill the sheet protectors with scrapbook pages.

sources

3L Corp
(800) 828-3130
3lcorp.com

3M Stationary
(800) 364-3577
3m.com

7 Gypsies
(800) 588-6707
7gypsies.com

Altered Pages
alteredpages.com

AMACO
(800) 374-1600
amaco.com

American Crafts
(800) 879-5185
americancrafts.com

American Tag Co.
(800) 642-4314
americantag.net

Anna Griffin
(888) 817-8170
annagriffin.com

Artistic Wire Ltd.
(630) 530-7567
artisticwire.com

Autumn Leaves
(800) 588-6707

Avery Dennison
averydennison.com

Bazzill
(480) 558-8557
bazzillbasics.com

Bead Heaven
(410) 789-2153
beadheaven.com

Bisous
(905) 502-7209
bisous.biz

Bo-Bunny Press
(801) 770-4010
bobunny.com

Canson, Inc.
(800) 628-9283
canson-us.com

Card Connection
card-connection.co.uk

Carolee's Creations
(435) 563-1100
caroleescreations.com

Chatterbox, Inc.
(888) 416-6260
chatterboxinc.com

Clearsnap, Inc.
(800) 448-4862
clearsnap.com

Close To My Heart
closetomyheart.com

Cloud 9 Design
(763) 493-0990
cloud9design.biz

Coats & Clark
coatsandclark.com

Craf-T Products
(800) 530-3410
craf-tproducts.com

Crafts Etc!
(800) 888-0321
craftsetc.com

Creating Keepsakes
(888)-247-5282
creatingkeepsakes.com

Creative Imaginations
(800) 942-6487
cigift.com

Darice
(800) 321-1494
darice.com

DCWV
(801) 224-6766
diecutswithaview.com

Delta Crafts
(800) 423-4135
deltacrafts.com

Deluxe Designs
(480) 497-9005
deluxecuts.com

Disney
go.disney.com

DMC
(973) 589-9890
dmc-usa.com

DMD Industries
(800) 805-9890
dmdind.com

Dollar Tree
757-321-5000
dollartree.com

Doodlebug
Designs Inc.
801-966-9952
timelessmemories.ca

Dress It Up!
dressitup.com

Dymo
dymo.com

EK Success
(800) 524-1349
eksuccess.com

Ever After
Scrapbook Co.
(800) 646-0010

Family Treasures
(949) 643-9526
familytreasures.com

Fibers by the Yard
fibersbytheyard.com

Foofala
(402) 758-0863
foofala.com

Frances Meyer, Inc.
francesmeyer.com

Halcraft
212-376-1580
halcraft.com

Heidi Grace Designs
(253) 973-5542
heidigrace.com

Herma Fix
herma.co.uk.com

Hero Arts
Rubber Stamps, Inc.
(800) 822-4376
heroarts.com

Hot Off The Press
(800) 227-9595
paperpizazz.com

Impress
Rubber Stamps
(206) 901-9101
impressrubberstamps.
com

Jolee's Boutique
joleesbyyou.com

JudiKins
(310) 515-1115

Junkitz
junkitz.com

K & Company
(888) 244-2083
kandcompany.com

Karen Foster Design
(801) 451-9779
karenfosterdesign.com

KI Memories
(972) 243-5595
kimemories.com

Lasting Impressions
lastingimpressions.safes-
hopper.com

LazerLetterz
lazerletterz.com

Magenta
Rubber Stamps
magentarubberstamps.
com

Magic Mounts
(800) 332-0050
magicmounts.com

Magic Scraps
(972) 238-1838
magicscraps.com

Making Memories
(800) 286-5263
makingmemories.com

Marvy Uchida
(800) 541-5877
uchida.com

Me & My Big Ideas
(949) 589-4607
meandmybigideas.com

Memories
in the Making
(800) 643-8030
leisurearts.com

Mrs. Grossmans
(800) 429-4549
mrsgrossmans.com

National Cardstock
(866) 452-7120
nationalcardstock.com

NRN Designs
nrndesigns.com

Offray & Son, Inc.
offray.com

Paper Adventures
(800) 727-0699
paperadventures.com

Paper Garden
(210) 494-9602
papergarden.com

Paper House
Productions
(800) 255-7316
paperhouseproductions.
com

Paper Patch, The
(801) 253-3018
paperpatch.com

Paper Pulp
Products Inc.
91-792-535-1715
pppi.vze.com

Paperfever Inc.
(800) 477-0902
paperfever.com

Pentel
(310) 320-3831
pentel.com

Pixie Press
(702) 646-1156
pixiepress.com

Provo Craft
(888) 577-3545
provocraft.com

PSX Design
(800) 782-6748
psxdesign.com

RA Lang
Card Company
(800) 648-2388
lang.com

Ranger Industries
(800) 244-2211
rangerink.com

Rebecca Sower
mississippipaperarts.com

Rusty Pickle, The
(801) 274-9588
rustypickle.com

Sandylion
sandylion.com

Scrapbook Wizard, The
(801) 947-0019
scrapbookwizard.com

Scrap-Ease
(800) 272-3874
scrap-ease.com

Scrapfindings
(780) 417-0161
scrapfindings.com

ScrapLovers
scraplovers.com

Scrapvillage
scrapvillage.com

Scrapworks
scrapworksllc.com

ScrapYard 329
(775) 829-1227
scrapyard329.com

SEI
(800) 333-3279
shopsei.com

Simply Stamped
(925) 417-2264
simplystamped.com

Sizzix
sizzix.com

Stamp Craft
stampcraft.com.au

Stampa Rosa
stamparosa.com

Stampendous!
(800) 869-0474
stampendous.com

Stampin' Up
(800) 782-6787
stampinup.com

Sticker Studio
stickerstudio.com

Susan Branch
susanbranch.com

Suze Weinberg
(732) 761-2400
schmoozewithsuze.com

Therm O Web, Inc.
(800) 323-0799
thermoweb.com

Tsukineko
(800) 769-6633
tsukineko.com

Two Mom's
Scrap n Stamp
281-550-6155
twomomsscrapnstamp.
com

Two Peas in a Bucket
twopeasinabucket.com

Uni-ball
uniball-na.com

Westrim Crafts
(800) 727-2727
westrimcrafts.com

Wordsworth Stamps
(719) 282-3495
wordsworthstamps.com

Xyron, Inc.
(800) 793-3523
xyron.com

Memory Albums *for all*

12 PROJECTS

395

Table of Contents

Memory Albums for all

Your precious memory albums are filled with **EXCITING AND CREATIVE** pages that chronicle your LIFE AND TIMES. Now you can make the covers of your scrapbooks as personal and appealing as the pages inside. This "gotta-have-it" treasury of **12 ALBUM COVERS** offers great ideas for newborns, athletes, school days, weddings, family heritage and more! You'll have fun using **SCRAPBOOKING SUPPLIES AND CRAFTY TRIMMINGS** to fashion breathtaking album covers with professional polish. EASY INSTRUCTIONS and **FULL-COLOR PHOTOGRAPHS** guide you step by step and inspire you to add your own novel embellishments. Just gather up your scrapbooking supplies and **JUMP INTO THE FUN!**

PICTURE THIS!
Album

Supplies

8" x 6" spiral journal

blue acrylic paint

brown scrapbook paper

silver paint pen

double-stick tape

$^3/_4$" square silver button

20" length of silver cord

hot glue gun

paintbrush

Instructions

1. Paint the front cover of the journal; allow to dry. Highlight the edges of the cover with the paint pen.

2. Cut assorted size squares from scrapbook paper (ours vary from 1" to $1^1/_2$"). Outline the edges of the squares with the paint pen. Cut one 2" square from scrapbook paper; cut a $1^1/_2$" square from center leaving a $^1/_2$" frame.

3. Tape the frame to the center right side of the journal. Randomly tape the squares to the journal.

4. Sew the cord through the holes of the button; glue the ends to the back of the button. Glue the button to the center of the frame.

5. Fold the cord in half to form a loop; knot the cord ends. Wrap the loop around the button, then glue the knot to the back of the journal.

Your LIFE in PICTURES Album

Supplies

10³/₄" x 11³/₄" x 2"
   three-ring binder

¹/₄ yd of white satin

¹/₄ yd each of 2 shades of
   champagne colored satin

¹/₄ yd of beige satin

³/₈ yd of lining fabric

3 yds of ³/₈"w chocolate brown
   grosgrain ribbon

batting

poster board

fabric glue

Instructions

1. Cut a piece of batting the same size as open binder. Glue batting to the outside of the binder.

2. Cut six 9" squares of satin. Matching right sides and raw edges and using a ¹/₂" seam allowance, sew squares into a block three squares wide and two squares high.

3. Center the binder, batting side down, on the wrong side of your sewn fabric 2" from bottom. Draw around the binder; cut out 2" outside drawn lines.

4. Fold corners of fabric diagonally over corners of the binder. Clipping top and bottom edges to fit under binding hardware, fold edges of fabric over edges of the binder; glue corners if necessary.

5. Weaving ribbons at seam intersection, cover seams with two lengths of ribbon. Fold and glue ends to inside of the binder; spot glue ribbon on outside of the binder.

6. To line the inside of the binder, cut two pieces of poster board slightly smaller than the inside covers. Cut two pieces of lining fabric 1" larger on all sides than poster board.

7. Center one piece of poster board on wrong side of one piece of fabric. Glue fabric corners diagonally over corners of poster board. Glue fabric edges over edges of poster board. Repeat with remaining poster board and fabric.

8. With fabric side up, glue covered poster board to inside covers of the binder.

A Very Special *Lady* ALBUM

Supplies

8" x 9¼" three-ring binder

⅓ yd of lavender silk

2 sheets of lavender cardstock

large white monogram

spray adhesive

fabric glue

Instructions

1. To cover binder, draw around open binder on wrong side of silk; cut out silk 2" outside drawn lines. Apply spray adhesive to wrong side of fabric; center open binder on fabric. Close binder; smooth fabric on front and back of binder.

2. Re-open binder; fold corners of fabric diagonally over corners of binder. Clipping top and bottom edges to fit under binding hardware, fold edges of fabric over edges of binder; glue corners if necessary.

3. Center and glue monogram to the front of the binder.

4. To line the inside of the binder, cut two pieces of cardstock ½" smaller than the inside covers. Glue the liners to the inside binder covers, scoring as necessary at the bends of the binder spine.

Tip:
If the binding hardware is attached to the front or back cover instead of the spine, cut an extra piece of inside liner material to cover the spine on the inside or cut one liner to cover the spine and the cover and score it at the bends of the spine.

Man of the Hour Album

Supplies

12" x 12" scrapbook with post binding system

$3/4$ yd of faux pressed leather

$1/4$ yd of faux suede

3" gold tassels with 28" length of cording between tassels

tape

4" wooden letter

gold spray paint

craft glue

awl

Instructions

1. Separate parts of scrapbook; set pages aside. Tape center of tassel cord and cut apart at tape.

2. For each cover, cut a 12" x $14^1/2$" piece of pressed leather and a 6" x $14^1/2$" piece of faux suede. Overlapping long edges 1", glue one suede piece to one leather piece.

3. Aligning suede edge with outer fold of binding flap, center and glue cover on wrong side of leather piece.

4. Make a clip in suede at inner fold of binding flap to $1/4$" from edge of cover at top and bottom of cover. Trim away suede along binding flap $1/4$" past edge of cover.

5. Pleating suede and leather at corners as necessary, glue suede and leather over edges of cover.

6. Cover spine of scrapbook with suede. Use awl to poke holes for posts through spine and binding flaps.

7. Beginning with tassel at bottom edge, glue cording along edge of suede. Trim end of cord and glue to inside of cover.

8. Fold binding flap to inside of one cover. Measure inside cover between outer edge and edge of folded flap. Cut 2 pieces of leather $1/2$" less than each measurement.

9. Glue leather to inside covers of scrapbook. Reassemble scrapbook.

10. Paint letter gold; allow to dry. Center letter on leather section of front cover and glue in place.

Supplies

12" x 12" scrapbook with 4" x 5" photograph opening and post binding system

1 yd of cream striped fabric

$^1/_4$ yd of blue & green checked satin

batting

$^7/_8$ yd of $1^1/_4$"w mint green grosgrain ribbon

$^5/_8$ yd of $^3/_8$"w mint green grosgrain ribbon

$^7/_8$ yd of 1"w cream satin ribbon

$^5/_8$ yd of $^1/_2$"w cream satin ribbon

$^5/_8$ yd of $^1/_8$"w pale green satin ribbon

white beading string

mixed pearls

clear glass beads

silver lined "E" beads

silver lined bugle beads

poster board

fabric glue

liquid fray preventative

awl

Wedding Bells are Ringing Album

Instructions

1. Separate parts of scrapbook; set pages and inside front cover aside.

2. For each cover, cut a 14" x $12^1/_2$" piece of batting. Glue batting to the outside of scrapbook covers. Trim batting around outer edges of photograph opening.

3. For each cover, cut a 6" x 14" piece of checked satin and a 13" x 14" piece of striped fabric. Overlapping long edges 1", glue checked piece to striped piece.

4. Aligning checked edge with outer fold of binding flap, center and glue cover on wrong side of fabric piece.

5. Make a clip in fabric at inner fold of binding flap to $^1/_4$" from edge of cover at top and bottom of cover. Trim away fabric along binding flap $^1/_4$" past edge of cover.

6. Pleating fabric at corners as necessary, glue fabric over edges of cover.

7. Wrapping ends to inside of cover, glue $1^1/_4$"w mint, then 1"w cream ribbon over seam of fabrics.

8. Cut an "X" in fabric at opening on front cover. Fold fabric to inside of cover, trim points, and glue in place.

9. Mitering at the corners, glue $^1/_2$"w cream, $^3/_8$"w mint, then $^1/_8$"w pale green ribbon around edges of opening. Secure photo behind opening.

10. Fold binding flap to inside of one cover. Measure inside back cover between outer edge and edge of folded flap. Cut 2 pieces of poster board $^1/_2$" less than each measurement.

11. Cut a piece of striped fabric 1" larger on all sides than poster board. Center poster board on wrong side of fabric. Glue fabric over corners of poster board. Glue remaining fabric edges to poster board.

12. Cover spine of scrapbook with checked fabric. Use awl to poke holes for posts through spine and binding flaps. Apply liquid fray preventative to raw edges of holes; allow to dry. Reassemble scrapbook.

13. Knotting each end, string 12$\frac{1}{2}$" of assorted beads onto beading string. Wrapping ends to inside of front cover, glue strand down center of ribbon. Knotting each end, string 10" of beads onto beading string. Shape into a bow and glue to album front.

14. Knotting each end, string 16" of assorted beads onto beading string. Glue strand along inside of photograph opening.

It's all in the Name

Instructions

1. Separate parts of scrapbook; set pages and front cover insert aside.

2. Piecing cardstock as needed, cut a piece of cardstock $1/2$" larger on all sides than each cover. Cut jewel toned papers into 3" squares. Arrange and glue onto cardstock pieces, leaving $1/8$" between squares.

3. Fold and glue covered cardstock over the edges of the covers, folding, pleating, and trimming corners as necessary.

4. Cut an "X" in cardstock over openings in front cover. Fold cardstock to inside of cover and glue in place.

5. Fold binding flap to inside of back cover. Measure inside back cover between outer edge and edge of folded flap. Cut a piece of cardstock $1/2$" less than measurement and $1/2$" less than height. Glue to inside back cover.

6. Cut a piece of cardstock 1" larger on all sides than front cover insert. Glue cardstock over corners of insert. Glue remaining edges to insert. Glue insert to inside front cover. Reassemble scrapbook.

7. Cut a $5/8$"w frame for each of the openings from cardstock. Cut a $1/2$"w frame for each of the openings from poster board.

8. Repeat Steps 3-4 to cover the poster board frames with striped paper. Layer and glue cardstock frames and covered frames around openings.

9. Cut a $2^1/4$" length of grosgrain ribbon. Tie through eyelet of tag. Adhere framed flower to tag. Center and adhere completed tag to upper opening using foam dots.

10. Use alphabet stickers to spell out family name in bottom opening.

11. Cover spine of scrapbook with paper. Reassemble scrapbook.

Supplies

12" x 12" scrapbook with 2 openings and post binding system

various jewel tone colored papers

coordinating striped paper

coordinating $3^1/4$" x $2^1/2$" tag

$1^1/2$" square framed flower sticker

$1/8$"w white grosgrain ribbon

dimensional foam dots

white cardstock

green alphabet stickers

poster board

craft glue

Baby's First Album

Supplies

12" x 12" scrapbook with post binding system

$1/2$ yd of yellow chenille

$3^1/2$" x 5" gold oval frame

light blue acrylic paint

$1/4$" – $1/2$" assorted heart-shaped buttons

$3/4$" yellow heart-shaped button

1 yd of $1/8$"w green silk ribbon

$2/3$ yd of $7/8$"w light blue satin ribbon

1 yd of $1/8$"w light blue mini dot satin ribbon

ribbon needle

paintbrush

awl

fabric glue

soft cloth

liquid fray preventative

Instructions

1. Separate parts of scrapbook; set pages aside.

2. For each cover, cut two pieces of chenille $1/2$" larger on all sides than cover including spine.

3. Leaving one short end open, match right sides and raw edges and use a $1/2$" seam allowance to sew chenille pieces together in pairs.

4. Turn right side out and insert covers; slipstitch openings closed.

5. Cover spine of scrapbook with chenille. Use awl to poke holes for posts through spine and binding flaps. Apply liquid fray preventative to raw edges of holes; allow to dry.

6. Fold binding flap to inside of cover. Reassemble scrapbook.

7. Paint frame. While paint is still wet, wipe paint away from raised areas with soft cloth. Allow to dry.

8. Cut photo to fit frame. Insert photo; glue frame to center front of scrapbook.

9. Thread assorted buttons, evenly spaced, onto silk ribbon. Form ribbon into an oval 1" away from frame. Glue buttons to cover to secure. Trim any excess ribbon.

10. Tie a bow with wide satin ribbon; notch ends and glue to center bottom of oval.

11. For tie closure, cut narrow ribbon in half. Thread one end of ribbon through needle then through fabric at center right edge of scrapbook back cover. Remove needle.

12. Thread other end of ribbon half through needle and repeat Step 12, moving down $1/4$". Knot ends together on inside cover to secure.

13. With remaining ribbon length, repeat Steps 11-12 for front cover, taking needle through $3/4$" button.

411

R&ck-a-Bye Baby Album

Supplies

12" x 12" scrapbook with post binding system

$^1/_2$ yd of pink chenille

$^1/_8$ yd of pink gingham

$^1/_8$ yd of dark pink print fabric

assorted white $^1/_2$" dia. buttons

$^1/_8$ yd of green printed fabric

polyester fiberfill

green embroidery floss

$2^1/_3$ yds of $^5/_8$"w green grosgrain ribbon

awl

liquid fray preventative

Instructions

1. Follow Steps 1-6 of Baby's First Album, page 410, to cover scrapbook with pink chenille.

2. For each flower, use pattern, page 422, to cut flower front and back from gingham.

3. With right sides together, sew flower front to flower back. Cutting through **only** one layer of fabric, cut a small slash in flower back. Turn flower right side out. Lightly stuff with fiberfill; hand sew opening closed.

4. For each flower center, cut a 3" dia. circle from dark pink fabric. Thread a needle with doubled thread. Finger press a $^1/_8$" hem and make running stitches around circle close to folded edge. Pull stitches tightly to close the center of the circle. Smooth and flatten circle with the hole in the center. Place circle in center of flower; secure by sewing a button through all layers.

5. Repeat Steps 2-3 with green fabric for leaves. Use embroidery floss to stitch a vein on each leaf.

6. Cut grosgrain ribbon into 3 equal lengths. Wrap lengths around front cover, twisting ribbon on front of cover and overlapping ends on inside of front cover. Secure ribbon ends by tacking a button through ribbon and fabric. Tack buttons at random along ribbon to hold pictures and notes.

7. Tack flowers and leaves along twisted ribbon on front cover.

413

Class Act
ALBUM

Supplies

6" x 6" white fabric album

poster board

scrapbook papers: plaid, denim, white flecked, and black

red alphabet stickers

school bus die-cut

Paperkins®

two $^3/_4$" dia. silver buttons

$1^1/_8$" x 1" x $^1/_2$" wooden apple

black extra-fine-point permanent marker

green ponytail holder

acrylic paints: white, green, and red

dimensional foam dots

craft glue

paintbrushes

Instructions

1. Cut a piece of poster board $^1/_4$" smaller on all sides than front of scrapbook. Cover with plaid paper, folding, pleating, and trimming corners as necessary. Center and glue covered poster board to front of scrapbook.

2. For school bus tires, cut two 1" dia. circles from black paper. Glue buttons to center of circles. Glue tires to school bus die-cut. Assemble Paperkins according to manufacturer's instructions. Glue the children's heads in the bus windows. Apply foam dots to the back of the bus and tires; adhere to scrapbook.

3. Cut a $2^3/_8$" x 6" piece of poster board. Cut a rectangle from center, creating a $^1/_2$"w frame. Cover frame with denim paper. Cut an "X" in paper over opening. Fold paper to back side of frame and glue in place. Glue a piece of white flecked paper to back of frame. Use alphabet stickers to add name to white paper. Glue frame to bottom of scrapbook.

4. Paint apple red. Paint the leaf and stem green. Add your child's age with white. Outline leaf and stem with black marker. Allow to dry; glue apple to scrapbook.

5. For closure, glue ponytail holder to inside back cover. When glue dries, loop ponytail holder around apple.

Terrific Teens
Album

Supplies

12" x 12" scrapbook with post binding system

1 ounce white Sculpey oven-bake clay

4" x 5" piece of balsa wood

three 1" wooden squares from Forster® Woodsies™

acrylic paints: gold, white, and black

scrapbook papers: purple, green, black, and striped

striped frame die-cut

purple alphabet stickers

scrap of lightweight purple velvet

craft glue

paintbrushes

toothpick or stylus

double-stick tape

Instructions

1. Separate parts of scrapbook; set pages aside.

2. For each cover, adding extra paper as necessary, tape together a piece of purple paper 1" larger on all sides than each cover.

3. Fold paper over the edges of the covers, folding, pleating, and trimming corners as necessary; glue to secure.

4. Cut two strips of striped paper 3"w and $^{1}/_{2}$" less than height of scrapbook. Center one strip of paper along side of front cover with 2" on front of cover and the rest wrapped to the back. Repeat to glue second strip to back cover.

5. Cut a strip of green paper 1"w and $^{1}/_{2}$" less than height of scrapbook. Glue next to striped paper on front cover.

6. Apply purple alphabet stickers to green strip.

7. Paint the balsa wood piece gold. Center and glue the die-cut frame on wood piece. Refer to photo, page 417, to glue wood in place on front cover.

8. Cover wooden squares with green paper and apply stickers. Glue to center of die-cut frame.

9. Cut team name out of velvet; glue above and below wood piece.

10. For soccer ball, knead the clay, roll into a ball, then flatten into a circle approximately $^3/_8$" thick. Use a small toothpick or stylus to draw outlines into ball. Bake according to manufacturer's instructions. Paint black and white; allow to dry, then glue to front cover.

11. Cut black paper into 1" x $^1/_8$" pieces for dashes. Refer to photo and glue in place.

12. Fold binding flap to inside of cover. Measure inside cover between outer edge and edge of folded flap. Cut two pieces of purple paper $^1/_2$" less than measurement and $^1/_2$" less than height.

13. Glue purple paper to inside covers of scrapbook. Cover spine of scrapbook with purple paper. Reassemble scrapbook.

A Joyous Christmas Album

Supplies

6" x 6" scrapbook

$^1/_3$ yd of maroon designer fabric

maroon acrylic paint

1 yd of $1^3/_8$"w sheer gold-edged ribbon

maroon cardstock

16mm gold bell

20" length of 20-gauge gold wire

4mm gold beads

$2^1/_2$" x 1" brass plate engraved with date or family name

needle-nose pliers

paintbrush

craft glue

maroon thread

Instructions

1. Separate parts of scrapbook; set pages aside.

2. Paint spine and inside flaps of scrapbook maroon; allow to dry.

3. Cut two 10" x 9" pieces of fabric. Turn raw edge of left side of each fabric piece under $^1/_2$" and glue to left edge of scrapbook covers.

4. Fold corners of fabric over corners of scrapbook; glue in place.

5. Fold and glue edges of fabric to inside edges of scrapbook.

6. For ties, cut ribbon length in half. Glue one end of each piece to center of inside front and back covers.

7. Measure inside cover. Cut two pieces of cardstock $^1/_2$" less than width and $^1/_2$" less than height.

8. Glue cardstock to inside covers of scrapbook. Reassemble scrapbook.

9. Thread beads onto wire; add bell to end of wire at top. Curl wire ends with pliers to secure. Use pliers to shape beaded wire into word using pattern, page 422.

10. Tack beaded word to scrapbook front.

11. Glue plate to center bottom of scrapbook front.

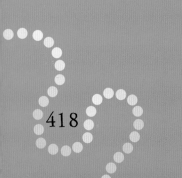

Your Family Heritage Album

Supplies

12" x 12" scrapbook with post binding system

$1/2$ yd of tapestry fabric

$3/8$ yd of faux suede

8" x 10" frame with a 4" x 6" opening

batting

1 yd of $5/8$"w gold woven trim

4 metal photo corners

awl

Two 2" tassels

heavy-duty thread

decorative button

$3/8$" dia. clear button

liquid fray preventative

fabric glue

poster board

Instructions

1. Separate parts of scrapbook; set pages aside.

2. For each cover, cut a piece of batting $1/2$" smaller on all sides than scrapbook covers.

3. Measure around frame. Cut an opening in batting for front cover $1/2$" larger than frame.

4. Glue batting to outside of scrapbook covers.

5. Center covers, batting side down, on the wrong side of tapestry fabric. Draw around covers; cut out 1" outside drawn line.

6. Cut an opening in front cover tapestry $1/2$" smaller on all sides than frame.

7. Center cover on tapestry piece. Glue front cover tapestry in place along edges of opening.

8. Make a clip in tapestry at inner fold of binding flap to $1/4$" from edge of cover at top and bottom of cover. Trim away tapestry along binding flap $1/4$" past edge of cover.

9. Pleating tapestry at corners as necessary, glue tapestry over edges of cover.

10. Cover spine of scrapbook with suede. Use awl to poke holes for posts through spine and binding flaps. Apply liquid fray preventative to raw edges of holes; allow to dry.

11. Fold binding flap to inside of cover. Measure inside cover between outer edge and edge of folded spine. Cut two pieces of poster board $1/2$" less than measurement and $1/2$" less than height.

12. Cut two pieces of faux suede 1" larger on all sides than poster board. Center one piece of poster board on wrong side of one piece of suede. Glue suede over corners of poster board. Glue remaining suede edges to poster board. Repeat with remaining poster board and suede.

13. With suede side up, glue covered poster board to inside covers of scrapbook. Reassemble scrapbook.

14. Glue woven trim around opening. Glue photo corners to outside corners of trim.

15. Place photo in frame; glue frame in opening.

16. Use awl to punch a small hole along center of right edge of back cover. Pull tassel cording through hole; then slip tassel through cording to secure.

17. Use awl to punch a small hole along center of right edge of front cover. Using heavy-duty thread, sew through decorative button and tassel cording, then through hole and clear button to secure.

patterns

A Joyous Christmas Album

Rock-a-Bye Baby Album

sources

SCRAPBOOKS

Hobby Lobby®
7707 SW 44th Street
Oklahoma City, OK 73179
www.hobbylobby.com

K & Company, LLC
8500 N. W. River Park Drive
Pillar #136
Parkville, MO 64152
(888) 244-2083
www.kandcompany.com

Perfect Fit Albums™
Making Memories
1168 West 500 North
Centerville, UT 84014
(801) 294-0430
www.makingmemories.com

Pioneer® E-Z Load Memory Book
Pioneer® Photo Albums, Inc.
P. O. Box 2497
Chatsworth, CA 91313
(818) 882-2161
www.pioneerphotoalbums.com

We R Memory Keepers, Inc.
P. O. Box 16509
Salt Lake City, UT 84116
(877) 742-5937
www.weronthenet.com

SUPPLIES

Memories in the Making®
  Denim Purple #61113
  Denim Green #61105
  Denim Stripe #61100
  Striped Frame Purple #66004
  Denim Alpha. Purple #64136

  Madras Plaid Yellow/Blue #61094
  Chambray Blue #61019
  Appliqué Alpha. Red #64021

Paperkins®
  Toddling Tina, Hiking Hayden, and
    Little Liza

S.E.I.
  Assorted jewel tone colored papers
  Coordinating striped paper tag

Stickopotamus®
  Framed flower

Mrs. Grossman's
  Green alphabet stickers

Sculpey
  Polymer clay

Metric Conversion Chart

Inches x 2.54 = centimeters (cm)
Inches x 25.4 = millimeters (mm)
Inches x .0254 = meters (m)

Yards x .9144 = meters (m)
Yards x 91.44 = centimeters (cm)
Centimeters x .3937 = inches (")
Meters x 1.0936 = yards (yd)

Standard Equivalents

1/8"	3.2 mm	0.32 cm	1/8 yard	11.43 cm	0.11 m
1/4"	6.35 mm	0.635 cm	1/4 yard	22.86 cm	0.23 m
3/8"	9.5 mm	0.95 cm	3/8 yard	34.29 cm	0.34 m
1/2"	12.7 mm	1.27 cm	1/2 yard	45.72 cm	0.46 m
5/8"	15.9 mm	1.59 cm	5/8 yard	57.15 cm	0.57 m
3/4"	19.1 mm	1.91 cm	3/4 yard	68.58 cm	0.69 m
7/8"	22.2 mm	2.22 cm	7/8 yard	80 cm	0.8 m
1"	25.4 mm	2.54 cm	1 yard	91.44 cm	0.91 m

IT'S ALL ABOUT
CARDS
& TAGS

The hottest trends and techniques for creating cards and tags for all occasions

a true friend
is a RARE
Blessing

miss yancy...

We have had so much fun designing *It's All About Cards & Tags*! As card makers and scrapbookers, how could we not enjoy the process of creating and selecting cards and tags from our exceptionally talented team of designers and submitters!

A hand made card is often a gift in itself—and most of us don't throw out a personalized card with the gift-wrap. Of all the cards and tags we could have featured on this page, we chose a card given to me by a very special neighborhood teenager with a quick wit and darling personality. It isn't the ornate quality of the paper or the use of design principles that makes me love this card; it's simply reflective of her fun personality. At 15 years old, her choice of combining a simple graphic with a grown up message is endearing. Cards such as these are treasures that become part of my "save forever" collection of memorabilia!

From simple to complex, we have chosen a variety of examples you can gather ideas from or "lift" onto your own cards and tags. Design tips, creative ideas, techniques and step-by-step processes have been included to assist in improving your card making skills.

Added features are our template and sentiment sections. The templates can be copied or traced to make cards, tags, envelopes and boxes, and for those of us who are truly at a "loss for words" our quotes can be copied for use right on your cards!

So, from all of us at NanC and Company to all of you who enjoy expressing yourself through handmade cards and tags – ENJOY!

Nancy

Nancy M. Hill

Table of Contents

Expressions of Friendship

A True Friend

Designer: Bea Elizalde

SUPPLIES Cardstock: DCWV • Patterned
Paper: The Paper Co., Memories in
the Making • Stickers: NRN Designs •

Eyelets: Making Memories

Beyond Basics

Create a matching envelope to go with your card.
This shows the recipient you have taken extra
time to make the note thoughtful.

Bamboo Card

Designer: Brenda Nakandakari

SUPPLIES Stamp: Hero Arts
• Adhesive: Hermafix

Asian Gift Bag

NanC and Campany Design

SUPPLIES Cardstock:
DCWV • Ribbon: Offray
& Son, Inc. • Charm:
Memories in the Making

CREATE A MINI BOOKLET

1. Cut a thin piece of cardboard into a rectangle (7 1/8 x 3 1/4 inches).
2. Fold the cardboard in half.
3. Cut a patterned piece of paper 1 inch longer and 1 inch wider than the cardboard.
4. Place the patterned paper right side down on a table.
5. Apply adhesive to the wrong side of the patterned paper.
6. Center the rectangular piece of cardboard onto the patterned paper with the point of the fold facing down.
7. Smooth the paper onto the cardboard.
8. Fold the excess paper to the inside, miter the corners, and adhere.
9. Cut a sheet of cardstock into three rectangles (6 1/4 x 2 7/8 inches).
10. Fold the rectangles in half.
11. Adhere the first half of the first cardstock rectangle to the inside of the front cover with the point of the fold facing down.
12. Adhere the second half of the first rectangle to the first half of the second rectangle with both points of the folds facing down.
13. Continue adhering the pages together in this manner.
14. Finish by adhering the wrong side of the second half of the last rectangle to the inside back cover of the booklet.

Change the dimensions of the booklet to meet your needs. You can also add more pages by cutting more rectangles of cardstock.

harmony

Asian Booklet

Designer: Brenda Nakandakari

SUPPLIES Mini Scrapbook: Pixie
Press • Stamp: Stampin' Up •
Ink Pad: Colorbok

431

Template on page 58

Forever Friends

Template Design: Phyllis Ducote
NanC and Company Design

SUPPLIES   Cardstock: DCWV •
Vellum Quote: DCWV • Stickers:
Memories in the Making • Button:
Making Memories • Small Flower
Embellishment: Jolee's Boutique

Flowers

NanC and Company Design

SUPPLIES A2 Card: DCWV • Metal Letters:
Making Memories • Felt Embellishments:
Jolee's Boutique

432

Best Friends

Designer: Camille Jensen

SUPPLIES Cardstock: Bazzill • Watermark
Pad: Versamark by Tsukineko • Brads: Lasting
Impressions for Paper • Embellishment:
Carolee's Creations

Friends are a Gift from God

Designer: Brindy Adams

SUPPLIES Cardstock: DCWV, Bazzill • Patterned
Paper: Memories in the Making • Vellum: DCWV •
Stamp: Stampin' Up • Ink Pad: Stampin' Up

Friends

Designer: Bea Elizalde

SUPPLIES Patterned Paper: Creative Memories •
Die Cuts: Sizzix • Button: Making Memories •
Metallic Accents: DCWV

Keeping in Touch

I Miss You

Designer: Miranda Isenberg

SUPPLIES Card Template: Deluxe Cuts
• Cardstock: Creative Imaginations •
Scrabble Tiles: Making Memories •
Eyelet Letter: Making Memories • Heart
Embellishments: Sarah Heidt Photo Craft
• Button: Dress It Up! • True Love Cut
Out: SEI • Charms: Embellish It!

434

Tried & True Technique

THEMED COLLAGE

Creating a themed collage is a great way to make a card. Use
many different mediums (paper, stickers, beads, charms,
buttons, metals, thread, fabric) to create the look you love.

Just Bee Yourself

Designer: Bea Elizalde

SUPPLIES Cardstock: DCWV
• Patterned Paper: DCWV,
Frances Meyer, Inc. • Bee
Stamps: Great Impressions,
Rubber Stamps, Inc., Rubber
Stampede, Stampabilities •
Font: Jenn Penn

Beyond Basics

Make a tag to match your card.
This is a great way to enhance a
simply wrapped gift.

Bee Tag

Designer: Bea Elizalde

SUPPLIES Cardstock: DCWV
• Patterned Paper: Frances
Meyer, Inc. • Stamp: Rubber
Stampede

Flower Card

Designer: Susan Stringfellow

SUPPLIES Patterned Paper: Memories
in the Making • Ink Pad: Stampin'
Up • Adhesive: Judikins • Flower
Embellishment: ScrapYard 329

If I had a rose for every time I thought of you, I'd walk through a garden forever.

Autumn Wreath

Designer: Bea Elizalde

SUPPLIES Cardstock: DCWV • Stamp: Anna Griffin

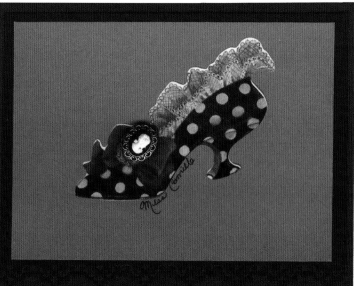

Miss Camille

Designer: Bea Elizalde

SUPPLIES A2 Card: DCWV • Sticker: Colorbok • Border Punch: Fiskars

delight in beauty

Delight in Beauty

Designer: Phyllis Ducote

SUPPLIES Paper: The Crafter's Workshop • Title: Magic Scraps • Fiber: Ties That Bind • Buttons: SEI • Punch: EK Success

CREATE A POTPOURRI CARD AND TAG

1. Cut out a window in a card or tag for the potpourri to show through the card.
2. Trace and cut the same window out of a second card or tag.
3. Cut a sheer ribbon or fabric to just over double the size of the window.
4. Fold fabric in half and sew two sides to create a pocket.
5. Fill the pocket with flowers, potpourri, seeds or whatever you can imagine.
6. Sew the top closed.
7. Sew, hand stitch, tape or adhere the potpourri pocket to the backside of the window.
8. Adhere the second card or tag to cover your handiwork. If the card is too bulky, cut off the back half of the first card. For variation, cut an oval, rectangular or circular window, or cut multiple small windows. You can also stitch a pocket of potpourri to the front of a card without the window.

Flower Potpourri
NanC and Campany Design

SUPPLIES   A2 Card: DCWV •
Floss: Making Memories • Pressed
Flowers: Nature's Pressed

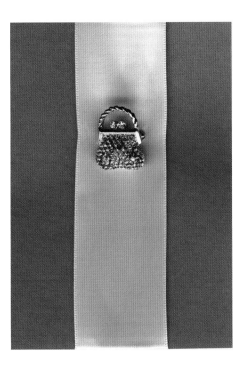

Purse
NanC and Company Design

SUPPLIES   Double
Dipped Cardstock:
DCWV • Ribbon:
Offray & Son, Inc.
• Purse Charm:
Austrian Crystal

Thinking of You
Designer: Susan Stringfellow

SUPPLIES   Patterned Paper:
Karen Foster Design, NRN
Designs • Stamps: Stampin'
Up • Ink Pad: Versamark by
Tsukineko • Mesh: Magic Mesh
• Chalks: Craf-T Products
• Wire: Artistic Wire Ltd. •
Brad: Making Memories

Memorable Moments

Flowers

Designer: Bea Elizalde

SUPPLIES Flower Stamps: Hero Arts Rubber Stamps, Inc. • Dot Stamps: Stamps by Judith

Way to Go

Designer: Brindy Adams

SUPPLIES Cardstock: DCWV • Patterned Paper: Memories in the Making • Stamps: Stampin' Up • Ink Pad: Stampin' Up • Floss: Making Memories

Design Tip

Color a stamp with different color inkpads. Stamp a second time (without re-inking) just to the side of the original stamp to create a shadow.

Lantern

Designer: Camille Jensen

SUPPLIES Mulberry Paper: DCWV • Patterned Paper: Memories in the Making • Ink Pad: Stampa Rosa

Tried & True Technique

WATER COLORING

Embellish your card with watercolors for a unique look that is simple to create. Just stamp with a watercolor stamp pad onto watercolor paper and watercolor.

Dare to Dream

Designer: Krista Fernandez

SUPPLIES Cardstock: Paper Adventures • Patterned Paper: Making Memories • Tag Template: Deluxe Cuts • Slide Mount: ScrapWorks 329 • Star Embellishments: Making Memories, Emagination Crafts Inc. • Letters: 7 Gypsies • Eyelets: Making Memories • Ribbon: Offray & Son, Inc. • Font: Doodle Cursive

Sandals

NanC and Campany Design

SUPPLIES A2 Card: DCWV • Floss: Making Memories • Sandal Embellishments: Marcel Schurman Collection

Design Tip

Use pop dots to make the letters in the middle of the slide mount the same height as the letters attached to the slide mount.

Terms of Endearment

with all my heart...

With All My Heart
Designer: Bea Elizalde
SUPPLIES Double Sided Cardstock: Making
Memories • Rub-ons: Making Memories •
Floss: Making Memories

440

You Hold the Key to My Heart

Designer: Miranda Isenberg

SUPPLIES Tag: SEI • Scrabble Tiles: Making Memories • Eyelet Letters: Making Memories • Sticker: SEI • Dog Tag: Clare Ultimo Inc. • Charm: Embellish It!

the more you give away, the more you have.

Believe

Designer: Tonia Borrosch

SUPPLIES Patterned Paper: Provo Craft, Daisy D's Paper Co. • Definition: Making Memories • Heart Vellum Tag: Making Memories • Ink: Making Memories Love Circle Embellishment: Keeping Memories Alive

Bryan

Designer: Camille Jensen

SUPPLIES Patterned Paper: Memories in the Making • Letters: Memories in the Making

I Love You

Designer: Krista Fernandez

SUPPLIES Patterned Paper: Making Memories • Punches: EK Success • Pen: ZIG by EK Success • Metal Rimmed Tag: Making Memories • Heart Shaped Clip: Making Memories • Ribbon: Offray & Son, Inc.

Love, Love, Love

Designer: Susan Stringfellow

SUPPLIES Tag Template: Deluxe Cuts • Rubber Stamp: All Night Media • Key Rubber Stamp: Stampabilities • Heart Rubber Stamp: Stampin' Up • Ink: Stampin' Up • Fibers: Fibers by the Yard • Gold Cord: Westrim Crafts • Gold Beads: Westrim Crafts • Glass Beads: All The Extras • Fonts: Black Jack Regular, Scriptina, Spring, Pegsanna, Mariah Regular, Ancient

I Love You . . .

Designer: Brindy Adams

SUPPLIES Cardstock: DCWV • Patterned Paper: Memories in the Making • Mulberry Paper: DCWV • Stamps: Stampin' Up • Ink Pad: Stampin' Up

You're Invited

Baby Shower

Designer: Brande Juber

SUPPLIES A2 Card: DCWV • Cardstock: DCWV • Patterned Paper: Memories in the Making

Tried & True Technique

CREATE A TORN AND CURLED WINDOW

1. Tear the opening in the paper smaller than the finished size of the window to allow for curling.
2. Snip the corners to the finished size with scissors.
3. Curl the edges by dampening the paper with water and curling back with your fingers.
4. When the paper dries the curl will remain.

444

House Warming

Designer: Camille Jensen

SUPPLIES Cardstock: DCWV •
Patterned Paper: Memories in the
Making • Stamp: Magenta Rubber
Stamps • Key Chain: Memories in
the Making • Floss: DMC • Font:
CK Sloppy

You're Invited

Designer: Camille Jensen

SUPPLIES Patterned Paper: Memories in the Making • Metal Tags: DCWV
• Round Metal Tag: Making Memories • Metal Stamps: Foofala • Brads:
All My Memories • Eyelets: Making Memories • Floss: DMC • Paper Tags:
Memories in the Making • Stickers: Memories in the Making

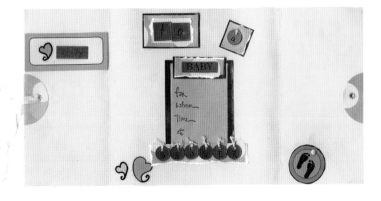

Design Tip

If you are nervous about ruining a card by
making a mistake with your handwriting,
use a transparency. You can practice your
handwriting until you get it right or you
can use a computer font and print onto a
transparency. The transparency will fade
away into the background of the card.

All Aboard . . .

NanC and Company Design

SUPPLIES A2 Card: DCWV •
Ribbon: Making Memories

445

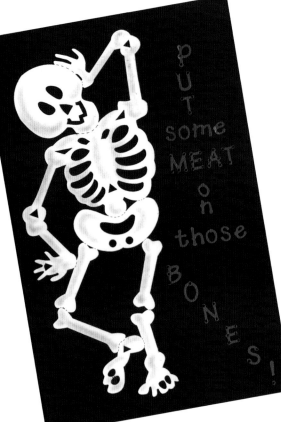

Put Some Meat on Those Bones

Designer: Eleanor Howse

SUPPLIES Cardstock: DCWV •
Stickers: Frances Meyer, Inc. •
Die Cut: Deluxe Cuts

Beyond Basics

A fun die cut can make an invitation a snap to create.

446

Shhhhhh . . .

Designer: Camille Jensen

SUPPLIES   Patterned Paper: Memories in
the Making • Stamp: PSX Design • Frame:
DCWV • Star: DCWV • Oil Pastels: Crayola
• Circle Tags: Making Memories • Paper
Wire: DMD Industries

Tried & True Technique

HOW TO USE CRYSTAL LACQUER

1. Squeeze crystal lacquer onto the area to be highlighted.
2. Let sit for three hours to dry.

Day at the Park

Designer: Miranda Isenberg

SUPPLIES   Border Sticker: Memories in
the Making • Brads: Making Memories

What a beautiful day
to spend at the park
for a picnic
or a ride
down the slide
I'll go around and around
and high on the swing
It's so fun
when we're playing outside.

Mums the Word

Designer: Maridawn Mayer

SUPPLIES   Letters: EK
Success • Circle Tags: EK
Success

447

Wedding & Anniversary

Angel

NanC and Company Design

SUPPLIES Thread: Sulky
of America • Pocket Angel:
Vilmaine

Wreath

NanC and Company Design

SUPPLIES   A2 Card: DCWV • Stamp:
Provo Craft • Embossing Pad: Tsukineko
• Embossing Powder: Ranger Industries •
Ribbon: Offray & Son, Inc.

448

Bride and Groom

Designer: Jenny Sanders

SUPPLIES Cardstock: Walmart • Patterned Paper: Treehouse Designs, Inc.

Love Bag

NanC and Company Design

SUPPLIES Page Pebbles: Making Memories

Beyond Basics

Try folding a card differently so the opening is in the middle of the front of the card.

Tried & True Technique

HEAT EMBOSSING

1. Press a rubber stamp onto an embossing stamp pad.
2. Press the stamp onto the paper you wish to emboss.
3. Cover the stamped area of the paper with embossing powder.
4. Shake off the excess powder.
5. With an embossing gun heat the embossing powder on the paper until the consistency changes from a powder to a smooth finish.

Use an embossing pen to write letters or draw your own pictures to be heat embossed.

Silver Pattern

NanC and Company Design

SUPPLIES A2 Card: DCWV • Stamp: Stampendous! • Embossing Pad: Tsukineko • Embossing Powder: Ranger Industries

Cards of Gratitude

Thank You

Designer: Bea Elizalde

SUPPLIES   Card: The Paper Co. •
Cardstock: DCWV • Patterned Paper:
DCWV • Brads: Making Memories •
Stamp: Hero Arts • Flower Punch: Marvy
Uchida • Small Flowers: EK Success

Thank You

NanC and Company Design

SUPPLIES   A2 Card: DCWV •
Beads: Bluemoon Beads

Design Tip

Beads are a wonderful embellishment
for cards and tags. They can be sewn
on with a needle and thread or, for a
faster result, glued on.

Thanks

Designer: Maridawn Mayer

SUPPLIES Patterned Paper: DCWV •
Page Pebble Letters: Making Memories

Thank You

NanC and Company Design

SUPPLIES A2 Card: DCWV •
Papers: DCWV, Memories in the
Making • Metal Letters: DCWV

Thanks

NanC and Company Design

SUPPLIES A2 Card: DCWV • Wire Letters:
Making Memories • Ribbon Charm:
Making Memories

451

Cards of Gratitude

Thank You

Designer: Brindy Adams

SUPPLIES Brad: Making Memories • Button: Making Memories • Chalk: Stampin' Up

Thank You

Designer: Camille Jensen

SUPPLIES Cardstock: DCWV • Patterned Paper: DCWV • Metal Letters: DCWV • Metal Words: DCWV • Brads: Lasting Impressions for Paper • Charm Embellishments: Making Memories

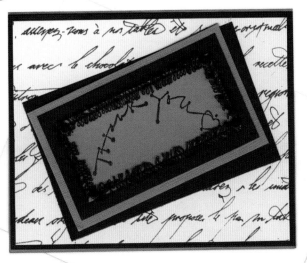

Beyond Basics

Create pockets for tags to fit into on your card. The receiver can pull out the tags to read individual messages.

Thank You

Designer: Maridawn Mayer

SUPPLIES Patterned Paper: DCWV • Stamp: Stampin' Up • Fiber: Ties That Bind

452

Thanks

Designer: Amanda Goodwin

SUPPLIES Cardstock: Keeping
Memories Alive • Pens: EK
Success • Embossing Powder:
UTEE by Ranger • Butterfly
Sticker: Colorbok

Tried & True Technique

ACCENT A STICKER WITH ULTRA THICK EMBOSSING ENAMEL (UTEE)

1. Affix a sticker to cardstock and trim around the sticker.
2. Rub the right side of the sticker on an embossing pad.
3. Cover with UTEE and shake off the excess powder.
4. With an embossing gun heat the UTEE until the consistency changes from a powder to a smooth, shiny finish.
5. Repeat steps two through four until the sticker shines to your liking.

Alter embellishments, accent words, or just add shine to your pages with UTEE.

Thank You Tag

Designer: Bea Elizalde

SUPPLIES Patterned Paper: The Paper Co. •
Stamp: Hero Arts • Flower Punch: Marvy Uchida
• Buttons: Making Memories • Brads: Making
Memories • Wire: Making Memories

Mini Thank You

Designer: Camille Jensen

SUPPLIES Patterned Paper: Memories
in the Making • Page Pebble: Making
Memories • Font: CK Sloppy

Thanks

Designer: Sheila Hansen

SUPPLIES A2 Card: DCWV
• Patterned Paper: Memories
in the Making • Button
Stickers: Memories in the
Making • Alphabet Stickers:
Provo Craft • Denim Pocket
Die Cut: Memories in the
Making • Tags: Pebbles in
my Pocket

New Arrival

Baa

NanC and Company Design

SUPPLIES A2 Card: DCWV •
Thread: Making Memories

Tried & True
Technique

HOW TO STITCH LETTERS

1. Print or handwrite letters the same size as you would like to stitch on a piece of paper.
2. Temporarily adhere the paper to your card or tag over the area to be stitched.
3. With a needle punch holes along the letters.
4. Remove the paper after all the holes have been punched.
5. Back stitch along the holes.

You can stitch designs in the same fashion as the letters. If you would like to add beads or other embellishments to the stitches, just thread a bead on the needle when the needle is positioned at the front side of the card.

454

It's a Boy

Designer: Bea Elizalde

SUPPLIES Card: The Paper Co. • Metallic
Letters: DCWV • Rub-ons: Making Memories •
Brads: Making Memories

B is for Boy

Designer: Maureen Spell

SUPPLIES Cardstock: Bazzill • Patterned Paper:
SEI • Die Cuts: Quickutz • Buttons: Dress It
Up! • Pen: ZIG by EK Success • Fibers: Fibers
by the Yard • Ink: All Night Media • Eyelet:
Making Memories

Tried & True Technique

INKING

Ink gives a weathered look to a card or just takes
away that brand new feel. To ink a card, tag or
embellishment gently rub the edges and center
with an ink pad.

Of all nature's gifts
to the human race,
what is sweeter to a man
than his **children**?

Blue

NanC and Company Design

SUPPLIES A2 Card: DCWV • Ribbon:
Offray & Son. Inc.

455

Happy New Baby

Designer: Camille Jensen

SUPPLIES   Paper: Memories in the Making • Metal Frame: DCWV • Flower: Dress It Up!

Mini Happy New Baby

Designer: Camille Jensen

SUPPLIES   Paper: Memories in the Making

Beyond Basics

Create mini cards and tags from your scraps. They are fun to give and receive.

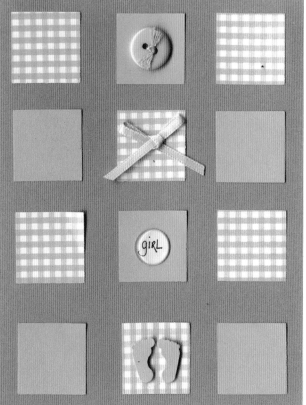

Sugar & Spice

Designer: Susan Stringfellow

SUPPLIES   Cardstock: Bazzill • Tag Template: Deluxe Cuts • Ink: Stampin' Up • Thread: Coats & Clark • Fibers: Fibers by the Yard • Ribbon Pinwheel: Offray & Son, Inc. • Flower: Dress It Up! • Embossed Vellum: K & Company • Charms: Westrim Crafts • Glass Beads: All The Extras • Brad: Magic Scraps • Diamond Glaze Adhesive: Judikins • Font: Scriptina

Girl

Designer: Melissa Deakin

SUPPLIES   Patterned Paper: Making Memories • Page Pebble: Making Memories • Punch: Marvy Uchida • Button: Dress It Up! • Ribbon: Offray & Son, Inc.

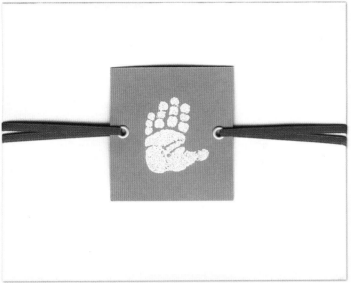

Handprint

NanC and Company Design

SUPPLIES   A2 Card: DCWV • Cardstock:
DCWV • Stamp: Inkadinkado • Embossing
Pad: Tsukineko • Embossing Powder: Ranger
Industries • Eyelets: Making Memories •
Ribbon: Offray & Son, Inc. • Tag – Floss: Two
Busy Moms • Metal Embellishment: Memories
in the Making

Lion

NanC and Company Design

SUPPLIES A2 Card: DCWV • Cardstock:
DCWV • Label: DCWV • Wire Accent:
Pier 1 Imports

Beyond Basics

Crimp paper, cardstock or embellishments
to add texture and interest to your cards
and tags. To crimp, simply run paper
through a crimping machine.

Ducks

NanC and Company Design
SUPPLIES A2 Card:
DCWV • Cardstock:
DCWV

457

Mother's Day

Mother

NanC and Company Design

SUPPLIES A2 Card:
DCWV • Thread:
Making Memories

Tried & True
Technique

CREATE TASSELS WITH BEADS AND FLOSS

1. Wrap embroidery floss around a card or tag.

2. Separate the strands of the floss to make more tassels.

3. With a needle, thread the beads onto the floss.

4. To secure the beads, loop the floss through the last bead and tie a knot.

5. Have the beads fall to different heights and trim off the excess floss.

Mothers

Designer: Camille Jensen

SUPPLIES Cardstock: DCWV
• Patterned Paper: Memories
in the Making • Page Pebble:
Making Memories • Button:
Making Memories • Ribbon:
Offray & Son, Inc.

Mother

NanC and Company Design

SUPPLIES A2 Card: DCWV • Metallic
Frames: DCWV • Buttons: Making
Memories • Ribbon: Offray & Son, Inc.

Beyond Basics

Embellish a card with coordinating tags.

#1 Mom

Designer: Ashley Smith

SUPPLIES A2 Card: DCWV • Tag:
DCWV • Beads: Me & My Big Ideas

459

Father's Day

Dad Gift and Card

NanC and Company Design

SUPPLIES Cardstock: DCWV • Ribbon
Offray & Son, Inc.

Tried & True
Technique

CONVERTING COLOR PHOTOS TO BLACK AND WHITE OR SEPIA

1. If the photo is not digital, scan it.
2. Open the photo in a photo manipulation software program.
3. Change the image from color to black and white or sepia.

4. Save the new image.
5. Print the image.

This is a useful technique if a black and white photo will compliment the theme of your card or tag.

RLB

NanC and Company Design

SUPPLIES A2 Card: DCWV • Metal
Letters: Making Memories

Design Tip

Don't throw away your scraps! They
can be paper pieced to create wonderful
cards and tags.

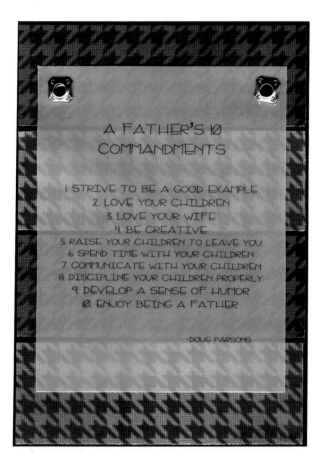

Happy Fathers Day

Designer: Camille Jensen

SUPPLIES A2 Card: DCWV • Cardstock: DCWV • Patterned
Paper: Memories in the Making • Letter Stickers: Memories
in the Making • Brads: Lasting Impressions for Paper •
Circle Tag: Making Memories

A Father's 10 Commandments

Designer: Miranda Isenberg

SUPPLIES Patterned Paper: Memories in
the Making • Eyelets: Making Memories •
Font: Two Peas in a Bucket Architect

461

Valentine's Day

2004

NanC and Company Design

SUPPLIES Cardstock: DCWV • Patterned Paper: Memories in the Making • Vellum Quote: DCWV • Metal Letters: Making Memories

Bee Mine

Designer: Miranda Isenberg

SUPPLIES Letter Stickers: Creative Imaginations • Diecut: Quickutz

Button Heart

NanC and Company Design

SUPPLIES Cardstock: DCWV • Buttons: ScrapArts • Thread: Two Busy Moms

Tried & True Technique

MACHINE STITCHING

1. Make sure your machine is properly threaded.
2. Always practice on a scrap piece of paper of the same thickness you will be stitching on for your card or tag.
3. Adjust the tension or needle as necessary.
4. It may be helpful to temporarily adhere what you will be stitching so there won't be any movement as you stitch.
5. Stitch your card or tag.

Easter Egg

NanC and Company Design

SUPPLIES Cardstock: DCWV •
Wire: Making Memories

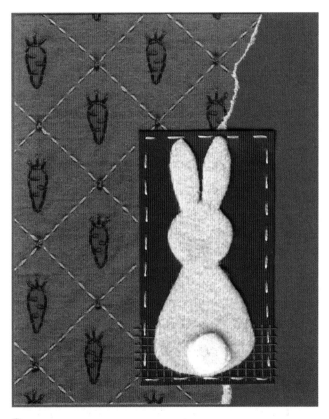

Design Tip

Use different fabrics and materials when
making cards and tags. The textures
add interest to the card or tag. Many
different materials can be used: felt, velvet,
corduroy, linen, satin and cheesecloth.

Bunny

Designer: Susan Stringfellow

SUPPLIES Patterned Paper: Daisy D's Paper Co. • Velveteen Fabric:
Hancock Fabrics • Floss: DMC • Mesh: Magic Mesh

Easter Tag

NanC and Company Design

SUPPLIES Tag: DCWV • Wire: Making
Memories • Metal Embellishment:
Making Memories • Button: Making
Memories • Thread: Making Memories
• Ribbon: Offray & Son, Inc.

Fourth of July

Red, White and Blue

NanC and Company Design

SUPPLIES   A2 Card: DCWV •
Cardstock: DCWV • Star Buttons:
Making Memories

Freedom Tag

NanC and Company Design

SUPPLIES   Tag: DCWV •
Buttons: Making Memories •
Floss: Making Memories

464

Tried & True Technique

THE MANY WAYS TO USE MICRO BEADS

1. Double sided tape —dip a cut
    piece of tape into a bag of
    micro beads to coat the adhesive
    side of the tape. Then remove
    the protective paper to reveal
    the second adhesive side.
    Adhere to your card or tag.
2. Glue — apply glue to the area
    where the micro beads will go.
    Sprinkle the wet glue with the
    micro beads. Allow the glue to
    dry.
3. Watch crystal — fill a watch
    crystal with micro beads and
    adhere to your card or tag.
4. Shadow box — fill a shadow box
    with micro beads and attach the
    shadow box to your card or tag.

Boo

Designer: Susan Stringfellow

SUPPLIES Patterned Paper: Provo Craft •
Embossing Powder: Stamps 'n' Stuff • Circle
Clip: Making Memories • Stickers: Bo-Bunny
Press, All The Extras • Fibers: Fibers by the
Yard • Eyelet: BagWorks Inc. • Foam Tape:
Magic Mounts

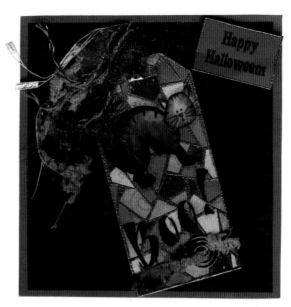

Pumpkins

NanC and Company Design

SUPPLIES Cardstock: DCWV, Bazzill • Metal
Word: DCWV • Floss: All My Memories, Daisy
D's Paper Co. • Eyelet: Making Memories

Happy Halloween

Designer: Brenda Nakandakari

SUPPLIES Tag Template: Deluxe Cuts •
Adhesive: Hermafix • Bat: Sizzix • Chalk:
Craf-T Products • Font: Horror

Tried & True
Technique

CREATE A MOSAIC LOOK WITH PATTERNED PAPER AND EMBOSSING POWDER

1. Cover a tag with two-way glue.
2. Cut patterned paper into shapes.
3. Place shapes onto glued tag, leaving space in-between each shape.
4. Sprinkle tag with embossing powder and shake off the excess powder.
5. With an embossing gun heat the embossing powder until the consistency changes from a powder to a smooth finish.

Enhance any embellishment or paper with embossing powder.

Thanksgiving

A Season of Change

Designer: Bea Elizalde

SUPPLIES   Double Sided Cardstock: The Paper Co. • Rub-ons: Making Memories

Give Thanks

Designer: Bea Elizalde

SUPPLIES   Double Sided Cardstock: The Paper Co. • Rub-ons: Making Memories • Wreath: Jolee's Boutique • Leaf Border Punch: Fiskars

Design Tip

If you don't like the look of your handwriting or would like a variety of lettering, use rub-ons as a fast and easy alternative.

Shalom

Designer: Camille Jensen

SUPPLIES   Cardstock: DCWV • Letter
Stencil: Words Worth Stamps • Snowflakes:
Provo Craft • Metal: Art Emboss • Prisma
Glitter: Close To My Heart

Shalom Box

Designer: Camille Jensen

SUPPLIES   Brush Marker:
Tombow • Brads: Lasting
Impressions for Paper •
Metal Letters: DCWV

Template on page 488

Tried & True
Technique

METAL EMBOSSING

1. Buy sheets of metal that can
   be embossed.
2. Trace or draw your own design
   on the metal or place a pattern
   onto the sheet of metal.
3. Trace the pattern with a stylus
   or, for a fuller look, the eraser
   of a pencil.
4. Cut the pattern or design out
   and attach to a card or tag.

You can simply cut the metal,
cut out letters, or even use your
punches on the metal (if it is soft
enough) for a nice embellishment
to a card or tag.

Happy Hanukkah

Designer: Camille Jensen

SUPPLIES   Cardstock: DCWV • Patterned Paper:
DCWV • Stamp: Hero Arts • Sparkle Powder: All
Night Media • Adhesive: Xyron Machine • Gold
Vellum: DCWV • Prisma Glitter: Close To My Heart

Christmas Joy

Designer: RoseMarie Sutton

SUPPLIES Card: The Paper Co.
• Paper: Bo-Bunny Press, Hobby
Lobby • Stamp: Inkadinkado

Beyond Basics

Stamp a pattern onto a die cut.

Happy Holidays

Designer: Brindy Adams

SUPPLIES A2 Card: DCWV • Cardstock:
DCWV • Stamps: Stampin' Up • Ink Pad:
Stampin' Up • Floss: Making Memories

Beyond Basics

Use a border punch with double
sided cardstock to have the
second color show through to
the front of a card.

Christmas Tree Tag

Designer: Miranda Isenberg

SUPPLIES Mosaic Tiles: Sarah
Heidt Photo Craft

Oh Christmas Tree

Designer: Bea Elizalde

SUPPLIES Double Sided Cardstock:
The Paper Co. • Mulberry Paper:
DCWV • Border Punch: Fiskars •
Font: Script

469

Do You See What I See?

Designer: Susan Stringfellow

SUPPLIES Patterned Paper: Memories in the Making • Snowflake Vellum: Memories in the Making • Stamp: Close To My Heart • Eyelets: All The Extras • Mesh: Magic Mesh

Snow

Designer: Susan Stringfellow

SUPPLIES Patterned Paper: Memories in the Making • Sticker: Memories in the Making • Punch: Marvy Uchida • Foam Tape: Magic Mounts • Wire: Artistic Wire Ltd. • Glitter: Creative Beginnings • Ribbon: Offray & Son, Inc.

Twelve Days of Christmas

Designer: Susan Stringfellow

SUPPLIES   Stamps: Stampin' Up • Ink: Stampin' Up • Fibers: Fibers by the Yard • Gold Mesh: Hancock Fabrics • Eyelets: All The Extras • Diamond Glaze Adhesive: Judikins

Beyond Basics

Making a tag for each of the twelve days of Christmas is a wonderful idea. They can be used on each page of a mini book or can be attached to a gift, especially if you are doing the twelve days of Christmas for a friend or neighbor.

Christmas

How to Dry Emboss Vellum

1. Place vellum on a soft surface like a mouse pad.
2. Position a stencil under the vellum.
3. Using a stylus, trace the stencil or create your own design, being careful not to push too hard.
4. Use either side of the embossed vellum.

Try dry embossing on cardstock and other papers.

Silver Pattern

Designer: Ashley Smith

SUPPLIES A2 Card: DCWV • Cardstock: DCWV

Snowman Tag

Designer: Stacy Frandsen

SUPPLIES Snowman Template: Making Memories • Stamp: Stampin' Up • Glitter: Stampin' Up • Glue Pen: ZIG by EK Success

Merry Christmas from Our Home to Yours

Designer: Leah Fung

SUPPLIES Patterned Paper: Making Memories • Corrugated Cardboard: DMD Industries • Eyelets: Making Memories • Holly Vine Wire: Westrim Crafts • Font: CK Chemistry

Happy Holidays

Designer: Ashley Smith

SUPPLIES A2 Card: DCWV • Cardstock: DCWV • Stamps: Hero Arts • Brads: Making Memories • Charms: Jolee's Boutique

Birthday Wishes

Happy Birthday
To You

Designer: Camille Jensen

Supplies A2 Card: DCWV • Patterned
Paper: Memories in the Making •
Thread: Coats & Clark

Design Tip

Use items you wouldn't
expect to find on a card or
tag. For example: a candle,
a page from a children's
book or jewelry.

Birthday Tags

Designer: Susan Stringfellow

SUPPLIES Patterned Paper: Memories in the Making • Letter Stickers: Memories in the Making: Mesh: Magic Mesh • Stamp: Hero Arts • Ink: Stampin' Up • Fibers: Fibers by the Yard • Foam Tape: Magic Mounts

Make a Wish

Designer: Camille Jensen

SUPPLIES Cardstock: Bazzill, DCWV • Stamp: Rubber Stampede • Eyelets: Making Memories

Design Tip

Use a variety of threads and fibers to embellish cards and tags.

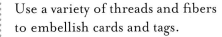

Happy Birthday

Designer: Jenny Sanders

SUPPLIES Cardstock: Walmart • Glue: Mono by Tombow

PAPER TEARING

Tearing paper is one of the most often used techniques in card and tag making. To have more control when you tear your paper, wet the area of the paper you want to tear and tear while the paper is still wet.

Happy Birthday

Designer: Maridawn Mayer

SUPPLIES Patterned Paper: Bazzill • Stamp: Stampin' Up

Candle

Designer: Miranda Isenberg

SUPPLIES A2 Card: DCWV • Cardstock: DCWV • Patterned Paper: Paper Adventures • Candle Die Cut: Sizzix • Font: DJ Squared

Happy Boo? Day

Designer: Miranda Isenberg

SUPPLIES Card Template: Deluxe Cuts • Cardstock: Creative Imaginations • Buttons: Dress It Up! • Ladybug Charm: Embellish It!

Happy Birthday, Dad

Designer: Sheila Toppi

SUPPLIES Cardstock: Bazzill • Patterned Paper: Rebecca Sower, PSX Design • Paper Frame: Provo Craft • Buttons: Dress It Up! • Stamps: PSX Design • Cork: Hygloss Products, Inc. • Ink: Brilliance by Tsukineko • Floss: DMC • Adhesive: Xyron, ZIG by EK Success

Tried & True Technique

HOW TO WALNUT INK

1. Mix walnut crystals with water according to package directions.
2. Apply walnut ink with a brush, q-tip or cotton ball.
3. Allow ink to dry.

There are other ways to accomplish an aged look: ink, crumpled paper, chalk or tea dye.

Wanted: Cool Hand Jake

Designer: Camille Jensen

SUPPLIES Patterned Paper: Karen Foster Design, Memories in the Making • Stamps: Hero Arts • Ink Pad: Staz-on by Tsukineko • Walnut Ink: 7 Gypsies • Horse Charm: Memories in the Making

Susan

Designer: Sheila Hansen

SUPPLIES A2 Card: DCWV • Patterned Paper: Memories in the Making • Sticker: Memories in the Making

475

Health & Happiness

Herbs

NanC and Company Design

SUPPLIES A2 Card: DCWV

Bee Happy

Designer: Bea Elizalde

SUPPLIES Double Dipped Cardstock:
DCWV • Alphabitties: Provo Craft •
Bee Stamp: Great Impressions Rubber
Stamps Inc.

Bouquet of Flowers

Designer: Bea Elizalde

SUPPLIES Cardstock: Bazzill • Punches:
EK Success • Beads: Making Memories

Flower

Designer: Susan Stringfellow

SUPPLIES Patterned Paper: NRN Designs • Die Cut:
NRN Designs • Stamps: Hero Arts • Border Stickers:
NRN Designs • Ribbon: All The Extras • Ink: Stampin'
Up • Glitter: Creative Beginnings

Beyond Basics

Use different size and style
punches to create your own
embellishment.

477

Flowers

Designer: Camille Jensen

SUPPLIES Cardstock: DCWV •
Patterned Paper: Memories in
the Making • Stamp: Magenta
Rubber Stamps • Buttons: Making
Memories

Smile

Designer: Susan Stringfellow

SUPPLIES Patterned Paper: Daisy
D's Paper Co., Making Memories,
Colorbok • Stamps: Stampin'
Up • Ink: Stampin' Up • Word
Stickers: Bo-Bunny Press • Fibers:
Fibers by the Yard

Design Tip

Ribbons add a nice
texture and the
finishing touch to any
card or tag.

478

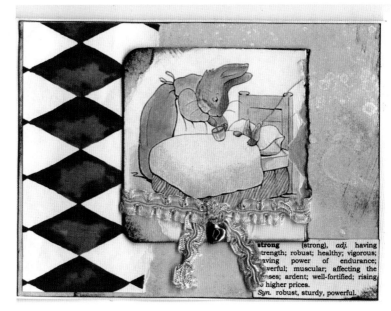

Get Well

Designer: Tonia Borrosch

SUPPLIES Patterned Paper: Provo Craft • Ink: Making Memories • Definitions: Foofala

Beyond Basics

Use a page from a children's book to embellish a card.

Teacup

Designer: Susan Stringfellow

SUPPLIES Patterned Paper: Making Memories • Charms: Memories in the Making • Punches: Creative Memories • Thread: Coats & Clark • Adhesive: Judikins

Got a Bug?

Designer: Brande Juber

SUPPLIES Cardstock: DCWV • Stickers: Memories in the Making • Eyelets: Making Memories

Wish You Were Here

NanC and Company Design

SUPPLIES Cardstock: DCWV • Patterned Paper:
Memories in the Making • Metal Letters: Making
Memories

Bridal Shower

NanC and Company Design

SUPPLIES Cardstock: DCWV • Patterned
Paper: Memories in the Making • Ribbon:
Offray & Son, Inc.

The Magic of Christmas

Designer: Ashley Smith

SUPPLIES A2 Card: DCWV • Cardstock: DCWV • Rub-ons: Making Memories

the magic of Christmas

Mother's Day

NanC and Company Design

SUPPLIES Cardstock: DCWV • Patterned Paper: Memories in the Making • Buttons: Making Memories

Happy

Mother's Day

Design Tip

Photos tell what words cannot say and are a welcome addition to any card or tag. Personalize your greetings with a favorite photo.

---

to: Grandma

♥McCall

Grandma Tag

NanC and Company Design

SUPPLIES Cardstock: DCWV • Metallic Frame: DCWV

Tags

School

Designer: Leah Fung

SUPPLIES Corrugated Cardboard: DMD
Industries • Tassel: American Tag Co.
• Brads: Carolee's Creations • Wire:
Carolee's Creations • Sticker: Jolee's
Boutique • Charm: Carolee's Creations

Design Tip

Use a fabric for the
background of a tag to
add texture and interest.

Grandparent's Love

Designer: Dee Gallimore-Perry

SUPPLIES Stamps: PSX Design, Hero Arts
• Chalk: Craf-T Products • Mesh: Magic
Mesh • Button: Hillcreek Designs

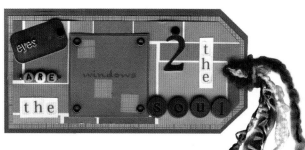

Eyes are the Windows to the Soul

Designer: Miranda Isenberg

SUPPLIES Patterned Paper: Chatterbox, Inc., SEI
• Letter Stickers: SEI • Eyelet Letters: Making
Memories • Dog Tags: Clare Ultimo Inc.

Sugar

Designer: Melissa Smith

SUPPLIES Metal: Art Emboss •
Vintage Label: Paperphernalia •
Specialty Paper: Paperphernalia

You Make My Heart Leap

Designer: Miranda Isenberg

SUPPLIES Tag Template: Deluxe Cuts • Cardstock:
Bazzill • Letter Stickers: SEI • Eyelet Letters: Making
Memories • Alphabet Nail Heads: Scrapworks,
LLC • Heart Eyelet: Creative Imaginations • Frog
Embellishment: Sarah Heidt Photo Craft

Don't Bug Me

Designer: Miranda Isenberg

SUPPLIES Tag: SEI • Scrabble
Tiles: Making Memories • Eyelet
Letters: Making Memories •
Charm: Embellish It!

Beyond Basics

Stitch pockets in tags and cards to
hold notes or special mementos.

483

Cowboy

Designer: Sara Horton

SUPPLIES Cardstock: Bazzill • Patterned Paper: Karen Foster Design • Brads: Jest Charming • Stickers: Tumblebeasts

Beyond Basics

Adhere a window on a tag or card with pop dots to make the contents of the window look like they are in a shadow box.

Be Happy

Designer: Miranda Isenberg

SUPPLIES Cardstock: Bazzill • Brad: Making Memories • Mesh: Magic Mesh • Charm: Embellish It!

All Boy

Designer: Susan Stringfellow

SUPPLIES Patterned Paper: Memories in the Making • Eyelets: Making Memories • Vellum: Paper Adventures • Rope: Two Busy Moms • Thread: Coats & Clark

All Boy!

Frogs and Snails, and Puppy Dog Tails

Tags

For You

Designer: Phyllis Ducote

SUPPLIES Cardstock: Bazzill, The Crafter's Workshop • Vellum Metal Tag: Making Memories • Stickers: Mrs. Grossmans, ScrapYard 329 • Lettering: The Crafter's Workshop • Ribbon: EK Success

To My Friend Rhonda

Designer: Melissa Smith

SUPPLIES Patterned Paper: Paper Adventures • Envelopes: Foofala • Pen: Hunt Corporation • Silver Clip: Westrim Crafts • Font: Albemarle Swash

Beyond Basics

Create a tag booklet with vellum envelopes. Each envelope in the booklet can hold a tag with a special note or picture on it.

Swim Like a Fish

Designer: Miranda Isenberg

SUPPLIES Alphabet Nail Heads: Scrapworks, LLC

Family Travels

Designer: Martha Crowther

SUPPLIES Patterned Paper: Karen Foster Design • Tag: Rebecca Sower • Stickers: Rebecca Sower Nostalgiques • Metal Embellishments: Li'l Davis Designs • Font: Antique

Template on page 487

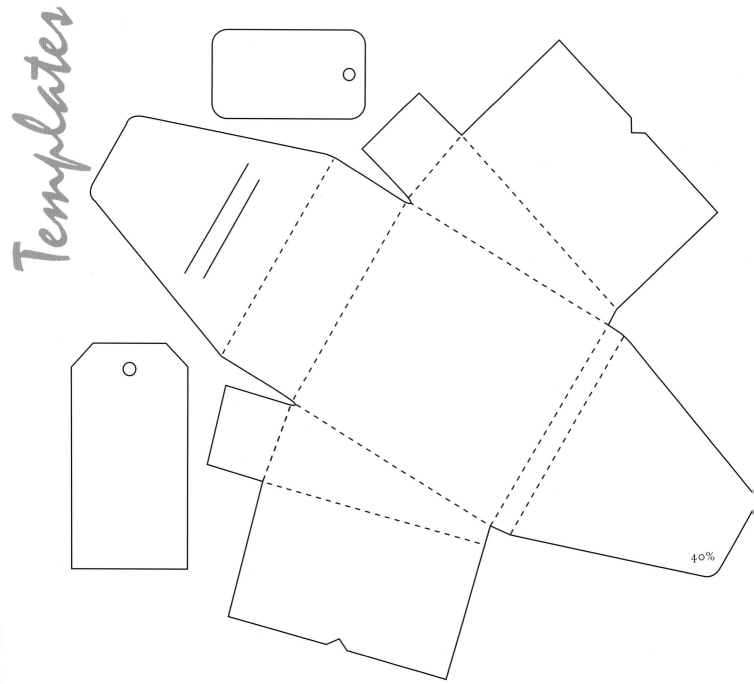

Templates

40%

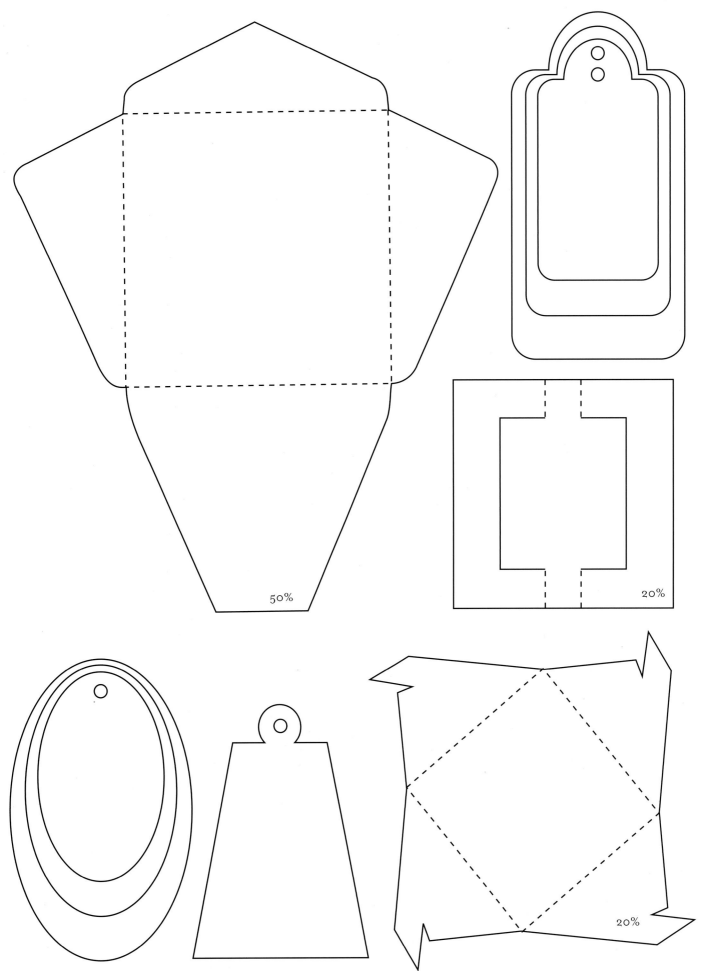

50%

20%

20%

487

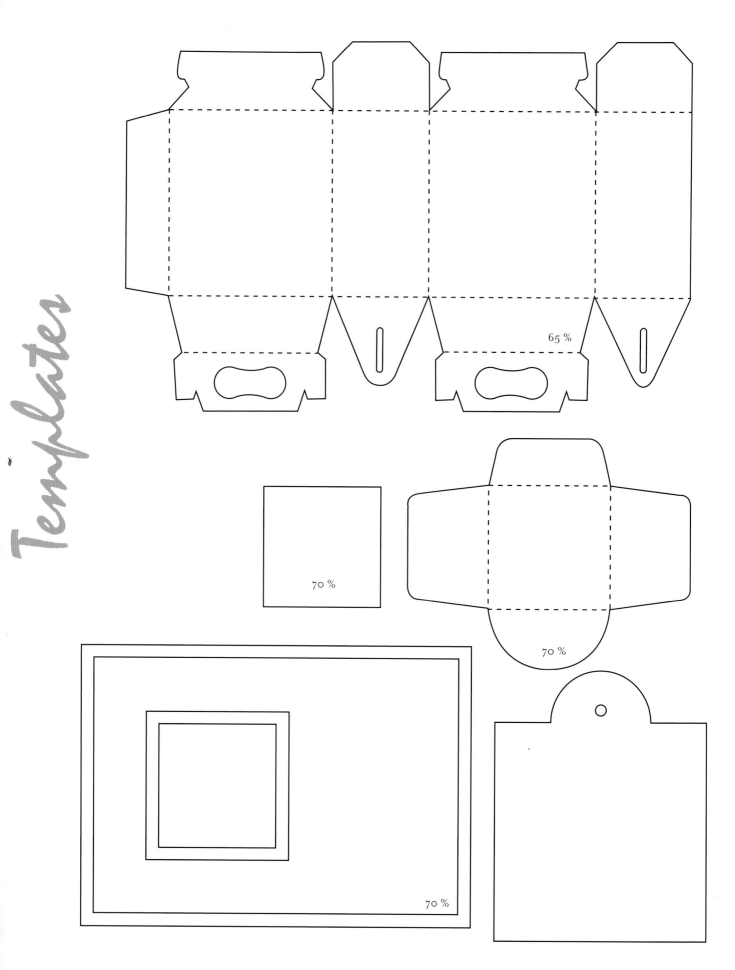

Templates

65 %

70 %

70 %

70 %

488

50%

70%

70%

489

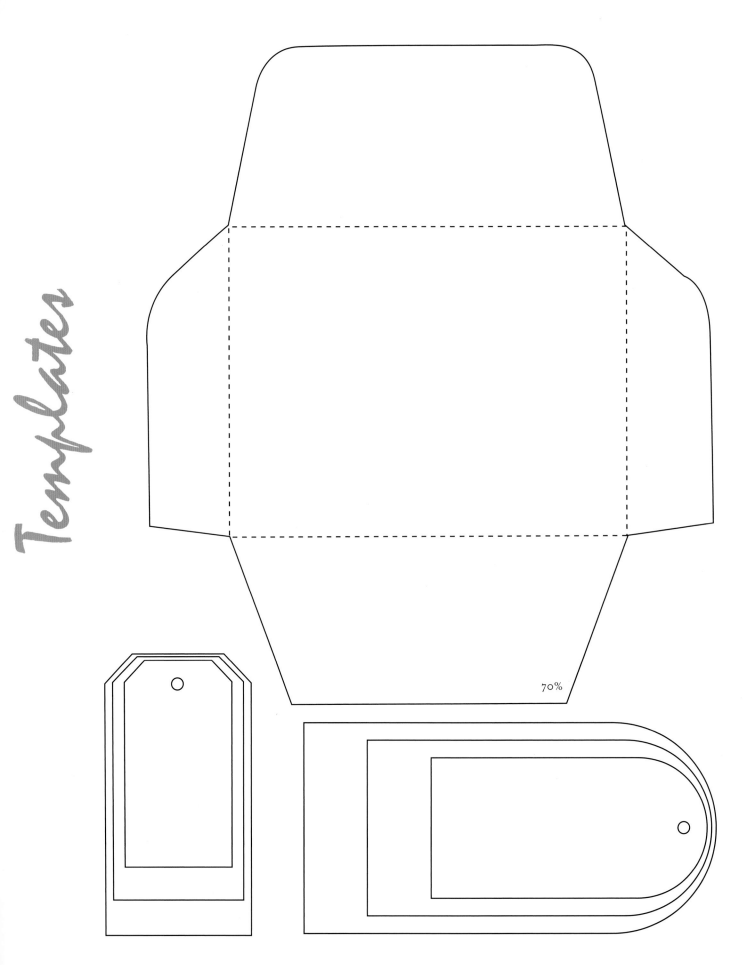

Templates

70%

490

3L Corp.
(800) 828-3130
3lcorp.com

3M Stationary
(800) 364-3577
3m.com

7 Gypsies
(800) 588-6707
7gypsies.com

All My Memories
(801) 619-8838
allmymemories.com

All Night Media
(800) 842-4197
allnightmedia.com

All The Extras
alltheextras.com

American Tag Co.
(800) 642-4314
americantag.net

Anna Griffin
(888) 817-8170
annagriffin.com

Art Emboss
amaco.com

Artistic Wire Ltd.
(630) 530-7567
artisticwire.com

BagWorks Inc.
(817) 446-8105
bagworks.com

Bazzill
(480) 558-8557
bazzillbasics.com

Bluemoon Beads
(800) 377-6715
bluemoonbeads.com

Bo-Bunny Press
(801) 770-4010
bobunny.com

Carolee's Creations
(435) 563-1100
caroleescreations.com

Chatterbox, Inc.
(888) 416-6260
chatterboxinc.com

Clare Ultimo Inc.
(212) 777-6973
clareultimo.com

Close To My Heart
closetomyheart.com

Coats & Clark
coatsandclark.com

Colorbok
(800) 366-4660
colorbok.com

Craf-T Products
(800) 530-3410
craf-tproducts.com

Crafter's Workshop, The
(877) CRAFTER
thecraftersworkshop.com

Crafts Etc!
(800) 888-0321
craftsetc.com

Crayola
(800) 272-9652
crayola.com

Creative Beginnings
(800) 367-1739
creativebeginnings.com

Creative Imaginations
(800) 942-6487
cigift.com

Creative Memories
(800) 341-5275
creativememories.com

Daisy D's Paper Co.
(888) 601-8955
daisydotsanddoodles.com

DCWV
(801) 224-6766
diecutswithaview.com

Deluxe Cuts
(480) 497-9005
deluxecuts.com

DMC
(973) 589-9890
dmc-usa.com

DMD Industries
(800) 805-9890
dmdind.com

Dress It Up!
dressitup.com

EK Success
(800) 524-1349
eksuccess.com

Emagination Crafts Inc.
(866) 238-9770
emaginationcrafts.com

Embellish It!
(702) 312-1628
embellishit.com

Fibers by the Yard
fibersbytheyard.com

Fiskars
(800) 950-0203
fiskars.com

Foofala
(402) 758-0863
foofala.com

Frances Meyer, Inc.
francesmeyer.com

Great Impressions
Rubber Stamps Inc.
(360) 807-0014
greatimpressionsstamps.com

Hancock Fabrics
(877) 322-7427
hancockfabrics.com

Herma Fix
herma.co.uk.com

Hero Arts Rubber
Stamps, Inc.
(800) 822-4376
heroarts.com

Hillcreek Designs
(619) 526-5799
hillcreekdesigns.com

Hunt Corporation
(800) 663-4868
hunt-corp.com

Hygloss Products, Inc.
(973) 458-1745
hygloss.com

Inkadinkado
(781) 938-6100
inkadinkado.com

Jest Charming
(702) 564-5101
jestcharming.com

Jolee's Boutique
joleesbyyou.com

Judikins
(310) 515-1115

K & Company
(888) 244-2083
kandcompany.com

Karen Foster Design
(801) 451-9779
karenfosterdesign.com

Keeping Memories Alive
(469) 633-9665
kimemories.com

Lasting Impressions
for Paper
(800) 936-2667

Li'l Davis Designs
(949) 838-0344
lildavisdesigns.com

Magenta Rubber Stamps
magentarubberstamps.com

Magic Mesh
(651) 345-6374
magicmesh.com

Magic Mounts
(800) 332-0050
magicmounts.com

Magic Scraps
(972) 238-1838
magicscraps.com

Making Memories
(800) 286-5263
makingmemories.com

Marcel Schurman
Collection
(707) 428-0200
shurman.com

Marvy Uchida
(800) 541-5877
uchida.com

Memories in the Making
(888) 257-7548
business.leisurearts.com

Mrs. Grossmans
(800) 429-4549
mrsgrossmans.com

Nature's Pressed
(800) 850-2499
naturespressed.com

NRN Designs
nrndesigns.com

Offray & Son, Inc.
offray.com

Paper Adventures
(800) 727-0699
paperadventures.com

Paperphernalia
(408) 736-5159
paperphernalia.com

Pixie Press
(702) 646-1156
pixiepress.com

Provo Craft
(888) 577-3545
provocraft.com

PSX Design
(800) 782-6748
psxdesign.com

Quickutz
(888) 702-1146
quickutz.com

Ranger Industries
(800) 244-2211
rangerink.com

Rebecca Sower
mississippipaperarts.com

Rubber Stampede
(800) 423-4135
rubberstampede.com

Sarah Heidt Photo Craft
(734) 424-2776
sarahheidtphotocraft.com

ScrapArts
(503) 631-4843
scraparts.com

Scrapworks, LLC
scrapworksllc.com

ScrapYard 329
(775) 829-1227
scrapyard329.com

SEI
(800) 333-3279
shopsei.com

Sizzix
sizzix.com

Stampa Rosa
stamparosa.com

Stampabilities
(800) 888-0321
stampabilities.com

Stampendous!
(800) 869-0474
stampendous.com

Stampin' Up
(800) 782-6787
stampinup.com

Stamps by Judith
stampsbyjudith.com

Stamps 'n' Stuff
stampsnstuff.com

Sulky of America
sulky.com

The Paper Co.
(800) 449-1125
papercompany.com

Ties That Bind
(505) 762-0295
tiesthatbindfiber.com

Tombow
(800) 835-3232
tombowusa.com

Treehouse Designs, Inc.
(877) 372-1109
treehouse-designs.com

Tsukineko
(800) 769-6633
tsukineko.com

Tumblebeasts
(505) 323-5554
tumblebeasts.com

Two Busy Moms
twobusymoms.com

Two Peas in a Bucket
twopeasinabucket.com

Un-Du
un-du.com

Westrim Crafts
(800) 727-2727
westrimcrafts.com

Words Worth Stamps
(719) 282-3495
wordsworthstamps.com

Xyron
(800) 793-3523
xyron.com

FEAR LESS, HOPE MORE;

WHINE LESS, BREATHE MORE;

TALK LESS, SAY MORE;

HATE LESS, LOVE MORE;

AND ALL GOOD THINGS

ARE YOURS.

-SWEDISH PROVERB

A new baby

is like the

beginning

of all things:

wonder, hope,

and a dream of

possibilities.

THERE IS NO MORE

LOVELY, FRIENDLY,

AND CHARMING

RELATIONSHIP,

COMMUNION,

OR COMPANY THAN

A GOOD MARRIAGE.

—Martin Luther

FRIENDSHIP

Friendship isn't a big thing - it's a million little things.

LOVE

IS BORN OF FAITH,

LIVES ON HOPE,

AND DIES OF CHARITY.

—UNKNOWN

A
Happy Marriage
is a
Long Conversation
which always
Seems too short.

—ANDRÉ MAUROIS

MY

HEART

IS

EVER AT

YOUR

SERVICE.

-Shakespeare

Some people come

into our lives,

leave footprints

in our hearts,

and we are never

ever the same.

492

baby

a new hand to hold
new heart to love
new life to lead

The
Highest Happiness on Earth
is in Marriage.

—WILLIAM LYON PHELPS

they say that **age** is all in your mind.

the **trick** is keeping it from creeping down

into your **body.**

thanks
for the
memories

**take
pride**

in how far
you've come,

**have
faith**

in how far
you can go.

*I
love thee,
I love but thee
With a love
that shall not die
Till the sun grows cold
And the stars grow old...*

...

—BAYARD TAYLOR

I WOULD
MAINTAIN THAT
THANKS ARE THE
HIGHEST FORM
OF THOUGHT;
AND THAT
GRATITUDE IS
HAPPINESS
DOUBLED BY
WONDER.

- G.K. CHESTERTON

Today you can be anything you

imagine

493

It's all in your imagination

how to be creative with scrapbooking papers and embellishments

495

introduction

We have all known a small child with a very vivid imagination. The type who can make up a completely fictitious 'story' and then convince you it is true. I have a grandchild who is a master at this. She could tell a whopper with the first sentence she strung together and not even know she was lying. While we all hope she will someday learn to be truthful, we also hope she will not let time stifle her imagination.

Over the past ten years as I have traveled the country teaching and talking with scrapbookers, I have observed that the more scrapbookers use their creativity and imagination to create a scrapbook page the more those pages become expressions of themselves.

It is not by chance that this section is entitled _It's All In Your Imagination_. Our goal has been to create pages that will spark your imagination and expand your capacity for developing your own exciting and creative pages. Remember, there are very few rules in Scrapbooking. Other than acid-free and preservation issues, Scrapbooking is like any other art form and the possibilities are endless. We are limited only by our own imagination.

This Idea and Technique section is unique because of the opportunity we were given to showcase the Leisure Arts _Memories in the Making Collection_ of paper designs and accessories. Our sample page layouts and creativity were greatly enhanced by the exciting mix-and-match coordinates of this line.

I wish you joy, creativity and pleasant memories as you review, read, and learn from the examples, techniques and tips shared here.

Remember, if you're looking for what to do with these great ideas,

It's All In Your Imagination,

Nancy

Nancy M. Hill

It's all in your imagination

table of contents

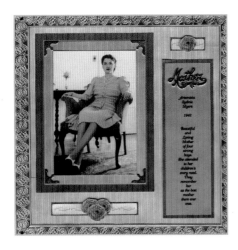

imagine those who...

imagine the adventure...

imagine what...

Rome In The Fall

imagine the joy of...

imagine traditions...

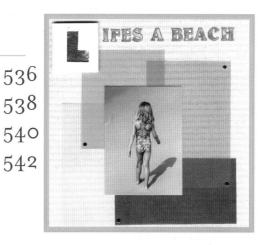

imagine the beauty of...

imagine our love...

LEISURE ARTS
Memories in the Making COLLECTION

This Technique and Idea book showcases the Leisure Arts *Memories in the Making Collection* of innovative Scrapbooking paper designs with matching accessories. These exciting mix–and–match coordinates, popular color ways and distinctive themes were exciting to work with and allowed us to present a variety of design techniques and creative ideas that are applicable across many product lines.

For those of you who have "more photos than time" you will definitely love the ease of coordination within these lines. No more searching aimlessly for coordinating papers and embellishments – Leisure Arts has done all the work for you!

Debra Jordan Bryan
Lighthearted, whimsical designs featuring playful flowers and wonderful sayings. These adorable papers and accessories offer the perfect themes for babies.

Heartwarming Memories by

Gooseberry Patch
An exciting new way of collecting favorite family recipes, photos and fond memories of grandma's kitchen. Heart warming designs also include a Recipes and Memories Album. With dozens of handy accessories, such as papers, stickers, recipe cards and more.

cards designed by Shelley Wallace

Denim

Denim

A casual, comfortable look for memory making. Blue jean-inspired paper and designs feature unique accessories resembling jean pockets, rivets and overall suspenders.

BASIC

Basic

A great selection of basic colors that mix well with other lines, available in various "textures." From the look of crackle to bead board and natural fabric weaves, these designs are perfect for basic backgrounds and simple color schemes.

The Art of
GLYNDA TURLEY
Romancing the Home®

Glynda Turley

Beautiful designs from the cottage-style floral paintings of internationally-known artist, Glynda Turley. This exclusive line of papers and accessories is perfect for heritage and wedding albums.

haberdashery

Haberdashery

Innovative papers and accessories, capturing the warmth and colors of fine men's wear. Realistic-looking accents include ties, buckles, luggage tags and three-dimensional embellishments.

designs by Cyndi

Groovy

Bright and colorful 1960's-inspired papers and accessories, featuring plenty of mod flowers, funky stickers, and new Spring colors. Perfect for tweens and babies.

imagine *those who loved us and left a*

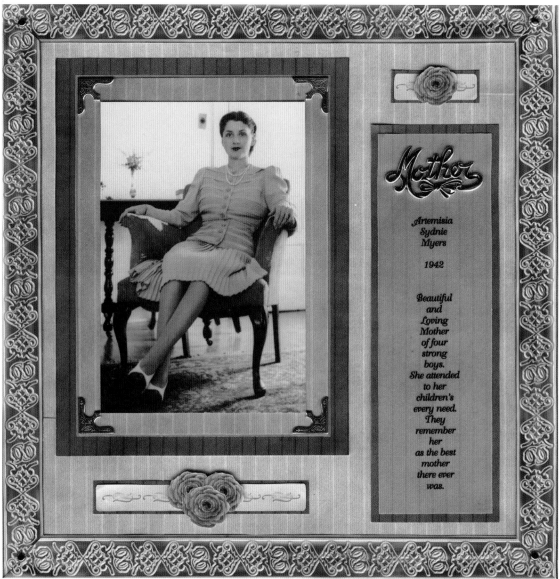

Sheila Hansen

haberdashery

Mother

This page began with a blue-gray striped paper from the Haberdashery line. Complementary borders and accents were chosen from the same line to build the page. There is an ever so slight edge of pink vellum peeking out from under the photo that matches the roses.

Reunion 1937

A sheet of patterned paper can have a dramatic effect with a clever but simple technique of a scalloped border. This designer understands the concept of color, scale, accent and simplicity. When they are all combined they have an incredibly dramatic outcome.

Shelley Wallace

haberdashery

legacy of honor to follow

Shelly Wallace

Grabeteria 1940

Masculine pages can often be a challenge. This page utilizes khaki, shades of green, and tan that give a guy-look to any old time 1940's photo. Tags are hung with white embroidery floss. True to the times, the fonts used are Mom's Typewriter and Typist.

haberdashery

503

imagine *those who* have gone before

Lest We Forget,

My Grandfather, Clark Mann was drafted from the "fishbowl" into World War II in 1940. As a very young man he left his childhood home in Salt Lake City, Utah and traveled to Ft. Sill, Oklahoma where he became a member of the United States 1st Cavalry Division.

He served in the South Pacific in Australia, New Guinea, The Solomon Islands, The Admiralties, Leyte, The Philippines, and Tokyo. He was severely burned in Leyte when a tank blew up on him and he spent several months on a hospital ship recovering before returning to the war.

His greatest reward was the privilege of riding with the cavalry into Tokyo with General Douglas McArthur in celebration of victory! General McArthur commended the 1st Cavalry as follows:

"No greater record has emerged from the War than that of the 1st Cavalry Division—swift and sure in attack, tenacious and durable in defense, and loyal and cheerful under hardship. It has written its own noble history. My personal connection with it in many moments of crisis has especially endeared it to me."

Jeremy Clark Smith,
Proud Grandson

Sheila Hansen

• Sgt. Clark Mann •

haberdashery

Lest We Forget
Paper embellishments resembling military ribbons were folded over and secured with eyelets and metal charms were wired into place. The nametag of Lt. Clark Mann was raised with foam core and glued into place. The silver brads on the name-plate are purely decorative.

Brothers 1918

The simplicity of this design matches the scant and hard life these early immigrants certainly had. It would seem strange to portray this photo in any other way. The tattered and torn vellum and dark colors reflect the era. Who would have thought paper could help portray so much feeling.

1918

haberdashery

Candice Snyder

leaving freedom at our door

Martin Joseph Hermansen

Black and White photos take on a whole new look when surrounded by color. The designer used peach vellum to do the journaling, and after attaching the vellum to the matting she wrapped the journaling with tan scrapbook string to give it that "navy" rope and sea feeling.

Martin Joseph Hermansen
1964

This photograph was taken one week before my grandfather entered the United States Naval Academy. His dream was to one day become an Admiral in the United States Navy. He achieved reaching this goal many years later. He graduated from the Academy four years later. Then he served in the Navy for twenty more years. He received lots of medals for loyalty and bravery. I look up to my grandfather as one of my many heros.

haberdashery

Sheila Hansen

imagine *those who* *tamed the wild west*

Teresa
on her
horse,
Sir
Walter
Franklin.

Taryn Evans

THE DENIM COLLECTION

Riding Side Saddle
This simple page illustrates the use of pre-
designed embellishments and the concept of
memories in minutes. With matching papers
and embellishments available in coordinated
sets, it is easy to create pages in no time at all.
Charms are affixed with pop-up dots and tied
on with embroidery floss.

Ride Um Cowboy

There is no end to the versatility of denim. The uniqueness of this page is found in the woven and stitched fence in the bottom right-hand corner. The designer cut strips of paper to create a fence and then stitched the pieces together — a loving touch for her daughter who dreamed of "Jessie" in Toy Story!

and those we would like to "tame"

"Wanted"

This torn and tattered denim theme is perfect for these "jail birds." The designer has done everything but set the page on fire to create the feeling of the old west. The longer you look at this page design the more you see how creative it really is — journaling, layering, eyelets, colorful embroidery floss, matting, charms and "strategic paper tearing."

Camille Jensen

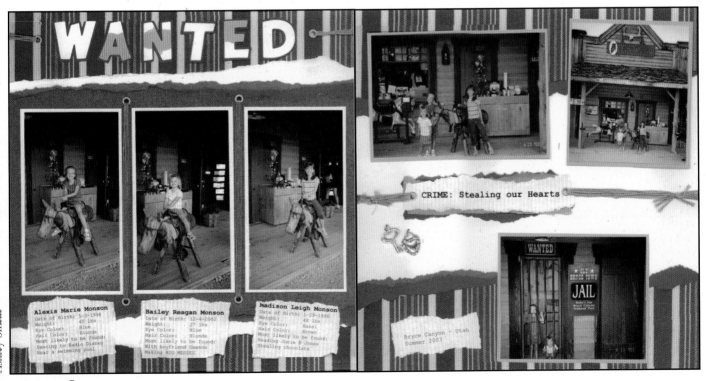

imagine *those who* *color our lives*

Brande Juber

Best Friends
After placing photos on the page, the designer created a "connecting border" by cutting strips of paper pieces and using embroidery floss to sew them together. The designer pokes a hole in the paper before the sewing actually begins to make sure the needle hits the right spot!

BASIC

Michael
These old bead board weathered frames are perfect for displaying black and white photos. A second mat is added inside the frame for a truly authentic look. To create a "hanger" use embroidery floss and mini brads for nails.

michael

was as cute as a button

with memories

Serena and Sydnie with Uncle David

Fun in the SUN

Sheila Hansen

Fun in the Sun
KISS KISS – this is scrapbooking for the time-challenged!! A plain sheet of paper for matting and all the matching embellishments available for you! The designer's task is simple – find photos that match the paper colors! This designer's technique is simple - put pop-dots behind the daisies and back the journaling!

The Groovy COLLECTION

imagine *those who* scatter sunshine

My little Ray of

Sunshine

GAP

GAP

Ansley Nichole Lucas, Age 1. We went to visit Aunt Kristie & Uncle Chris in West Plains, MD. We were at the park Playing on the toys. She loved the horse. Right after we took the picture, she fell & crashed to the ground.

Brande Juber

THE DENIM COLLECTION

Little Ray of Sunshine
This eclectic page is pulled together with plastic mesh. The journaling strip on the bottom of the page was chalked after the white cardstock was torn. The sunshines were hand cut out of yellow mulberry paper.

It's a Whipping Cream Tradition!

Not only is there whipping cream flowing out of the children's mouths, but the designer has it flowing across the bottom and top of the page by embossing the vellum with white embossing powder. The quilled hearts and shaker box full of tiny silver spoons are indeed 'one of a kind' designs. Creating shaker boxes with tags, transparencies and foam core is an easy technique when you simply glue it to the page. The silver beading is "micro beads" which are sprinkled on glue.

Candice Snyder

everywhere they go

Faces of the People I Love

Faces are the theme of this two-page spread. To add variety to your scrapbook pages, pick a feature and highlight it – eyes, ears, smiles, hands, feet, and of course, faces!

Camille Jensen

imagine *the adventures of*
Grandma's Treasures

Happy Birthday

Maddie's 4th Birthday! She had a Monsters Inc cake, her favorite movie.

Celebrating

Brande Juber

Happy, Happy Birthday
The designer trimmed down a sheet of 12x12 paper and then tore it about 1 inch down from the top of the page. Using gold embroidery floss the designer widely stitched the torn page back together. The Happy Birthday and Celebrating metallic words (DieCuts With a View) capture the theme of the page!

Sheila Hansen

THE GROOVY COLLECTION
Designs by Cyndi

Miss Attitude Maddie
This fun and groovy design is quick and easy to make. The daisy flowers are stacked on top of each other with pop-up squares to add height. (Make your own pop-up squares by cutting foam core into squares and use your favorite adhesive to glue into place.)

and how they never end

Brande Juber

The creative titling and play on words of "SHORE things" is the highlight of this page. The word "SHORE" was created with CK Fun Boxes font and an eye applicator was used to apply blue chalk in the squares. CK Bella font was used for the word "things." Strips of cardstock were place under the vellum title to add dimension.

imagine *the adventure*
of a Safari

Busch Gardens

Spring 2003

We were able to go on a safari during our trip to Busch Gardens.

It was so neat to get up close and personal with animals.

Watch out for those horns.

Candice Snyder

haberdashery

All Tied up at Busch Gardens
Nothing adds texture to your scrapbook pages quite like twine. The pieces of this page are stitched and tied together using eyelets, wire and twine. This mimmicks the stitching on the buttons and lashes and coordinates with the animal hides.

514

Motorbike Tour

A triage of dark to light color creates a great "guy page". So simple and yet the focus is on the photos. The "oh so popular" tag has been given a new look with charm, a hanging string and journaling. The mixed textures on this page are very cozy.

haberdashery

or any journey that sets us "free"

Kanta in Tokyo

For the time-challenged scrapbooker, many popular paper lines are now accompanied by coordinating accessories and embellishments. The Leisure Arts Haberdashery line has stickers, tags, journaling papers as well as the journaling pocket shown in this page. Look how easy it has become to make great pages without spending all your time shopping for matching components.

haberdashery

imagine *the adventure of*
Snow White and the little dwarfs

Another family tradition . . .
Grand Children's Trip
Orlando Disney World
November 2001

A visit from Snow White
Brought such pure delight,
To our Grand Children
Who are always on the run!!

Sheila Hansen

Heartwarming Memories by

Snow White
The designer began with a solid sheet of blue
and white checked paper from the Goosberry
Patch collection and worked inward with trim,
zig-zag and stickers. The finished result, with
journaling and red eyelets, is a delightfully fun
page of a visit with Snow White!

Sheila Hansen

Spinning
in the
Teacups
with
Uncle John

Spinning in the Tea Cups
Mulberry paper is a popular matting medium as it offers both color and texture. It tears very easily when slightly wet. Notice how the designer has selectively chosen not to mat everything on the page to keep the design from blending into itself. The stickers have been mounted on foam core and adhesive has been used to raise and give them dimension on the page.

and the magical memories of Disneyland

The Magic of Disneyland
Angles are dominant throughout this design. From the angle of the photos to the slant of the journaling and stitching, there appears to be no pattern to the variety of directions on this page — and yet it all works together in a eye-pleasing way. The mix-matched fonts from Creating Keepsakes add a finishing touch of variety to the page.

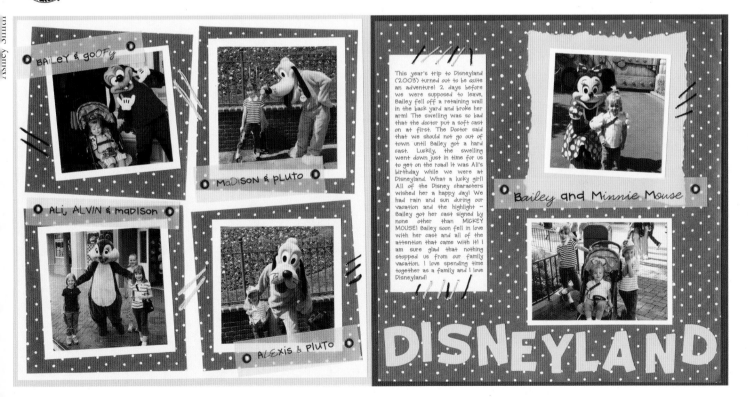

BAILEY & gOOFy

MaDISON & PLUTO

ALi, ALVIN & maDISON

ALEXiS & PLUTO

This year's trip to Disneyland (2003) turned out to be quite an adventure! 2 days before we were supposed to leave, Bailey fell off a retaining wall in the back yard and broke her arm! The swelling was so bad that the doctor put a soft cast on at first. The Doctor said that we should not go out of town until Bailey got a hard cast. Luckily, the swelling went down just in time for us to get on the road! It was Ali's birthday while we were at Disneyland. What a lucky girl! All of the Disney characters wished her a happy day! We had rain and sun during our vacation and the highlight — Bailey got her cast signed by none other than MICKEY MOUSE! Bailey soon fell in love with her cast and all of the attention that came with it! I am sure glad that nothing stopped us from our family vacation. I love spending time together as a family and I love Disneyland!

Bailey and Minnie Mouse

DISNEYLAND

imagine *the adventure of an* *adrenaline rush*

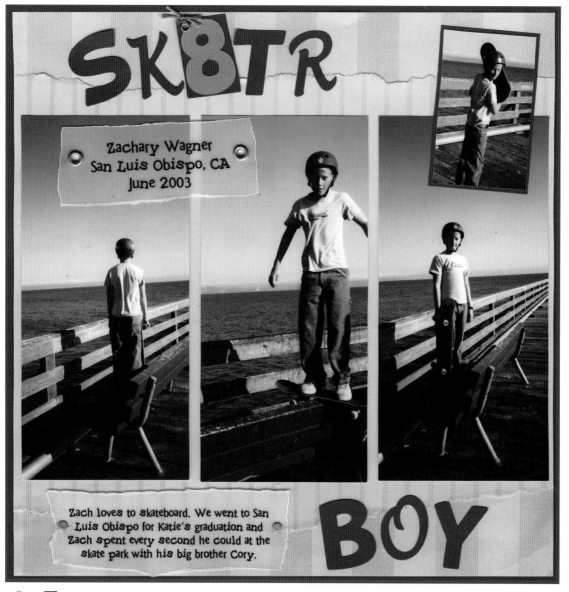

Sk8tr Boy

Clever page, clever title, not-so-clever boy! (Is he really going to board right into the ocean?) This page layout is a great way to use several photographs that expose the same subject (Zachary) from different points of view. CK Evolution font and QwicKutz lettering add the finishing touches to this page.

or the water fight waiting to happen

Snake River Rafting

A monochromatic theme was chosen to display these high adventure river rafting photos. Designer paper was used as the base and layered torn pieces of green and white vellum papers were added to simulate the river moving down the page. Even the journaling is floating down the river.

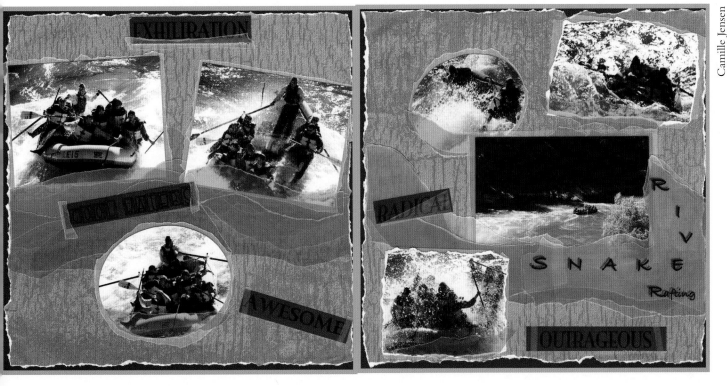

Camille Jensen

imagine *what can develop when the same photos are scrapped in* Sepia

Positively Pretentious Posing Princesses

Camille Jensen

Please note:
These two pages displa
the same four photos
printed in Sepia, Black
and White and Color.
Even though the photo
are the same, please
notice the contrast and
diversity that is availabl
when using black and
white and sepia tone
photos.

Girls in Sepia
The monochromatic tones of the sepia coloring
allows for more color in the background. Our
designer chose the Glynda Turley pansy paper
and backed the photos in torn mulberry shades
of pastel. Little rosebud charms were sewn into
place with forget-me-not embroidery stitches.
Notice the fun alliteration in the journaling.

Camille Jensen

Strawberry Delights...

...in black and white!

Black & White

Girls in Black and White
Who would have thought to just glue them together and tie a ribbon around um!   It works – and oh so easy. The narrow matting in the polka dot print, the red and white matching check bring it all together. This would not work if these photos were not black and white. Something would clash!

Girls in Color
This page began with a DieCuts with a View overlay laid on top of the Debra Jordan Bryan paper. The designer has matted the photos in green mulberry paper and used the Provo Craft shadow letter fonts to cut out the word Easter.

Color

EASTER

traditions

Pretty in Purple

Candice Snyder

Spring is my favorite season. It is a time when I think about love, beauty, new beginnings and especially family. I love spending time with my grandbabies – these photos were taken in April 2003. Madison (7), Alexis (4), Bailey (2), Sydnee (9), & Issac (3).

imagine
what Spring
would be like
without
flowers

Easter Hearts and Blossoms
Memorable times and whimsical papers combine to make great layouts. In this two-page spread, the elegance of quilling is used in a variety of colors to add dimension to the border design.

Easter 2003

Ashley Smith, Quilling by Candice Snyder

Sheila Hansen

Easter in Purple

This light and airy page has used purple and white vellum for matting photos, for the journal space and for the design box at the bottom of the page. The design box has been wrapped with coordinating colors of embroidery floss as a finishing touch.

and the innocence of children

Sheila Hansen

Grow Your Heart

Two sheets of design paper have been combined to make a cohesive page that requires very little additional embellishment. A soft pink mulberry paper has been used to mat the journaling and photo. The photo has also been backed with vellum. The designer has cut out hearts from a matching sheet of paper and used foam core to mount on top of the backing sheet.

imagine *what "fleurs"*
bring to romance

Ashley Smith

A walk through the streets of France
No adhesive is needed for this unique
journaling, which is simply sewn on with a
single stitch using three strands of embroidery
thread. The metallic letters (by DieCuts With a
View) are also stitched to the page.

Sheila Hansen

This Ring
The linear layout pattern of this two-page design is consistent and flows smoothly. The eye easily moves across and down the page.

Brian Matthew Olmetti
And
Emily Anne Dobbins

June 1, 2001

in such subtle ways

With
this
ring

Our
promise
to each other
will
strengthen
through the
years
because we
know each
others heart
and soul

A symbol
of unending
love

This layout features shimmering vellum, which is positioned on top of the Glynda Turley pansy paper for an elegant dressed-up look. All of the photos and the quotes are linear adding to the simplistic design of the page. The silver corner embellishments from the Memories in the Making line are the added touch of elegance this page needs.

Sheila Hansen

imagine *what life would be like*
without jeans

THE
DENIM
COLLECTION

Hill Family 2002

Many of us would not immediately think of denim and lime green as coordinating colors – but look at this distinctive and attractive work of art. Torn paper with white inset, a tag layered with paper, tied with wire and embellished with a camera, simple journaling, a few eyelets, and metal paper clips pull it all together in an exquisite way.

526

Memories with Great Grandpa

The designer has chosen paper for this page carefully. The lines in the baby's socks, the sister's shirt and the house are certainly not lost in the choice of lined paper!

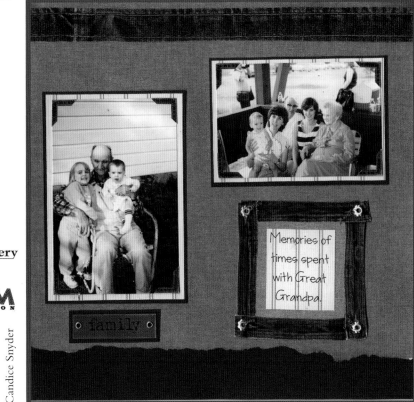

Candice Snyder

Reunion

Has there ever been a family picnic without denim? This rendering of the "blue-jean" is incredibly creative and the longer you look at the design the more you can see how simple it is to copy. The page has been made easier by embellishments from Memories in the Making line including stickers, buttons, letters, and belt loops.

...and family gatherings

imagine *the joy of* wearing blue

Pigtails and Ruffles

Sometimes when you have a photo as adorable as this all you need to do is frame it! The right-hand border was made by simply writing Maddie's name on the lines, so she would have a sample of Gammy's handwriting for years to come.

528

Sweet Dreams

Stitching pieces of torn paper together as if it were fabric for a quilt is a great technique to add design and interest to your page. The charms hanging from string secured by eyelets is a clever way to draw the eye into the heart of the photo.

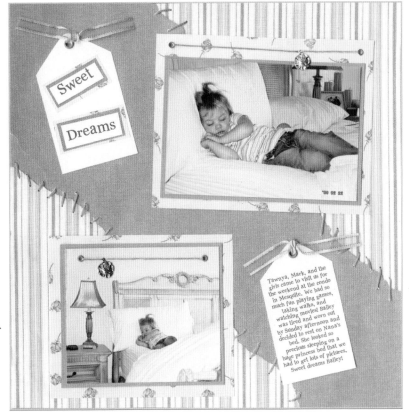

Ashley Smith

and sleeping and playing the whole day through
BASIC

Snow Baby

There is nothing better then clear vellum, torn and layered, to create the look of snow. In this design the vellum was layered to create a pocket for the photo and sign.

The cutest snowball in the yard.

imagine *the joy of*
photographing Rome

Rome in the Fall

The elegance of Rome needed the elegance of the Glynda Turley's line of papers. Charms, ribbon and borders also complement the sophisticated page theme.

Candice Snyder

530

and getting camera and film safely home

Mike is such a
wonderful
photographer. Rome
was his favorite city of
our European
Vacation. I even got
him to be in one of the
pictures.

imagine *the joy of a pile of falling leaves*

Candice Snyder

haberdashery

Counting Leaves

A combination of denim and checks creates a distinctive appearance. The technique of hanging letters from grommets, twine and wire is a clever addition. The letters are double matted then a hook is made with twisted wire, attached to the back of each letter and strung on the twine. The twine is then attached to the page with eyelets. Wire twisted into a spiral is a clever way of imitating a button and also a way to hang your journaling box. The combination of stitching and twine is not only unique but easier than it looks. Give it a try.

Candice Snyder

*and napping in
a pumpkin
patch*

haberdashery

And I think
we found the
best pumpkin
in the patch!

Pumpkin Pick'in

This designer loves texture and color. For the photo featured on the left, the artist has tied twine into knots and using mounting foam has affixed the knots so they hang against the outside of the mat. The pumpkin accent has been torn and sewn back together.

imagine *the joy of*
the weekend photographer

In the spring of 1994, on our way to a tradeshow, we took a side trip drive to Shreveport, Louisiana & down to New Orleans. Mike had just started doing photography. These are a few pictures he took while we were there.

•Louisiana•

Camille Jensen

THE
DENIM
COLLECTION

Louisiana
This patchwork overlay by DieCuts With a View was placed on top of a solid and a torn sheet of Denim paper. The tag utilizes embroidery floss colors that coordinate with the photos. The "Louisiana" title was made by running a piece of paper through a Xyron machine, cutting the pieces into strips and covering with a piece of vellum.

who captures such impressive images

South African Safari (sort of)
The Haberdashery papers are perfect for a safari at Busch Gardens. The designer used creative templates and stitching to focus on the main attraction of the safari "the animals."

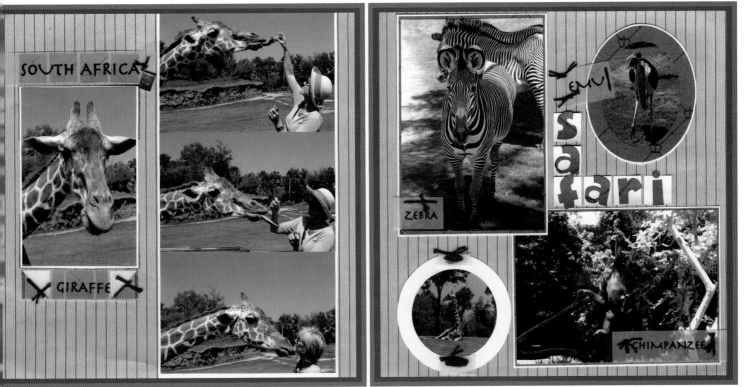

imagine *traditions that start in Grandma's Kitchen*

Candice Snyder

Memories of Grandma

A full solid sheet of cardstock with a smaller sheet of print, bordered with trim, is the foundation for this enticing page. The shadow box of kitchen tools is a window box with pieces of foam core down the sides. The charms are attached with small pieces of twisted wire.

...and end with a mess!

Anytime is Cookie Time
Zig-Zag stickers have been added to both of
these pages to enhance the design. Some of the
photos and journaling statements have been
backed with torn mulberry papers. Thin
matting borders show off the Gooseberry
background paper.

Heartwarming Memories by

Brande Juber

imagine *traditions that* surround the holidays

Camille Jensen

Christmas 2002 at Nana and Papa's Alexis age 3

Christmas at Nana and Papa's
An overlay from DieCuts With a View™ has been punched out and layed on top of this paper from Glynda Turley. The designer has added contrasting papers, textured threads, and a sticker border to bring it all together. The papers are elegant, but do not distract from the photos of Alexis.

538

Sheila Hansen

The colors of the season

The design interest in this page is created with the use of silk ribbon and designer stickers. Before the wide sticker strip was adhered to the page it was loosely wrapped with thin ribbon to give an "airy" effect. Additional ribbon and embellishments were added to draw the theme across the page. The colors of the ribbon, stickers and paper were chosen to bring out the holiday colors in the children's clothing.

and create more time for family

A trip to the Nutcracker with Nana and Papa

The best of all gifts around any Christmas tree: the presence of a happy family

Christmas Traditions

A rounded paper clip holds these photos in place. The designer has twisted green embroidery floss with red fibers that have been snipped and frayed. The journaling is done on white vellum and is secured with eyelets. The look is festive, simple and fun!

BASIC

Ashley Smith

539

Ashley Smith

Summer Fun

A color blocking technique has been used in this design. The procedure is very popular, as it is simple to do and allows for a great deal of creativity. In this case, several sheets of paper from a coordinating line (Groovy) have been pieced together in a patchwork motif and then the photo has been matted and placed on top. Running out of room on your page – simply journal on vellum and lay right over photos.

Brande Juber

Life's a Beach

This two-page beach spread is simple but elegant. Both pages begin with the same pale yellow chenille paper from the Denim line. On the title page the designer has overlaid 4 vellum squares with the pattern of the printed-paper peaking through the vellum. The vellum has been secured with silver brads and the photo has been mounted in the center. The shaker box has been filled with microbeads small enough to look like sand.

and endless days and rays

The second page in this two-page spread also has vellum squares on top of the yellow chenille paper, but the designer has also chosen a blue and gray striped pattern to tie in the lettering on the title page. The layout design in soft muted colors makes these pages particularly attractive.

Brande Juber

541

imagine *traditions* *that unite us*

the announcement

GLYNDA TURLEY

Mark & Tawnya

The lacing pattern on this page was made by tearing away a two inch strip from the printed hydrangea paper, and then overlaying it on a sheet of checked vellum. Pewter brads were attached and white scrapbook string was laced around the brads to pull the page together.

542

Engagement Pics

The use of mulberry paper as a matting accent on this design adds color and distinction. A small make-up size spray bottle can be used to moisten mulberry paper before tearing. This allows the damp paper to tear and fray in a much more controlled way.

the engagement

the event

Wedding by the Old Mill Pond

This two-page spread captures the story and photos from this beautiful wedding setting. The designer began with solid cardstock and used the printed paper and charms from the Memories in the Making as accents in a quasi-patchwork technique that is worth a second look.

Camille Jensen

Taryn Evans

543

imagine *the beauty of* the French Riviera

Southern France

The understated softness of this layout can be attributed in part to the designer's choice of matting materials. The photos were matted in ochre vellum and light august green cardstock.

Adding a jagged, torn edge to some of the mats contributed an ethereal look. The stitching on the journaling and placement of the charms is equally subdued and understated.

Ashley Smith

...and the quaintness of a stone walkway

Spending three weeks in Southern France last spring was a much-needed vacation. Mike and I enjoyed spending time together, relaxing, taking photographs, and enjoy the beautiful landscape of France.

imagine *the beauty of*
a sleeping child

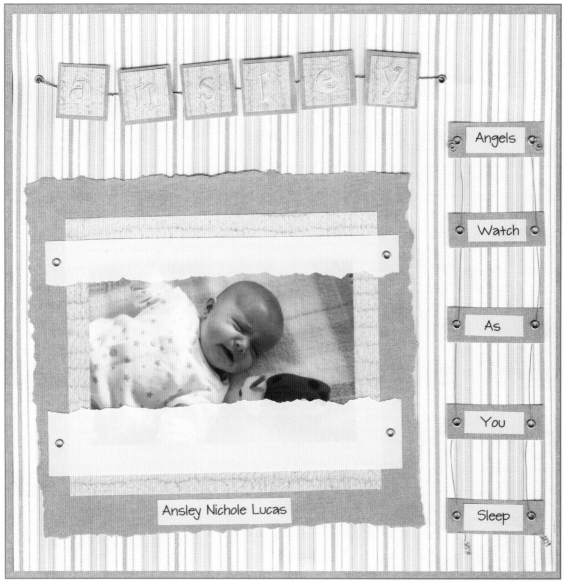

Rock–a–Bye Ansley

The designer of this page has very cleverly torn vellum and placed it in a frame motif around Ansley's face. A first glace at this page takes the observer's eye directly to the focal point – the baby's face. Notice also, the scale of the wire and eyelets. They are particularly delicate – very inline with the small features of the baby.

Brande Juber

As the Years Go By
Yes, vellum can be stitched. The uniqueness of this page is the vellum pocket that has been hand stitched (with stitches very close together) using five strands of yellow embroidery thread. Notice how the yellow stitching on the denim becomes visible by the simple addition of a yellow mat.

and the 'tolerance' for one with an ATTITUDE

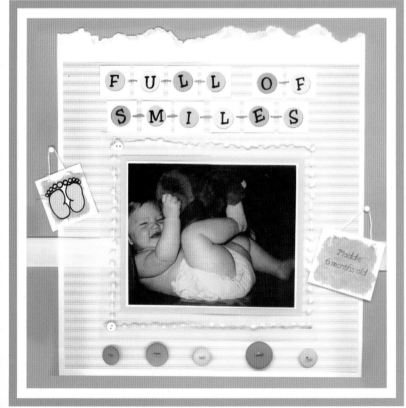

This page could win a prize for the most techniques used on a single page – and it doesn't diminish its validity one bit!! From stitched together letters, mulberry backed stickers and journaling, string hung faux photo frames, buttons, vellum, torn paper, ribbon and brads the baby in the photo is still the main attraction!

Brande Juber

imagine *the beauty*
of butterflies

'Mike's Butterflys'
Bush Gardens
Tampa, Florida
May 2003

Sheila Hansen

Butterflies

There was a perfect match between this collection of recent butterfly photos and the whimsical designed papers of Debra Jordan Bryan. The birdhouses and flowers were double layered and rolled inward around the edges to help them curl. The butterflies in the photos are real, while the birdhouses have been extended to overlap into a few of the photos. The butterfly charms that accompany this collection were the perfect ending to a beautiful page.

Bellagio Gardens
These beautiful garden photos were mounted on white cardstock, white mesh, and finally purple vellum. To add depth to the garden border, a second set of flowers were cut and mounted on pop-up dots.

flowers and lakefront gardens

All Things Grow With Love
In addition to the color blocking, stickers and the pattern on this fun paper, it is the embroidering that is so unusual. As if it were a dishtowel, our designer has hand stitched around photos and some of the flowers and bird houses to add depth, dimension and interest to the page.

imagine *the beauty of* *the world*

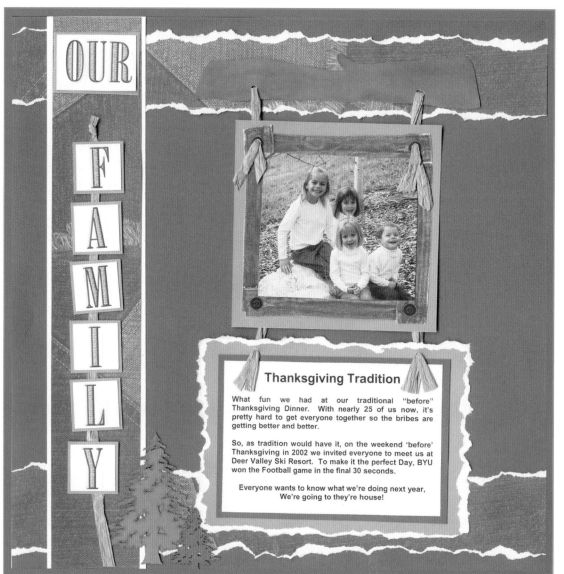

OUR

FAMILY

Thanksgiving Tradition

What fun we had at our traditional "before" Thanksgiving Dinner. With nearly 25 of us now, it's pretty hard to get everyone together so the bribes are getting better and better.

So, as tradition would have it, on the weekend 'before' Thanksgiving in 2002 we invited everyone to meet us at Deer Valley Ski Resort. To make it the perfect Day, BYU won the Football game in the final 30 seconds.

Everyone wants to know what we're doing next year,
We're going to they're house!

Brande Juber

THE DENIM COLLECTION

Thanksgiving Tradition
This page began with tearing the denim paper into strips and adhering the strips in a pattern on to matching cardstock. Accent pieces from the Denim line were used to complete the page. Natural colored raffia was the perfect texture and width for assembling the pieces. The raffia was easy to thread through the loops, tie into knots and mount letters on.

Ashley Smith

BASIC

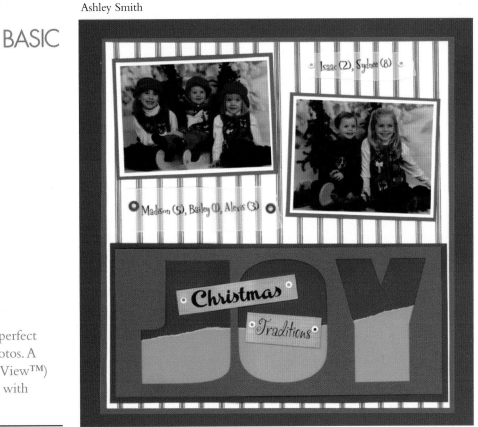

Christmas Joy
Red and white striped paper was a perfect choice for matting these holiday photos. A word overlay (from DieCuts With a View™) was trimmed down and embelished with metallic words and torn vellum.

around us and the children about us

The Best Things in Life aren't Things
This page utilizes a patchwork overlay from the DieCuts With a View line and showcases the Groovy papers. The designer chose to include several paper designs in each block adding greater interest and dimension. The layering, matting and diversity of techniques produced a charming page.

Candice Snyder

imagine *our love affair* *with the sea*

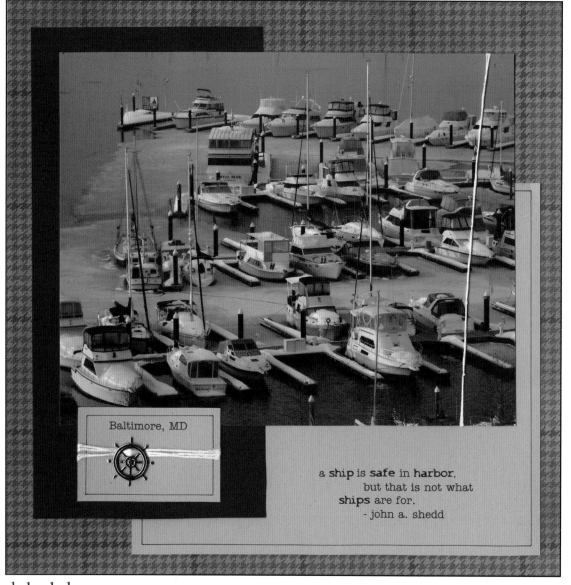

Baltimore, MD

a ship is **safe** in **harbor**, but that is not what **ships** are for. - john a. shedd

Shelley Wallace

haberdashery

Harbor

Subtly of color is the essence in this Baltimore Harbor page. The softness of the blue and the grey tones balance each other and the layout design off-sets the boat masts and height. The use of a single charm and a touch of embroidery thread mimicking a mast is all that is needed to give this page perfect balance.

552

Brande Juber

Down by the Sea

Yes, that's sandpaper "filling in" for the sand on the beach and doubling as photo corners. Tying the photos together (literally) with eyelets and wire is a great technique to make sure that everyone gets the idea that all these people are connected!

haberdashery

and its simplicity

In 1997 our family took a vacation to California. It was definitely a hit. The kids discovered the beach for the first time!

Grace, Abbi, and Conor

Taryn Evans

Stripes on the Beach

Creating a border with hand drawn lines is a simple way to add personality and cohesiveness to a page. The designer uses a ruler and an acid free marker to draw lines, dots, and dashes around the borders of her photos and journaling.

haberdashery

imagine *our love for*
sand castles in the sun

BASIC

Beach Babes

Through controlled tearing the artist of this page has created a beach scene that makes you want to "step right in." Starting with a solid sheet of basic tan, the large landscape pieces were added first and the palm tree, frames and embellishments were added last.

554

Fun in the Sand

Several coordinating papers in the Groovy line have been blocked together to create this great page. The designer began by matting and placing the photos then filled in the spaces with alternating designs.

Candice Snyder

Beach Bums

The title for these pages was made by first mounting letters on small squares, then threading copper wire through the squares and curling the extra wire on each end. A photo overlay (by DieCuts With a View) is used on one photo to accent two cute girls playing on the beach!

and children having fun

Brande Juber

555

imagine *our love for* *each new child*

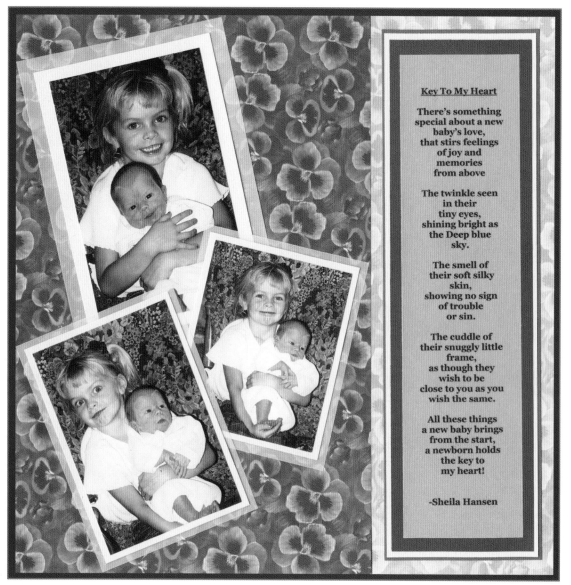

Sheila Hansen

Key To My Heart

There's something
special about a new
baby's love,
that stirs feelings
of joy and
memories
from above

The twinkle seen
in their
tiny eyes,
shining bright as
the Deep blue
sky.

The smell of
their soft silky
skin,
showing no sign
of trouble
or sin.

The cuddle of
their snuggly little
frame,
as though they
wish to be
close to you as you
wish the same.

All these things
a new baby brings
from the start,
a newborn holds
the key to
my heart!

-Sheila Hansen

Key to my Heart
This page takes advantage of similar paper patterns coordinating, as the dark pansies fade
into light pansies. The poem written by the
page designer is uniquely accented with layers
of matting and vellum.

556

Desmond TuTu on Family
This page began with a half sheet of checked paper and a half sheet of lined paper attached in the middle and enhanced with a torn strip. The perfect quote is used on this page to express the designer's feelings about family.

Brande Juber

who joins our family

All Things Grow With Love
Layers of red and white and then more red and white describe the process used in the delightful creation of this rendition of sisters clowning around for the camera. There are actually nine layers of either torn vellum or cardstock in assorted sizes between the large photo and the backing sheet. Heart shaped eyelets and metallic letters (by DieCuts With a View) are the perfect accent.

Ashley Smith

imagine *our love for the simple*

Shelley Wallace

Heartwarming Memories by
Gooseberry Patch

Sydnee Loves Strawberries
The black and white fonts on this page (DJ Sweet and PC Uneven) coordinate with the zig-zaggy look of this page. The title topper "Sydnee" was colored using chalks and a blending pen. Sydnee's dress was colored red on the computer. This designer knows when to keep a page simple and sweet!

558

Monson Family Tree
This is a sample of a simple page with snap! The page captures a moment in time for the Monson Family. Notice, the embellishments are faux and flat to keep things simple as well.

The Monsons

Mark • Tonya • Madison
Alexis • Bailey

Taryn Evans

THE DENIM COLLECTION

pleasures of life

BATH

May 2002

While staying at the Hilton in Orlando, we filled the bathtub with bubbles and cousins !

Bathtime
Bubble baths can get a little crazy and so can using busy papers. It is best to balance fun patterns with a simple layout. The bathtub die cut (by Ellison) has been chalked in complementary colors and then blended with a cotton ball.

THE Groovy COLLECTION

Shelley Wallace

It's All in Your Imagination
Sources

The following companies manufacture products featured in this section. Please check with your local retail store for these materials. We have made every attempt to identify and give proper credit for the materials used. If by chance we have missed giving the appropriate credit, we would appreciate hearing from you.

3L Corp.
(800) 828-3130
www.3lcorp.com

3M Stationary
(800) 364-3577
www.3m.com

Art Accents
(360) 733-8989
www.artaccents.net

Artistic Wire Ltd.
(630) 530-7567
www.artisticwire.com

Beadery, The Greene Plastics Corp.
(401) 539-2432

Carl Mfg. USA, Inc.
(800) 257-4771
www.carl-products.com

Craf-T Products
(507) 235-3996

Darice, Inc.
(800) 321-1494
www.darice.com

DieCuts with a View
(801) 224-6766
www.diecutswithaview.com

Ellison, Craft & Design
(800) 253-2238
www.ellison.com

Fibers by the Yard
www.fibersbytheyard.com

Fiskars, Inc.
(800) 950-0203
www.fiskars.com

Glue Dots International
(wholesale only)
(888) 688-7131
www.gluedots.com

Hero Art, Rubber Stamps, Inc.
(800) 822-4376
www.heroarts.com

Leisure Arts
(888) 257-7548
www.business.leisurearts.com

Making Memories
(800) 286-5263
www.makingmemories.com

Marvy, Uchida
(800) 541-5877
www.uchida.com

McGill, Inc.
(800) 982-9884
www.mcgillinc.com

Plaid Enterprises, Inc.
(800) 842-4197

QuicKutz
(888) 702-1146
www.quickutz.com

Sakura Hobby Craft
(801) 212-7878

Sakura of America
(800) 776-6257
www.sakuraofamerica.com

Xyron Inc.
(800) 793-3523
www.xyron.com

The following
BONUS SCRAPBOOK PAPERS
are from the
Memories in the Making Collection from Leisure Arts:

#61054 Patchwork Denim
(Denim Collection)

#61095 Red Bandana
(Denim Collection)

#61055 Stonewashed Blue Denim
(Denim Collection)

#61020 Stripe Pink/Denim
(Denim Collection)

#61064 Rusty Tin
(Elements Collection)

#61073 Reptile Rust
(Elements Collection)

#61070 Small Stripe Blue/Lime
(Groovy Collection)

#61074 Small Stripe Pink/Yellow
(Groovy Collection)

#61257 Blue Toile
(Baby Collection)

#61258 Pink Toile
(Baby Collection)

#61108 Four-Square Green
(Denim Collection)

#61105 Denim-Green
(Denim Collection)

#61076 Dots Blue Background
(Groovy Collection)

#61093 Stripe Chenille Yellow
(Denim Collection)

#61075 Dots Pink Background
(Groovy Collection)

#61053 Stripe Chenille Pink
(Denim Collection)

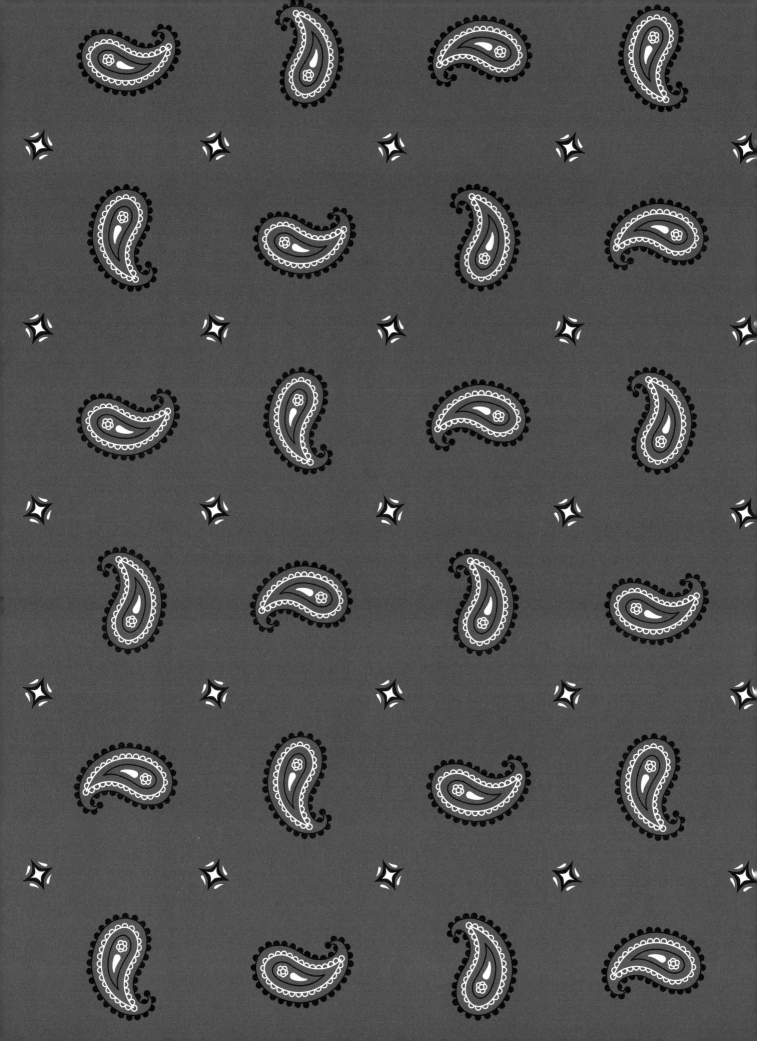

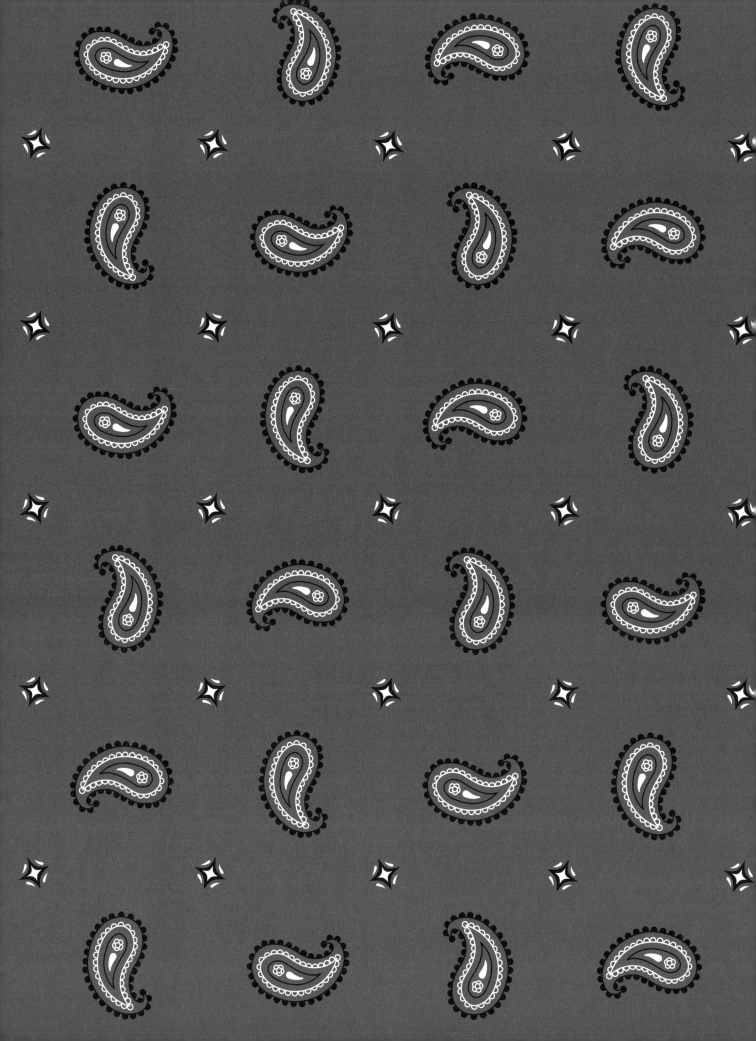